Shakespeare

*The Essential Guide to the Life
and Works of the Bard*

Encyclopædia Britannica

John Wiley & Sons, Inc.

Published by John Wiley & Sons, Inc., Hoboken, New Jersey
Published simultaneously in Canada

Design and composition by Navta Associates, Inc.

For general information about our other products and services, please contact our Customer Care Department within the United States at (800) 762-2974, outside the United States at (317) 572-3993 or fax (317) 572-4002.

Wiley also publishes its books in a variety of electronic formats. Some content that appears in print may not be available in electronic books. For more information about Wiley products, visit our web site at www.wiley.com.

Library of Congress Cataloging-in-Publication Data

Shakespeare : the essential guide to the life and works of the Bard / Encyclopaedia Britannica.
     p. cm.
   Includes bibliographical references.
   ISBN-13: 978-0-471-76784-8 (pbk.)
   ISBN-10: 0-471-76784-0 (pbk.)
   1. Shakespeare, William, 1564–1616—Encyclopedias. 2. Dramatists, English—Early modern, 1500–1700—Biography—Encyclopedias. I. Encyclopaedia Britannica, Inc.

PR2892.S55 2007
822.3'3—dc22

                                                        2006012523

Contents

Note to the Reader

In 2005 a special rendition of *Macbeth*, one told from the perspective of Lady Macbeth, had its world premiere at the Chicago Shakespeare Theater. Acclaimed director and cultural figure Shōzo Satō staged the production with American actors and English dialogue but melded it with the conventions of kabuki theater, including traditional Japanese music, makeup, costumes, and stage props; it was East-meets-West in a theater form known as "fusion kabuki." Staged at the same theater the following year was another unusual version of *Macbeth*. This time a single actor, the Canadian-born, classically trained thespian Rick Miller, performed Shakespeare's shortest tragedy in 50 strange but highly recognizable voices: all dead-on impersonations of Homer, Marge, Bart, Lisa, and many other wacky characters from *The Simpsons*, the hit animated TV series; the hilarious absurdity of combining Shakespeare and *The Simpsons* has led to sold-out shows around the world. Performances like these, especially ones as disparate as *Kabuki Lady Macbeth* and the inimitable *MacHomer*, only confirm the obvious: Shakespeare remains the quintessential "man for all seasons" whose far-flung influence is never hard to find. Or as Gail Kern Paster puts it in her wonderful introduction that follows, "The sun never sets on the Shakespeare industry."

Britannica is proud to contribute to this prolific industry with *Shakespeare: The Essential Guide to the Life and Works of the Bard*. Encyclopædia Britannica is one of the most trusted sources of information in the world, and its legendary print set, first published in 1768 and the basis for the first encyclopedia on the Internet in 1994, is the oldest continuously published and revised work in the English language. And so it is with great pleasure that we offer today, in conjunction with John Wiley & Sons, yet another way to access Britannica's wealth of information: the "Essential Guide" series.

The entries that follow derive from articles commissioned for the encyclopedia and largely edited by Britannica's senior editor for world literature, Kathleen Kuiper, and they make up but a fraction of Britannica's extensive coverage of Elizabethan life and letters. They are written by the world's leading authorities on Shakespeare. David Bevington of the University of Chicago, for example, is the main author of Britannica's large biography of Shakespeare, which has been broken up here into convenient short entries (such as "Assessment," "Authorship," "Criticism," and "Sexuality"), and he composed the summaries of each Shakespeare play; Stephen J. Greenblatt of Harvard University, author of the acclaimed *Will in the World: How Shakespeare Became Shakespeare*, wrote the biography of Elizabeth I; Alvin Kernan of Princeton University contributed "Shakespeare on Theater"; Kenneth Rothwell of the University of Vermont wrote "Shakespeare on Film"; and the introduction, by Gail Kern Paster, director of the Folger Shakespeare Library, surveys the social, cultural, and political factors contributing to Shakespeare's success and influence. These are but a few of the distinguished scholars featured in this volume. There are also discussions of various controversies—concerning Shakespeare's identity, the Bard's sexual orientation, and the mysterious "Dark Lady" and "fair youth"—as well as appendixes offering a chronology of Shakespeare's plays and an extensive filmography.

The entries are arranged alphabetically for easy access to specific subjects, but many readers will doubtless choose to read this book straight through, from beginning to end, and we have developed the entries with this in mind. So whether you choose to skip around or to read this book cover to cover, we trust you will find the information and explanations you are looking for.

The combination of these various article types, ranging from plot summaries to special essays, all organized in this easy-to-use format, will provide you with a quick, concise, and informative overview of Shakespeare's life and legacy. And if still more information on the Bard is desired, there is an extensive bibliography of additional sources at the end of this book. We also invite you to visit www.britannica.com, where authoritative answers—and even a multimedia "spotlight" on Shakespeare and his world—are just a click away.

Theodore Pappas
Executive Editor
Encyclopædia Britannica, Inc.

Introduction

Gail Kern Paster

"He was not of an age, but for all time!" exclaimed Ben Jonson in his poem "To the memory of my beloved, the Author Mr. William Shakespeare," one of several dedicatory poems prefacing the great 1623 Folio of *Comedies, Histories, and Tragedies*, the first collected volume of Shakespeare's works. Time has thus far supported this bold declaration: no writer before or since has equaled Shakespeare in influence, reverential acclaim, or enduring commercial and popular success. Although his work has been studied more than that of any other writer, the facts of his life remain maddeningly elusive: some skeptics claim that the son of a Stratford glover could not possibly have written such an unparalleled body of work. And in fact the sort of uncritical reverence that Shakespeare often receives can lead to disappointment. The apocryphal first-time reader of *Hamlet* who comes away disgusted because the play turned out to be "nothing but quotes" testifies to the level of Shakespeare's saturation of our culture—and to the understandable impulse to mock and debunk so iconic a figure. Today, as we know, Shakespeare's works are performed all over the world in almost every language, including Klingon, and in every imaginable medium including comic books and pornographic travesties. The sun never sets on the Shakespeare industry.

Indeed, Shakespeare's literary and cultural authority is now so unquestioned that it has taken on an aura of historical inevitability and has enshrined the figure of the solitary author as the standard bearer of literary production. It is all the more important, then, at the opening of a volume devoted to essential information about the greatest of all poets to suggest that Shakespeare had a genius for timing—managing to be born in

1

exactly the right place and at the right time to nourish his particular form of greatness. His birth occurred at a propitious moment in England for the history of the English language, education, the theater, the social and political structure, and for the dawning British Empire. While historical factors do not *determine* the cultural formation of any writer, they do help us to understand how writers emerge and why they come to choose one genre over others. Because Shakespeare was first and foremost a playwright, the historical factors necessary for his development are particularly worth enumerating.

It is indisputable that had Shakespeare been born even a half-century earlier—in 1514 rather than 1564—he could not and would not have written his plays, because they arose from specific historical conditions unique to his era. If there is no satisfactory explanation for the appearance of great genius, it is not too difficult to articulate the cultural conditions that extinguish it. Certainly it is unlikely that in 1514 the son of a Midlands tradesman would have been literate, let alone that he would have written poetry. Thus, first place among the necessary if not sufficient historical preconditions for the creation of Hamlet and Falstaff must go to the development of English as a serious literary language. Shakespeare wrote in what historical linguists now designate as early modern English (c. 1450–c.1700). For most modern readers, early modern English poses enough semantic and syntactic difficulties to require editorial annotation—that swift glance to the bottom of the page that informs us that many familiar words, such as *virtue*, and *honesty*, and *credit*, had different meanings then.

Most readers of Shakespeare do not realize how remarkably fortunate the poet was to come of age when English first blossomed as a great literary language. In Shakespeare's childhood, as the linguist Jonathan Hope has pointed out, Latin was still the language of theology and science, and a peculiar form of Anglo-Norman was used in legal contexts; written English had not yet achieved standardization in spelling, syntax, or grammatical forms. There was no English dictionary of English. By the end of the 16th century, English was ready for transformation into one of the greatest mediums for the representation of thought, emotion, and complex inner states ever created by any society.

Shakespeare played a huge role in expanding the expressive capacity of the language, especially in the verbal representation of thinking and subjectivity. But the language, written and spoken, relied on expansion through borrowing from Latin and the European vernacular tongues. Such borrowing, we now realize, was and continues to be a major reason for the expansiveness of English. For writers like Shakespeare, the ready absorption of foreign words must have been a powerful stimulus to stylistic and intellectual invention. The massive and relatively sudden explosion of great literary creativity during Shakespeare's lifetime supports this supposition, as does the appearance of works such as Richard Mulcaster's 1582 *Elementary*, which devotes itself, in part, to the defense of English as a literary tongue. Mulcaster believed that English had entered upon a formative golden age, writing, "Such a period in the Greke tung was that time, when Demosthenes lived, and that learned race of the father philosophers: such a period in the Latin tung, was that time, when Tullie [Cicero] lived, and those of that age: such a period in the English tung I take this to be in our daies."

The defeat of the Spanish Armada in 1588 and the nationwide glorification of Elizabeth I as the Virgin Queen in the wake of that fortuitous event also promoted the status of English—just when Shakespeare had arrived in London and was beginning his career as actor and playwright. Hope speculates that even Shakespeare's Midland origins facilitated his personal creation of a comparatively "richer linguistic palate." A writer born in London would have heard a more modern form of English in his linguistically formative early years than the rich mixture of older and newer forms that would have surrounded a Warwickshire youth. Perhaps hearing such variation and change stimulated Shakespeare's consciousness of language and a desire to play with it. Perhaps this is why Shakespeare's colleague and great rival, the London-born Ben Jonson, establishes himself instead as a linguistic purist and rule-setter—specifying in the Prologue to his *Every Man in His Humour* that the material of comedy be "deeds, and language, such as men do use." Shakespeare by contrast seems to revel in polyglot wordplay and neologism, allowing the intensely guilt-ridden Macbeth, for example, to worry that he can never wash off the murdered Duncan's blood; that "this my hand will rather / The multitudinous seas incarnadine, making the green one red." Shakespeare's use of this hyperbolic image of a murderer's bloody hand staining the ocean is not new; there are numerous classical antecedents. What is new in Shakespeare is his use of a massively polysyllabic monologue using two new Latinate words— *multitudinous* and *incarnadine*—that he may well have invented.

In addition to his good fortune at being born into a language exploding with expressive potential, Shakespeare was also deeply fortunate in his early education. Here too the timing of his birth played a part. It is almost certainly the case that Shakespeare's grandfather Richard Shakespeare was illiterate, and Shakespeare's father may have been as well; neither would have had the benefit of a grammar school education. Despite Ben Jonson's famous sneer at Shakespeare's "small Latine and less Greeke" in the First Folio's dedicatory poem, Shakespeare seems to have had a very substantial immersion in the standard Latin curriculum and an introduction to Greek at the excellent King's New School in Stratford-upon-Avon. (School records for this period are lost, but it is very likely that the son of a prosperous citizen like John Shakespeare would have been enrolled there.) The education was rhetorical and the language of pedagogy was Latin: grammar school students memorized key texts, practiced translating back and forth between Latin and English, and delivered speeches in Latin as well. They also sometimes took part in schoolboy Latin theatricals.

The proliferation of such grammar schools throughout the 16th century is one reason that so many of the great Elizabethan playwrights—including shoemaker's son Christopher Marlowe, bricklayer's son Ben Jonson, and William Shakespeare—were drawn from the middle ranks of English society. It was the bright, ambitious boys in such classes who gained the most from their grammar school training, even if—like Shakespeare and Jonson—they were unable to proceed to a university education at Oxford or Cambridge. It is clear from the plays that Shakespeare's imagination was a bookish one, perhaps inspired by this early education and certainly fired by his later reading. He returned to favorite books, such as Ovid's *Metamorphoses*— both in Latin and in English translation—and Sir Thomas North's English translation of Plutarch's *Parallel Lives of the Greeks and Romans*, over and over again for inspiration.

Apart from the state of the English language and an English grammar school education, the relative peacefulness of 16th-century England and the long reign of Elizabeth I were also crucial to Time's fostering of Shakespeare. The English polity had achieved a period of genuine stability by the mid 16th century after a century of destructive feudal wars, the fractious break from the Church of Rome occasioned by the divorce of Elizabeth's father, Henry VIII, and the troubled previous reigns of Elizabeth's half siblings, Edward VI and Mary I. The latter, known to subsequent ages as "Bloody Mary" Tudor, tried to restore England to Roman Catholicism. In the process she created many English Protestant martyrs who were burned at the stake and a lingering atmosphere of religious divisiveness. Elizabeth, returning the nation to a moderate form of Protestantism known as the Elizabethan settlement, tried unsuccessfully to quell this atmosphere of religious tension, but it lingered in the form of continued persecution and deep quarrels among Catholic recusants, radical Protestants, and more moderate Anglicans. Such religious division forced ordinary English people to choose between sharply contrasting forms of religious belief and practice. The greatest minds of the time engaged ferociously in destroying their opponent's basic religious beliefs, in demonstrating that the other's faith was based on illusion and chicanery. As Stephen Greenblatt points out in *Renaissance Self-*

Fashioning (1980), these debates produced sharp skepticism in many thinkers such as the iconoclastic Christopher Marlowe.

Paradoxically, though, this combination of political stability and religious controversy may have been quite fortuitous for the development of Shakespeare's intellect and narrative gifts and for the great theatrical tradition of which he was a part. Albert Camus, speculating about why there have been only two ages of great tragic theater (the theater of Aeschylus, Sophocles, and Euripides of 5th century BC Athens and the Renaissance theater of Shakespeare and Pierre Corneille), suggested that "great periods of tragic art occur, in history, during centuries of crucial change, at moments when the lives of whole peoples are heavy both with glory and with menace, when the future is uncertain and the present dramatic." In both ages, the bare stage of the theater represented the whole plane of human action. Hamlet is perhaps Shakespeare's most eloquent spokesman for this sense of the significance of theater when he tells the players that the purpose of playing is to hold "the mirror up to nature" and to show "the very age and body of the time his form and pressure" and when he asks Ophelia plaintively, "What should such fellows as I do crawling between earth and heaven?"

Shakespeare's own religious views cannot be known with certainty. But his plays suggest a deep interest in the efficacy of ritual and the status of symbolic language, matters clearly related to theater as a representational art. In Shakespeare's day, performance of public plays required state licensing—the express permission of a court officer known as the Master of the Revels—and punishment for violating theatrical censorship could be severe. Such censorship, it has been argued by such scholars as Annabel Patterson, is a powerful stimulus to developing "a system of communication in which ambiguity becomes a creative and necessary instrument, a social and cultural force of considerable consequence." Shakespeare became a master of such ambiguity, and if his plays encode topical allusions to religious controversy, as scholars have sometimes argued, they do so without sacrificing their purchase on timelessness.

It is clear, then, that good timing was also involved in the arrival of William Shakespeare to London sometime in the late 1580s, when public theatrical performance by professional actors in purpose-built playhouses was an emerging commercial enterprise looking for talent and as hungry for content as today's cable TV and World Wide Web. England had a rich theatrical heritage, not only of the religious plays produced by civic guilds that Shakespeare might have seen in his boyhood but also of theatrical performances in the colleges at Oxford and Cambridge and entertainments by players who, as members of noble households, regularly toured the countryside. Theater historians of the period have found a wealth of evidence in private libraries, guildhalls, and public record offices all over England of provincial performances of all kinds. Shakespeare was born into a society that valued popular theatrical entertainment and celebrated many festive holidays with singing, dancing, and theatricals. Although touring and provincial playing were thus well known, the explosion of theater construction and the formation of professional acting companies in London in the last two decades of the 16th century were unprecedented. The tremendous popularity of the new London playhouses represented a commercial and artistic opportunity that—we now recognize in hindsight—perfectly suited the expressive gifts of the talented and ambitious newcomer from Stratford.

Playwrights must write within the governing theatrical conventions of their time, and this fact would have been axiomatic for a consummate man of the theater like Shakespeare. Theater is perhaps the most collaborative and social of the arts, requiring a well-orchestrated network of artisans, financiers, actors, playwrights, playhouse functionaries, and, of course, paying audiences. It is important to recognize the inspiration that Shakespeare must have found in the other actors, his fellow playwrights, and the audience too. With the benefit of a more or less stable company of actors developing their talents over time, Shakespeare could write demanding roles such as Hamlet or Othello confident that they could be performed by Richard

Burbage, the company's leading actor. Though we do not know the names of the boy actors who played Rosalind and Celia in *As You Like It* or Viola and the lady Olivia in *Twelfth Night*, we can recognize—as Shakespeare must have—the histrionic talent required to perform those multilayered comic roles with grace and power. Tom Stoppard wittily recognizes the collaboration at the heart of theater in his screenplay for the film *Shakespeare in Love*, portraying Christopher Marlowe as Shakespeare's great rival and having Marlowe casually suggest in an alehouse conversation that Shakespeare reconsider "Ethel" as the name of his heroine in a forthcoming play tentatively entitled *Romeo and Ethel the Pirate's Daughter.* (This is a spoof, of course: Shakespeare found the lovers' names in Arthur Brooke's very dull 1562 poem entitled *The Tragical History of Romeo and Juliet.*) Elizabethan playwrights did find real inspiration in one another's work, and thanks in part to the public demand for novelty and new material they had a practical reason for collaboration. Scholars now think that Shakespeare was not an exception to the rule; he probably collaborated with others in the composition of *Titus Andronicus, Timon of Athens,* and *Pericles* and certainly with his successor John Fletcher in the late plays *Henry VIII* and *The Two Noble Kinsmen.* As William Hazlitt pointed out in his pioneering lectures for the general public printed in *Lectures on the Dramatic Literature of the Age of Elizabeth*, Shakespeare was part of a group of talented playwrights: "The sweetness of Decker [sic], the thought of Marston, the gravity of Chapman, the grace of Fletcher and his young-eyed wit, Jonson's learned sock, the flowing vein of Middleton, Heywood's ease, the pathos of Webster, and Marlowe's deep designs, add a double lustre to the sweetness, thought, gravity, grace, wit, artless nature, copiousness, ease, pathos, and sublime conceptions of Shakespeare's Muse. They are indeed the scale by which we can best ascend to the true knowledge and love of him." By means of such comparisons, an accurate picture of Shakespeare, not as a solitary genius, but as a supremely gifted and eminently practical theater professional—indebted to actors, to other playwrights, and to a demanding public audience—comes clear.

Finally, we cannot divorce Shakespeare's unique pre-eminence from the historical sweep of British imperialism. If the greatness of the English language comes in part from its permissive borrowings from other tongues, the worldwide recognition of Shakespeare's greatness arises in part from the global spread of English, and now American, culture. English is now the world's *lingua franca*. Shakespeare has inspired not only British and American actors and directors but also performers and filmmakers the world over. His plays are never appropriated by other cultures without change and transformation, but that too is a sign of their remarkable humanity.

To specify the historical conditions that nourished Shakespeare's development as a great poet and playwright is to take away nothing from Shakespeare's consummate artistic achievements. Giving them historical resonance and a global context offers instead strong resistance to current critical celebrations of Shakespeare as a transcendent figure, self-created if not self-begotten. In the strongest form of these descriptions—such as Harold Bloom's best-selling *Shakespeare: The Invention of the Human* (1998), Shakespeare becomes the titanic figure who "invented the human as we continue to know it" by creating characters such as Lear and Hamlet. Bloom describes Falstaff as "the mortal god of my imaginings," testifying with great eloquence to the power of Shakespeare's most compelling characters to move us and enlarge our imaginations. As Bloom rightly insists, supreme literary talent is the necessary precondition for the composition of *Hamlet, Lear*, the Sonnets, and Shakespeare's other great works that have shaped our language, embedded themselves in our individual and collective imaginations, and inspired so much work by other artists.

Yet the vagaries of historical contingency must be acknowledged. This is not a matter of making the banal point that Shakespeare might have succumbed to some childhood disease and died early, or of noting how many great poets die prematurely.

This is to make the more important case that Shakespeare's remarkable achievement—now recognized so widely—required the convergence of a number of historical forces. Had it not been for the efforts of editors John Heminge and Henry Condell, who published the First Folio, 18 of Shakespeare's 37 plays would have remained in manuscript form and probably would have been forever lost to posterity. These plays include *Macbeth*, *Julius Caesar*, *The Tempest*, and *Twelfth Night*. It is difficult to imagine our culture and our language without them: William Faulkner's *The Sound and the Fury* would have had a different title, a different way of alluding to existential despair; the science fiction classic *Forbidden Planet* would have taken a different form; no one would say "*Et tu, Brute*," when betrayed by a trusted friend.

Shakespeare's works matter in ways too many and too various to count. His cultural effect is like the largest place-name on a world map—difficult to see because it covers so much territory. And, like that map, his works have helped readers and playgoers for four centuries to get their bearings. Beautiful and profound in themselves, they have provided readers and theatergoers for four centuries with a world of stories and a language of unparalleled reach. More than any other single corpus of imaginative literature, his works prove the immortality and universality of secular art.

Gail Kern Paster is the director of the Folger Shakespeare Library in Washington, D.C.

All's Well That Ends Well

This comedy in five acts was written in 1601–1605 and published in the First Folio of 1623, seemingly from a theatrical playbook that still retained certain authorial features or from a literary transcript either of the playbook or of an authorial manuscript. The principal source of the plot was a tale in Giovanni Boccaccio's *Decameron*.

The play concerns the efforts of Helena, daughter of a renowned physician to the recently deceased count of Rossillion (i.e., Roussillon), to win as her husband the young new count, Bertram. When Bertram leaves Rossillion to become a courtier, Helena follows after, hoping to minister to the gravely ill king of France with a miraculous cure that her father had bequeathed to her. In return for her success in doing so, the king invites her to select a husband, her choice being Bertram. The young man, unwilling to marry so far below himself in social station, accedes to the royal imperative but promptly flees to military action in Tuscany with his vapid but engaging friend Parolles. By letter Bertram informs Helena that he may not be considered her husband until she has taken the ring from his finger and conceived a child by him. Disguised as a pilgrim, Helena follows Bertram to Florence, only to discover that he has been courting Diana, the daughter of her hostess. Helena spreads a rumor of her own death and arranges a nighttime rendezvous with Bertram in which she substitutes herself for Diana. In exchange for his ring, she gives him one that the king has given her. When Bertram returns to Rossillion, where the king is visiting the countess, the royal guest recognizes the ring and suspects foul play. Helena then appears to explain her machinations and claim her rightful spouse.

▮ *Antony and Cleopatra*

This tragedy in five acts was written in 1606–1607 and published in the First Folio of 1623 either from an authorial draft in a more finished state than most of Shakespeare's working papers or possibly from a transcript of those papers not yet prepared as a playbook. It is considered one of Shakespeare's richest and most moving works. The principal source of the play was Sir Thomas North's *Parallel Lives* (1579), an English version of Plutarch's *Bioi paralleloi*.

The story concerns Mark Antony, Roman military leader and triumvir, who is besottedly in love with Cleopatra, queen of Egypt and former mistress of Pompey and Julius Caesar. Summoned to Rome upon the death of his wife, Fulvia, who had openly antagonized his fellow triumvir Octavius, Antony heals the residual political rift by marrying Octavius's sister, Octavia. Word of the event enrages Cleopatra. Renewed contention with Octavius and desire for Cleopatra, however, send Antony back to his lover's arms. When the rivalry erupts into warfare, Cleopatra accompanies Antony to the Battle of Actium, where her presence proves militarily disastrous. She heads back to Egypt, and Antony follows, pursued by Octavius. Anticipating the eventual outcome, Antony's friend and loyal officer Enobarbus deserts him and joins Octavius. At Alexandria, Octavius eventually defeats Antony. Cleopatra, fearing for her life in light of Antony's increasingly erratic behavior, sends a false report of her suicide, which prompts Antony to wound himself mortally. Carried by his soldiers to the queen's hiding place in one of her monuments, he dies in her arms. Rather than submit to Roman conquest, the grieving Cleopatra arranges to have a poisonous snake delivered to her in a basket of figs. Attended by her faithful servants Charmian and Iras, she kills herself.

As You Like It

This five-act comedy was written and performed about 1598–1600 and first published in the First Folio of 1623. Shakespeare based the play on *Rosalynde* (1590), a prose romance by Thomas Lodge (c. 1557–1625).

The play has two principal settings: the court that Frederick has usurped from his brother, the rightful duke (known as Duke Senior), and the Forest of Arden, where the Duke and his followers (including the disgruntled Jaques) are living in exile. Rosalind, the Duke's daughter, who is still at court, falls in love with Orlando, who has been denied by his older brother Oliver the education and upbringing that should have been Orlando's right as a gentleman. To escape Oliver's murderous hatred, Orlando flees to the Forest of Arden with his faithful old servant Adam. Soon Rosalind is banished too, merely for being the daughter of the out-of-favor Duke Senior. She flees to Arden accompanied by her cousin Celia and the jester Touchstone. Disguised as a young man named Ganymede, Rosalind encounters Orlando, lovesick for his Rosalind, and promises to cure him of his lovesickness by pretending to be that very Rosalind, so that Orlando will learn something of what women are really like. Oliver appears in the forest intending to kill Orlando, but when Orlando saves his brother from a hungry lioness and a snake, Oliver experiences deep remorse. He then falls in love with Celia. Revelation of the girls' true identities precipitates a group wedding ceremony. When word arrives that Frederick has repented, the Duke's exile is at an end. A group of forest inhabitants—William, Audrey, Silvius, and Phoebe—and the courtier Le Beau further round out the cast of characters, and an abundance of song complements the play's amorous theme and idyllic setting. The play is considered to be one of Shakespeare's "great" or "middle" comedies.

Assessment

Shakespeare occupies a position unique in world literature. Other poets, such as Homer and Dante, and novelists, such as Leo Tolstoy and Charles Dickens, have transcended national barriers; but no writer's living reputation can compare to that of Shakespeare, whose plays, written in the late 16th and early 17th centuries for a small repertory theater, are now performed and read more often and in more countries than ever before. The prophecy of his great contemporary, the poet and dramatist Ben Jonson, that Shakespeare "was not of an age, but for all time," has been fulfilled.

It may be audacious even to attempt a definition of his greatness, but it is not so difficult to describe the gifts that enabled him to create imaginative visions of pathos and mirth that, whether read or witnessed in the theater, fill the mind and linger there. He is a writer of great intellectual rapidity, perceptiveness, and poetic power. Other writers have had these qualities, but with Shakespeare the keenness of mind was applied not to abstruse or remote subjects but to human beings and their complete range of emotions and conflicts. Other writers have applied their keenness of mind in this way, but Shakespeare is astonishingly clever with words and images, so that his mental energy, when applied to intelligible human situations, finds full and memorable expression, convincing and imaginatively stimulating. As if this were not enough, the art form into which his creative energies went was not remote and bookish but involved the vivid stage impersonation of human beings, commanding sympathy and inviting vicarious participation. Thus Shakespeare's merits can survive translation into other languages and into cultures remote from that of Elizabethan England.

▌Authorship

Readers and playgoers in Shakespeare's own lifetime, and indeed until the late 18th century, never questioned Shakespeare's authorship of his plays. He was a well-known actor from Stratford who performed in London's premier acting company, among the great actors of his day. He was widely known by the leading writers of his time as well, including Ben Jonson and John Webster, both of whom praised him as a dramatist. Many other tributes to him as a great writer appeared during his lifetime. Any theory that supposes him not to have been the writer of the plays and poems attributed to him must suppose that Shakespeare's contemporaries were universally fooled by some kind of secret arrangement.

Yet suspicions on the subject gained increasing force in the mid-19th century. One Delia Bacon proposed that the author was her claimed ancestor Sir Francis Bacon, Viscount St. Albans, who was indeed a prominent writer of the Elizabethan era. What had prompted this theory? The chief considerations seem to have been that little is known about Shakespeare's life (though in fact more is known about him than about his contemporary writers), that he was from the country town of Stratford-upon-Avon, that he never attended one of the universities, and that therefore it would have been impossible for him to write knowledgeably about the great affairs of English courtly life such as we find in the plays.

The theory is suspect on a number of counts. University training in Shakespeare's day centered on theology and on Latin, Greek, and Hebrew texts of a sort that would not have greatly improved Shakespeare's knowledge of contemporary English life. By the 19th century, a university education was becoming more and more the mark of a broadly educated person, but university training in the 16th century was quite a different matter. The notion that only a university-educated person could write of life at court and among the gentry is an erroneous and indeed a snobbish assumption. Shakespeare was better off going to London as he did, seeing and writing plays, listening to how people talked. He was a reporter, in effect. The great writers of his era (or indeed of most eras) were not usually aristocrats, who had no need to earn a living by their pens. Shakespeare's social background was essentially like that of his best contemporaries. Edmund Spenser went to Cambridge, it is true, but he came from a sail-making family. Christopher Marlowe also attended Cambridge, but his kindred were shoemakers in Canterbury. John Webster, Thomas Dekker, and Thomas Middleton came from similar backgrounds. They discovered that they were writers, able to make a living off their talent, and they (excluding the poet Edmund Spenser) flocked to the London theaters, where customers for their wares were to be found. Like them, Shakespeare was a man of the commercial theater.

Other candidates—William Stanley, 6th earl of Derby, and Christopher Marlowe among them—have been proposed, and indeed the very fact of so many candidates makes one suspicious of the claims of any one person. The late-20th-century candidate for the writing of Shakespeare's plays, other than Shakespeare himself, was Edward de Vere, 17th earl of Oxford. Oxford did indeed write verse, as did other gentlemen; sonneteering was a mark of gentlemanly distinction. Oxford was also a wretched man who abused his wife and drove his father-in-law to distraction. Most seriously damaging to Oxford's candidacy is the fact that he died in 1604. The chronology presented in this book, summarizing perhaps 200 years of assiduous scholarship, establishes a professional career for Shakespeare as dramatist that extends from about 1589 to 1614. Many of his greatest plays—*King Lear*, *Antony and Cleopatra*, and *The Tempest*, to name but three—were written after 1604. To suppose that the dating of the canon is totally out of whack and that all the plays and poems were written before 1604 is a desperate argument. Some individual dates are uncertain, but the overall pattern is coherent. The growth in poetic and dramatic styles, the development of themes and subjects, along with objective evidence, all support a chronology that extends to about 1614. To suppose alternatively that Oxford wrote the plays and poems before 1604 and then put them away in a drawer, to be brought out after his death and updated to make them appear timely, is to invent an answer to a nonexistent question.

When all is said, the sensible question one must ask is, why would Oxford want to write the plays and poems and then not claim them for himself? The answer given is that he was an aristocrat and that writing for the theater was not elegant; hence he needed a front man, an alias. Shakespeare, the actor, was a suitable choice. But is it plausible that a cover-up like this could have succeeded?

Shakespeare's contemporaries, after all, wrote of him unequivocally as the author of the plays. Ben Jonson, who knew him well, contributed verses to the First Folio of 1623, where (as elsewhere) he criticizes and praises Shakespeare as the author. John Heminge and Henry Condell, fellow actors and theater owners with Shakespeare, signed the dedication and a foreword to the First Folio and described their methods as editors. In his own day, therefore, he was accepted as the author of the plays. In an age that loved gossip and mystery as much as any, it seems hardly conceivable that Jonson and Shakespeare's theatrical associates shared the secret of a gigantic literary hoax without a single leak or that they could have been imposed upon without suspicion. Unsupported assertions that the author of the plays was a man of great learning and that Shakespeare of Stratford was an illiterate rustic no longer carry weight, and only when a believer in Bacon or Oxford or Marlowe produces sound evidence will scholars pay close attention.

Bacon, Sir Francis

A lawyer, statesman, philosopher, master of the English tongue, and contemporary of Shakespeare, Sir Francis Bacon (1561–1626) is remembered in literary terms for the sharp worldly wisdom of a few dozen essays; by students of constitutional history for his power as a speaker in Parliament and in famous trials and as James I's lord chancellor; and intellectually as a man who claimed all knowledge as his province and, after a magisterial survey, urgently advocated new ways by which man might establish a legitimate command over nature for the relief of his estate.

Bacon was born the younger of the two sons of the lord keeper, Sir Nicholas Bacon, by his second marriage. Nicholas Bacon, born in comparatively humble circumstances, had risen to become lord keeper of the great seal. Francis's cousin

Sir Francis Bacon, oil painting by an unknown artist.

through his mother was Robert Cecil, later earl of Salisbury and chief minister of the crown at the end of Elizabeth I's reign and the beginning of James I's. From 1573 to 1575 Bacon was educated at Trinity College, Cambridge, but his weak constitution caused him to suffer ill health there. His distaste for what he termed "unfruitful" Aristotelian philosophy began at Cambridge. From 1576 to 1579 Bacon was in France as a member of the English ambassador's suite. He was recalled abruptly after the sudden death of his father, who left him relatively little money. Bacon remained financially embarrassed virtually until his death.

In 1576 Bacon had been admitted as an "ancient" (senior governor) of Gray's Inn, one of the four Inns of Court that served as institutions for legal education, in London. In 1579 he took up residence there and, after becoming a barrister in 1582, progressed in time through the posts of reader (lecturer at the Inn), bencher (senior member of the Inn), and queen's (from 1603 king's) counsel extraordinary to those of solicitor general and attorney general. Even as successful a legal career as this, however, did not satisfy his political and philosophical ambitions.

Bacon occupied himself with the tract "Temporis Partus Maximus" ("The Greatest Part of Time") in 1582; it has not survived. In 1584 he sat as member of Parliament for Melcombe Regis in Dorset and subsequently represented Taunton, Liverpool, the County of Middlesex, Southampton, Ipswich, and the University of Cambridge. In 1589 a "Letter of Advice" to Queen Elizabeth and *An Advertisement Touching the Controversies of the Church of England* indicated his political interests and showed a fair promise of political potential by reason of their levelheadedness and disposition to reconcile. In 1593 came a setback to his political hopes: he took a stand objecting to the government's intensified demand for subsidies to help meet the expenses of the war against Spain. Elizabeth took offense, and Bacon was in disgrace during several critical years when there were chances for legal advancement.

Meanwhile, sometime before July 1591, Bacon had become acquainted with Robert Devereux, the young earl of Essex, who was a favorite of the queen, although still in some disgrace with her for his unauthorized marriage to the widow of Sir Philip Sidney. Bacon saw in Essex the "fittest instrument to do good to the State" and offered him the friendly advice of an older, wiser, and more subtle man. Essex did his best to mollify the queen, and when the office of attorney general fell vacant, he enthusiastically but unsuccessfully supported the claim of Bacon. Other recommendations by Essex for high offices to be conferred on Bacon also failed.

By 1598 Essex's failure in an expedition against Spanish treasure ships made him harder to control; and although Bacon's efforts to divert his energies to Ireland, where the people were in revolt, proved only too successful, Essex lost his head when things went wrong and he returned against orders. Bacon certainly did what he could to accommodate matters but merely offended both sides; in June 1600 he found himself as Elizabeth's learned counsel taking part in the informal trial of his patron. Essex bore him no ill will and shortly after his release was again on friendly terms with him. But after Essex's abortive attempt of 1601 to seize the queen and force her dismissal of his rivals, Bacon, who had known nothing of the project, viewed Essex as a traitor and drew up the official report on the affair. This, however, was heavily altered by others before publication.

After Essex's execution, Bacon, in 1604, published the *Apologie in Certaine Imputations Concerning the Late Earle of Essex* in defense of his own actions. It is a coherent piece of self-justification, but to posterity it does not carry complete conviction, particularly since it evinces no personal distress.

When Elizabeth died in 1603, Bacon's letter-writing ability was directed to finding a place for himself and a use for his talents in James I's service. He pointed to his concern for Irish affairs, the union of the kingdoms, and the pacification of the church as proof that he had much to offer the new king.

Through the influence of his cousin Robert Cecil, Bacon was one of the 300 new knights dubbed in 1603. The following year he was confirmed as learned counsel and sat in the first Parliament of the new reign in the debates of its first session. He was also active as one of the commissioners for discussing a union with Scotland. In the autumn of 1605 he published his *Advancement of Learning*, dedicated to the king, and in the following summer he married Alice Barnham, the daughter of a London alderman. Preferment in the royal service, however, still eluded him, and it was not until June 1607 that his petitions and his vigorous though vain efforts to persuade the Commons to accept the king's proposals for union with Scotland were at length rewarded with the post of solicitor general. Even then, his political influence remained negligible, a fact that he came to attribute to the power and jealousy of Cecil, by then earl of Salisbury and the king's chief minister. In 1609 his *De Sapientia Veterum* ("The Wisdom of the Ancients"), in which he expounded what he took to be the hidden practical meaning embodied in ancient myths, came out and proved to be, next to the *Essayes*, his most popular book in his own lifetime. About 1614 he wrote *The New Atlantis*, his far-seeing scientific utopian work, which did not get into print until 1626.

After Salisbury's death in 1612, Bacon renewed his efforts to gain influence with James, writing a number of remarkable papers of advice upon affairs of state and, in particular, upon the relations between Crown and Parliament. The king adopted his proposal for removing Sir Edward Coke (1552–1634) from his post as chief justice of the common pleas and appointing him to the King's Bench, while appointing Bacon attorney general in 1613. During the next few years Bacon's views about the royal prerogative brought him, as attorney general, increasingly into conflict with Coke, the champion of the common law and of the independence of the judges. It was Bacon who examined Coke when the king ordered the judges to be consulted individually and separately in the case of Edmond Peacham, a clergyman charged with treason as the author of an unpublished treatise justifying rebellion against oppression. Bacon has been criticized for having taken part in the examination under torture of Peacham, which turned out to be fruitless. It was Bacon who instructed Coke and the other judges not to proceed in the case of commendams (i.e., the holding of benefices in the absence of the regular incumbent) until they had spoken to the king. Coke's dismissal in November 1616 for defying this order was quickly followed by Bacon's appointment as lord keeper of the great seal in March 1617. The following year he was made lord chancellor and Baron Verulam, and in 1621 he was created Viscount St. Albans.

The main reason for this progress was his unsparing service in Parliament and the court, together with persistent letters of self-recommendation; according to the traditional account, however, he was also aided by his association with George Villiers, later duke of Buckingham, the king's new favorite. It would appear that he became honestly fond of Villiers; many of his letters betray a feeling that seems warmer than timeserving flattery.

Among Bacon's papers a notebook has survived, the *Commentarius Solutus* ("Loose Commentary"), which is revealing. It is a jotting pad "like a Marchant's wast booke where to enter all maner of remembrance of matter, fourme, business, study, towching my self, service, others, eyther sparsim or in schedules, without any maner of restraint." This book reveals Bacon reminding himself to flatter a possible patron, to study the weaknesses of a rival, to set intelligent noblemen in the Tower of London to work on serviceable experiments. It displays the multiplicity of his concerns: his income and debts, the king's business, his own garden and plans for building, philosophical speculations, his health, including his symptoms and medications, and an admonition to learn to control his breathing and not to interrupt in conversation. Between 1608 and 1620 he prepared at least 12 drafts of his most celebrated work, the *Novum Organum*, and wrote several minor philosophical works.

The major occupation of these years must have been the management of James, always with reference, remote or direct, to the royal finances. The king relied on his lord chancellor but did not always follow his advice. Bacon was longer sighted than his contemporaries and seems to have been aware of the constitutional problems that were to culminate in civil war; he dreaded innovation and did all he could, and perhaps more than he should, to safeguard the royal prerogative. Whether his policies were sound or not, it is evident that he was, as he later said, "no mountebank in the King's services."

By 1621 Bacon must have seemed impregnable, a favorite not by charm (though he was witty and had a dry sense of humor) but by sheer usefulness and loyalty to his sovereign; lavish in public expenditure (he was once the sole provider of a court masque); dignified in his affluence and liberal in his household; winning the attention of scholars abroad as the author of the *Novum Organum*, published in 1620, and the developer of the *Instauratio Magna* ("Great Instauration"), a comprehensive plan to reorganize the sciences and to restore man to that mastery over nature that he was conceived to have lost by the fall of Adam. But Bacon had his enemies. In 1618 he fell foul of George Villiers when he tried to interfere in the marriage of the daughter of his old enemy, Coke, and the younger brother of Villiers. Then, in 1621, two charges of bribery were raised against him before a committee of grievances over which he himself presided. The shock appears to have been twofold because Bacon, who was casual about the incoming and outgoing of his wealth, was unaware of any vulnerability and was not mindful of the resentment of two men whose cases had gone against them in spite of gifts they had made with the intent of bribing the judge. The blow caught him when he was ill, and he pleaded for extra time to meet the charges, explaining that genuine illness, not cowardice, was the reason for his request. Meanwhile, the House of Lords collected another score of complaints. Bacon admitted the receipt of gifts but denied that they had ever affected his judgment; he made notes on cases and sought an audience with the king that was refused. Unable to defend himself by discriminating between the various charges or cross-examining witnesses, he settled for a penitent submission and resigned the seal of his office, hoping that this would suffice. The sentence was harsh, however, and included a fine of £40,000, imprisonment in the Tower of London during the king's pleasure, disablement from holding any state office, and exclusion from Parliament and the verge of court (an area of 12 miles radius centered on where the sovereign is resident). Bacon commented to Buckingham: "I acknowledge the sentence just, and for reformation's sake fit, *the justest Chancellor that hath been in the five changes since Sir Nicolas Bacon's time.*" The magnanimity and wit of the epigram sets his case against the prevailing standards.

Bacon did not have to stay long in the Tower, but he found the ban that cut him off from access to the library of Charles Cotton, an English man of letters, and from consultation with his physician more galling. He came up against an inimical lord treasurer, and his pension payments were delayed. He lost Buckingham's goodwill for a time and was put to the humiliating practice of roundabout approaches to other nobles and to Count Gondomar, the Spanish ambassador; remissions came only after vexations and disappointments. Despite all this his courage held, and the last years of his life were spent in work far more valuable to the world than anything he had accomplished in his high office. Cut off from other services, he offered his literary powers to provide the king with a digest of the laws, a history of Great Britain, and biographies of Tudor monarchs. He prepared memorandums on usury and on the prospects of a war with Spain; he expressed views on educational reforms; he even returned, as if by habit, to drafting papers of advice to the king or to Buckingham and composed speeches he was never to deliver. Some of these projects were completed, and they did not exhaust his fertility. He wrote: "If I be left to myself I will graze and bear natural philosophy." Two out of a plan of six separate natural histories were composed—*Historia Ventorum* ("History of the Winds") appeared in 1622 and *Historia Vitae et Mortis* ("History of Life and Death") in the following year. Also in 1623 he published the *De Dignitate et Augmentis Scientiarum*, a Latin translation, with many additions, of the *Advancement of Learning*. He also corresponded with Italian thinkers and urged his works upon them. In 1625 a third and enlarged edition of his *Essayes* was published.

Bacon in adversity showed patience, unimpaired intellectual vigor, and fortitude. Physical deprivation distressed him, but what hurt most was the loss of favor; it was not until January 20, 1623, that he was admitted to kiss the king's hand; a full pardon never came. Finally, in March 1626, driving one day near Highgate (a district to the north of London) and deciding on impulse to discover whether snow would delay the process of putrefaction, he stopped his carriage, purchased a hen, and stuffed it with snow. He was seized with a sudden chill, which brought on bronchitis, and he died at the earl of Arundel's house nearby.

Beaumont, Francis

A poet and playwright, and a contemporary of Shakespeare, Francis Beaumont (c. 1585–1616) collaborated with John Fletcher on comedies and tragedies between about 1606 and 1613.

The son of Francis Beaumont, justice of common pleas, of Grace-Dieu priory, Charnwood Forest, Leicestershire, Beaumont entered Broadgates Hall (later Pembroke College), Oxford, in 1597. After his father died the following year, he abruptly left the university without a degree and later (November 1600) entered London's Inner Temple, where he evidently became more involved in London's lively literary culture than in legal studies.

In 1602 there appeared the poem *Salmacis and Hermaphroditus*, generally attributed to Beaumont, a voluptuous and voluminous expansion of the Ovidian legend, adding to the story humor and a fantastic array of episodes and conceits. At age 23 he prefixed to Ben Jonson's *Volpone* (1607) some verses in honor of his "dear friend" the author. John Fletcher contributed

Francis Beaumont, engraving by George Vertue, 1729.

verses to the same volume, and by about this time, the two were collaborating on plays for the Children of the Queen's Revels. According to John Aubrey, a 17th-century memorialist, "They lived together on the Banke side, not far from the Play-house, both batchelors; lay together . . . ; had one wench in the house between them . . . ; the same cloathes and cloake, &c., betweene them" (*Brief Lives*). Their collaboration as playwrights was to last for some seven years. In 1613 Beaumont married an heiress, Ursula Isley of Sundridge in Kent, and retired from the theater. He died in London in 1616 and was buried in Westminster Abbey.

It is difficult to disentangle Beaumont's share in the 35 plays published in 1647 as by "Beaumont and Fletcher" (to which another 18 were added in the 1679 collection). Scholars now believe that only 10 of these were by the two friends, while Beaumont's hand also appears in three plays substantially written by Fletcher and Philip Massinger. The rest are plays written by Fletcher alone, or in collaboration with other dramatists, except for *The Knight of the Burning Pestle*, which is Beaumont's unaided work. Attempts to separate the shares of Beaumont and Fletcher in any given work are complicated by the fact that Beaumont sometimes revised scenes by Fletcher, and Fletcher edited some of Beaumont's work. *The Knight of the Burning Pestle* parodies a then popular kind of play—sprawling, episodic, with sentimental lovers and chivalric adventures. It opens with the Citizen and his Wife taking their places on the stage to watch "The London Merchant"—itself a satire on the work of a contemporary playwright, Thomas Dekker. Citizen and Wife interrupt, advise, and insist that the play should be more romantic and their apprentice should take a leading part. Thereafter, these two contradictory plots go forward side by side, allowing Beaumont to have fun with bourgeois naiveté about art.

▮ Blackfriars Theatre

Two separate theaters bore the name Blackfriars Theatre, with the second famed as the winter quarters (after 1608) of the King's Men, the company of actors for whom Shakespeare served as chief playwright and also as a performer.

The name of the theaters derives from their location on the site of a 13th-century Dominican (the Black Friars) priory lying within the City of London between the River Thames and Ludgate Hill. The estates of the priory were split up in 1538 at the suppression of the English monasteries under Henry VIII, and in 1576, under Elizabeth I, Richard Farrant, Master of the Children of the Chapel, leased part of the buildings along the western side of the priory cloisters so that the Children could present their plays in this "private" theater before performing them at court. Other children's companies also acted there until 1584, when the buildings reverted to their owner.

In 1596 another part of the old monastery was bought by James Burbage (the father of actor Richard Burbage), who converted it into a theater. Opposition to the scheme forced him to lease it to children's companies. Richard Burbage, who was a principal actor with the Lord Chamberlain's Men, acted at the Globe Theatre. He inherited the second Blackfriars Theatre in 1597, and in 1608 formed a company of "owners" (called housekeepers) along the lines of that operating at the Globe Theatre. His company of players (by now called the King's Men) played at the Blackfriars during the winter seasons. Shakespeare's later plays were performed there, as were works by Beaumont and Fletcher.

The Blackfriars was forced to close on the outbreak of the English Civil Wars in 1642. It was demolished in 1655. Its site is today commemorated by Playhouse Yard.

A Closer Look
Theaters in the Liberties
by Steven Mullaney

In 1567 John Brayne went east of Aldgate to Stepney, where he erected a theater called the Red Lion. It was the first permanent building designed expressly for dramatic performances to be constructed in Europe since late antiquity; the civic authorities of London, already unhappy with playing in the streets and inn-yards of the city proper, were not pleased with this new development. Within two years they were complaining about the "great multitudes of people" gathering in the "liberties and suburbs" of the city. In 1576 Brayne's brother-in-law, James Burbage, joined the family enterprise by erecting the Theatre in the liberty of Shoreditch (it was here that William Shakespeare would find his first theatrical home when he went to London, sometime in the 1580s). The Theatre was joined by the Curtain in 1577, and in subsequent years the liberties across the River Thames would also become sites of civic complaint as they became host to the Rose (1587), the Swan (c. 1595), and the Globe (1599), which was fashioned from timbers of the original Theatre. By the turn of the century, when the Fortune had completed the scene, the city was ringed with playhouses posted strategically just outside its jurisdiction. "Houses of purpose built . . . and that without the Liberties," as John Stockwood remarked in a sermon delivered at Paul's Cross (a public site outside and adjacent to St. Paul's Cathedral, and a major crossroads of the city) in 1578, "as who would say, 'There, let them say what they will say, we will play.'"

The drama of Shakespeare and his contemporaries is regarded by modern audiences as one of the supreme artistic achievements in literary history; in its own day, however, it was viewed by many as a scandal and an outrage—a hotly contested and controversial phenomenon that religious and civic authorities strenuously sought to outlaw. In 1572, in fact, players were defined as vagabonds—criminals subject to arrest, whipping, and branding unless they were "liveried" servants of an aristocratic household. Burbage's company and others used this loophole in the law to their advantage by persuading various lords to lend their names (and often little more) to the companies, which thus became the Lord Chamberlain's or the Lord Strange's Men. Furthermore, "popular" drama, performed by professional acting companies for anyone who could afford the price of admission, was perceived as too vulgar in its appeal to be considered a form of art. Yet the animus of civic and religious authorities was rarely directed toward other forms of popular recreation, such as bearbaiting or the sword-fighting displays that the populace could see in open-air amphitheaters similar in construction to the Theatre and the Globe. The city regularly singled out the playhouses and regularly petitioned the court for permission to shut them down—permission that was granted only temporarily, most typically when such petitions coincided with an outbreak of plague. Elizabeth I liked to see well-written and well-rehearsed plays at court during Christmas festivities but was not inclined to pay for the development and maintenance of the requisite repertory companies herself. Her economy was inseparable from her political calculation in this instance, since the favor she showed the extramural playing companies served to keep the city of London—a powerful political entity on the doorstep of her own court—off-balance, properly subordinate to her own will, and thus, as it were, in its place.

Attacks on professional popular drama were variously motivated and sometimes revealed more about the accuser than the accused, yet they should not be discounted too readily, for they have a great deal to communicate about the cultural and historical terrain that Shakespeare's theater occupied in its own day. Nowhere is this more the case than in one of the most consistent focal points of outrage, sounded regularly from the pulpit and in lord mayors' petitions, toward these "Houses of purpose built . . . and that without the Liberties"—the place of the stage itself.

The "liberties or suburbs" of early modern London bear little resemblance to modern suburbs in either a legal or a cultural sense. They were a part of the city, extending up to 3 miles (5 km) from its ancient Roman wall, yet in crucial aspects they were set apart from it; they were also an integral part of a complex civic structure common to the walled medieval and Renaissance metropolis, a marginal geopolitical domain that was nonetheless central to the symbolic and material economy of the city. Free, or "at liberty," from manorial rule or obligations to the crown, the liberties "belonged" to the city yet fell outside the jurisdiction of the lord mayor, the sheriffs of London, and the Common Council, and they constituted an ambiguous geopolitical domain over which the city had authority but, paradoxically, almost no control. Liberties existed inside the city walls as well—it was in them that the so-called private, or hall, playhouses were to be found—but they too stood "outside" the city's effective domain. Whatever their location, the liberties formed an equivocal territory that was at once internal and external to the city, neither contained by civic authority nor fully removed from it.

Clearly, the freedom from London's legal jurisdiction was crucial to the survival of the playhouses in a pragmatic sense, but the city's outrage and sense of scandal cannot be fully explained by jurisdictional frustration alone. The liberties had for centuries performed a necessary cultural and ideological function in the city's symbolic economy, one that can be only briefly summarized here but that made them peculiarly apt ground for early modern drama to appropriate and turn to its own use and livelihood. Early modern cities were shaped, their common spaces inscribed with communal meaning and significance, by a wide variety of ritual, spectacle, and customary pastimes. Inside the city walls, ritual traditions were organized around central figures of authority, emblems of cultural coherence; the marginal traditions of the liberties, by contrast, were organized around emblems of anomaly and ambivalence. Whatever could not be contained within the strict order of the community, or exceeded its bounds in a symbolic or moral sense, resided there, and it was a strikingly heterogeneous zone. In close proximity to brothels and hospitals stood monasteries—markers, in a sense, of the space between this life and the next—until such church holdings were seized by the crown following Henry VIII's break with Rome; gaming houses, taverns, and bearbaiting arenas nestled beside sites for public execution, marketplaces, and, at the extreme verge of the liberties, the city's leprosariums. Viewed from a religious perspective, the liberties were marked as places of the sacred, or of sacred pollution in the case of the city's lepers, made at once holy and hopelessly contaminated by their affliction. From a political perspective, the liberties were the places where criminals were conveyed for public executions, well-attended and sometimes festive rituals that served to mark the boundary between this life and the next in a more secular fashion. From a general point of view, the margins of the city were places where forms of moral excess such as prostitution were granted license to exist beyond the bounds of a community that they had, by their incontinence, already exceeded.

This civic and social structure had been remarkably stable for centuries, primarily because it made room for what it could not contain. As the population of London underwent an explosive expansion in the 16th century, however, the structure could no longer hold, and the reigning hierarchy of London found the spectacle of its own limits thrust upon it. The dissolution of the monasteries had made real estate in the liberties available for private enterprises; the traditional sanctuary and freedom of the city's margins were thus opened to new individuals and social practices. Victims of enclosure, masterless men, foreign tradesmen without guild credentials, outlaws, and prostitutes joined radical Puritans and players in taking over and putting the liberties to their own uses, but it was the players who had the audacity to found a viable and highly visible institution of their own on the grounds of the city's well-maintained contradictions. And it was the players too who converted the traditional liberty of the suburbs into their own dramatic license, establishing a liberty that was at once moral, ideological, and topological—a "liberty" that gave the stage an impressive freedom to experiment with a wide range of perspectives on its own times.

Playhouses also existed within the city walls, but they operated on a more limited scale. Acting companies composed entirely of young boys performed sporadically in the city's intramural liberties from 1576 to 1608, until repeated offenses to the crown provoked James I to disband all boys' companies. After 1608 at Blackfriars, Whitefriars, and other hall playhouses, adult companies from the extramural liberties moved into the city as well and regularly performed in both the hall and the arena playhouses.

The boys' repertory was a highly specialized one: more than 85 percent of their dramatic offerings were comedies, largely satirical—a genre that was conversely rare on the arena stages. The difference is a significant one. Although satire frequently outraged its specific targets, its immediate topicality also limited its ideological range and its capacity to explore broad cultural issues. As dramatic genres, city comedy and satire were relatively contained forms of social criticism; in terms of repertory as well as topology, the hall playhouses produced what might be called an "interstitial" form of drama, one that was lodged, like the theaters themselves, in the gaps and seams of the social fabric.

In contrast to the hall theaters, the open-air playhouses outside the city walls evolved what Nicholas Woodrofe, lord mayor of London in 1580, regarded as an "incontinent" form of drama:

> Some things have double the ill, both naturally in spreading the infection, and otherwise in drawing God's wrath and plague upon us, as the erecting and frequenting of houses very famous for *incontinent rule* [author's italics] out of our liberties and jurisdiction.

Playhouses were regarded not merely as a breeding ground for the plague but as the thing itself, an infection "pestering the

City" and contaminating the morals of London's apprentices. Theaters were viewed as houses of Proteus, and in the metamorphic fears of the city, it was not only the players who shifted shapes, confounded categories, and counterfeited roles. Drama offered a form of "recreation" that drew out socially unsettling reverberations of the term, since playhouses offered a place "for all masterless men and vagabond persons that haunt the highways, to meet together and *to recreate themselves* [author's italics]." The fear was not that the spectators might be entertained but that they might incorporate theatrical means of impersonation and representation in their own lives—for example, by dressing beyond their station and thus confounding a social order reliant on sumptuary codes to distinguish one social rank from another.

What the city objected to was the sheer existence of the playhouses and the social consequences of any form of theatricality accessible to such a broad spectrum of the population. In contrast, religious antitheatricality, whether Anglican or Puritan, extended to issues of content and the specific means of theatrical representation employed by acting companies. Puritans were particularly incensed by the transvestite character of all English companies prior to the Restoration. Women onstage would have outraged them as well, but the practice of having boys don women's apparel to play female roles provoked a host of irate charges. Such cross-dressing was viewed by Puritans as a violation of biblical strictures that went far beyond issues of costuming. On the one hand, it was seen as a substantive transgression of gender boundaries; the adoption of women's dress contaminated, or "adulterated," one's gender, producing a hybrid and effeminate man. On the other hand, transvestite acting was assumed to excite a sodomitic erotic desire in the audience, so that after the play "everyone brings another homeward of their way very friendly and in their secret enclaves they play sodomite or worse."

Puritan charges tend to the rather imaginative, to say the least; they do serve as a reminder, however, that the transvestite tradition in English acting was not without controversy. Until the late 20th century, critics tended to explain it away, ascribing its origins to biblical prohibitions about women's public behavior and regarding its significance as minimal, except when a particular play (such as *As You Like It*) made thematic use of cross-dressing. Otherwise (so the argument went), it was a convention that the audience was trained not to perceive; boys were taken for women onstage and learned their craft by first serving such an apprenticeship. It now appears that male sexual practice in Renaissance England was often bisexual rather than strictly heterosexual and that sexual relations between males typically involved a disparity in age; in relations with the same as with the opposite sex, the sexual relationship was also a power relationship based on hierarchy and dominance by the (older) male. It is quite possible that boy actors were also the sexual partners of the adult actors in the company; when such boys played women, their fictive roles reproduced their social reality in terms of sexual status and subordination. To what degree the audience responded to the actor, the character portrayed, or an erotically charged hybrid of the two is impossible to say, but, as the Shakespeare scholar Stephen Orgel has noted, transvestite actors must have appealed to both men and women, given the large number of the latter who attended the theater.

The drama that developed in the arena playhouses of early modern London was rich in its diversity, aesthetically complex, and ideologically powerful in its far-reaching cultural and political resonance. And literacy was not the price of admission to Shakespeare's theater; consequently, the popular stage enjoyed a currency and accessibility that was rivaled only by the pulpit and threatened to eclipse it. Elizabethan and Jacobean drama is not normally thought of primarily in terms of the information it disseminated, but it gave the illiterate among its audience unprecedented access to ideas and ideologies, stories fictive and historical, all affectively embodied and drawn from an impressive repertoire that ranged from the classical to the contemporary. In doing so, the Renaissance stage combined with other forces (such as the rapid expansion of print culture and what is believed to have been a slow but steady rise in literacy) to alter the structure of knowledge by redefining and expanding its boundaries. Born of the contradiction between court license and civic prohibition, popular theater emerged as a viable cultural institution only by materially embodying this contradiction, dislocating itself from the strict confines of the social order and taking up a place on its margins. From this vantage point, as contemporaneous fears and modern audiences' continuing fascination testify, the popular stage developed a remarkable capacity to explore and realize, in dramatic form, some of the fundamental controversies of its time. In effect, the stage translated London's social and civic margins, the liberties of the city, into margins in the textual sense: into places reserved for a "variety of senses" (as the translators of the 1611 Bible described their own margins) and for divergent points of view—for commentary upon, and even contradiction of, the main body of their text, which in this instance means the body politic itself.

Steven Mullaney is associate professor of English and director of graduate studies in the Department of English, University of Michigan–Ann Arbor. He is the author of The Place of the Stage: License, Play, and Power in Renaissance England.

Burbage, Richard

An English actor, Richard Burbage (1567–1619) was the first player of Shakespeare's Richard III, Romeo, Henry V, Hamlet, Macbeth, Othello, and Lear.

The son of the actor and theater manager and owner James Burbage, Richard had attained wide popularity as an actor by age 20. He was a member of the Earl of Leicester's company and remained with it through its evolution into the King's Men

*Richard Burbage, oil painting
by an unknown artist.*

in 1603. He also prospered as a major shareholder in the Globe and Blackfriars theaters. Excelling in tragedy, Burbage was much in demand on the stage and performed in works by Thomas Kyd, Ben Jonson, and John Webster, as well as by Shakespeare.

Although short and stout, Burbage was apparently an impressive figure, and there are numerous praises of him in contemporary prose, verse, and plays. Burbage was a painter as well; a painting of a woman at Dulwich College, London, is undoubtedly by him, and the Chandos portrait of Shakespeare has sometimes been attributed to him. Shakespeare was closely associated with him during his career in London and in his will left Burbage a token remembrance.

▌Collaborations and Spurious Attributions

The Two Noble Kinsmen (c. 1612–1614) brought Shakespeare into collaboration with John Fletcher, his successor as chief playwright for the King's Men. (Fletcher is sometimes thought also to have helped Shakespeare with *Henry VIII*.) The story, taken out of Geoffrey Chaucer's *Knight's Tale*, is essentially another romance, in which two young gallants compete for the hand of Emilia and in which deities preside over the choice. Shakespeare probably had a hand earlier as well in *Edward III*, a history play of about 1590–1595, and he seems to have provided a scene or so for *The Book of Sir Thomas More* (c. 1593–1601) when that play encountered trouble with the censor. Collaborative writing was common in the Renaissance English stage, and it is not surprising that Shakespeare was called upon to do some of it.

Nor is it surprising that, given his towering reputation, he was credited with having written a number of plays that he had nothing to do with, including those that were spuriously added to the third edition of the Folio in 1664: *Locrine* (1591–1595), *Sir John Oldcastle* (1599–1600), *Thomas Lord Cromwell* (1599–1602), *The London Prodigal* (1603–1605), *The Puritan* (1606), and *A Yorkshire Tragedy* (1605–1608).

▌ *The Comedy of Errors*

This five-act comedy was written in 1589–1594 and first published in the First Folio of 1623 from Shakespeare's manuscript. It was based on *Menaechmi* by Plautus, with additional material from Plautus's *Amphitruo* and the story of Apollonius of Tyre. The play's comic confusions derive from the presence of twin brothers, unknown to each other, in the same town. Its twists of plot provide suspense, surprise, expectation, and exhilaration and reveal Shakespeare's mastery of construction.

Egeon, a merchant of Syracuse, is arrested in Ephesus because of hostilities between the two cities and, unable to pay the local ransom, is condemned to death. He tells the duke, Solinus, his sad tale: years earlier he and his wife had been shipwrecked with their infant sons, identical twins, and a pair of infant servants, also identical twins. The parents, each with a son and a servant, were rescued but then permanently separated. Antipholus of Syracuse, the son raised by Egeon, has for five years been seeking his mother and brother, while Egeon in turn has been seeking his missing son. Egeon's story wins from Solinus a day's respite to raise the ransom money.

Meanwhile, Antipholus of Syracuse (with his servant, Dromio) has arrived in Ephesus, not knowing that his brother, Antipholus of Ephesus (with his own servant, also named Dromio), is already there. A series of misidentifications ensue. Antipholus of Syracuse is entertained by his brother's wife and woos her sister; he receives a gold chain meant for his brother and is chased by a goldsmith for nonpayment. He and his servant hide in a priory, where they observe Egeon on his way to execution and recognize the priory's abbess as their mother, Emilia. The play ends happily with Egeon's ransom paid, true identities revealed, and the family reunited.

▌ *Coriolanus*

The last of the so-called political tragedies, *Coriolanus* was written about 1608 and published in the First Folio of 1623 seemingly from the playbook, which had preserved some features of the authorial manuscript. The five-act play, based on the life of Gnaeus Marcius Coriolanus, a legendary Roman hero of the late 6th and early 5th centuries BC, is essentially an expansion of the Plutarchan biography in *Parallel Lives*. Though it is Elizabethan in structure, it is markedly Classical in tone.

The action of the play follows Caius Marcius (afterward Caius Marcius Coriolanus) through several phases of his career. He is shown as an arrogant young nobleman in peacetime, as a bloodstained and valiant warrior against the city of Corioli, as a modest victor, and as a reluctant candidate for consul. When he refuses to flatter the Roman citizens, for whom he feels contempt, or to show them his wounds to win their vote, they turn on him and banish him. Bitterly he joins forces with his enemy Aufidius, a Volscian, against Rome. Leading the enemy to the edge of the city, Coriolanus is ultimately persuaded by his mother, Volumnia—who brings with her Coriolanus's wife, Virgilia, and his son—to make peace with Rome, and in the end he is killed at the instigation of his Volscian ally.

Coriolanus is in many ways unusual for Shakespearean drama: it has a single narrative line, its images are compact and striking, and its most effective moments are characterized by understatement or silence. When the banished Coriolanus returns at the head of the opposing army, he says little to Menenius, the trusted family friend and politician, or to Volumnia, both of whom have come to plead for Rome. His mother's argument is long and sustained, and for more than 50 lines he listens, until his resolution is broken from within. Then, as a stage direction in the original edition testifies, he "holds her by the hand, silent." In his own words, he has "obey[ed] instinct" and betrayed his dependence; he cannot "stand / As if a man were author of himself / And knew no other kin." Thus is his desire for revenge defeated. While his mother is hailed as "patroness, the life of Rome," Coriolanus stands accused of treachery by Aufidius and is cut down by Aufidius's supporters.

▌ Criticism

During his own lifetime and shortly afterward, Shakespeare enjoyed fame and considerable critical attention. The English writer Francis Meres, in 1598, declared him to be England's greatest writer of comedy and tragedy. Writer and poet John Weever lauded "honey-tongued Shakespeare." Ben Jonson, Shakespeare's contemporary and a literary critic in his own right, granted that Shakespeare had no rival in the writing of comedy, even in the ancient classical world, and that he equaled the ancients in tragedy as well, but Jonson also faulted Shakespeare for having a mediocre command of the classical languages and for ignoring classical rules. Jonson objected when Shakespeare dramatized history extending over many years and moved his dramatic scene around from country to country, rather than focusing on 24 hours or so in a single location. Shakespeare wrote too glibly, in Jonson's view, mixing kings and clowns, lofty verse with vulgarity, mortals with fairies.

Seventeenth Century

Jonson's Neoclassical perspective on Shakespeare was to govern the literary criticism of the later 17th century as well. John Dryden, in his essay *Of Dramatick Poesie* (1668) and other essays, condemned the improbabilities of Shakespeare's late romances. Shakespeare lacked decorum, in Dryden's view, largely because he had written for an ignorant age and poorly educated audiences. Shakespeare excelled in "fancy" or imagination, but he lagged behind in "judgment." He was a native genius, untaught, whose plays needed to be extensively rewritten to clear them of the impurities of their frequently vulgar style. And in fact most productions of Shakespeare on the London stage during the Restoration did just that: they rewrote Shakespeare to make him more refined.

Eighteenth Century

This critical view persisted into the 18th century as well. Alexander Pope undertook to edit Shakespeare in 1725, expurgating his language and "correcting" supposedly infelicitous phrases. Samuel Johnson also edited Shakespeare's works (1765), defending his author as one who "holds up to his readers a faithful mirror of manners and of life"; but though he pronounced Shakespeare an "ancient" (supreme praise from Johnson), he found Shakespeare's plays full of implausible plots quickly huddled together at the end, and he deplored Shakespeare's fondness for punning. Even in his defense of Shakespeare as a great English writer, Johnson lauded him in classical terms, for his universality, his ability to offer a "just representation of general nature" that could stand the test of time.

Romantic Critics

For Romantic critics such as Samuel Taylor Coleridge in the early 19th century, Shakespeare deserved to be appreciated most of all for his creative genius and his spontaneity. For Goethe in Germany as well, Shakespeare was a bard, a mystical seer. Most of all, Shakespeare was considered supreme as a creator of character. Maurice Morgann wrote such character-based analyses as appear in his book *An Essay on the Dramatic Character of Sir John Falstaff* (1777), where Falstaff is envisaged as larger than life, a humane wit and humorist who is no coward or liar but a player of inspired games. Romantic critics, including Charles Lamb, Thomas De Quincey (who wrote *Encyclopædia Britannica*'s article on Shakespeare for the eighth edition), and William Hazlitt, extolled Shakespeare as a genius able to create an imaginative world of his own, even if Hazlitt was disturbed by what he took to be Shakespeare's political conservatism. In the theater of the Romantic era, Shakespeare fared less well, but as an author he was much touted and even venerated. In 1769 the famous actor David Garrick had instituted a Shakespeare Jubilee at Stratford-upon-Avon to celebrate Shakespeare's birthday. Shakespeare had become England's national poet.

Twentieth Century and Beyond

The Increasing Importance of Scholarship

The late 19th and early 20th centuries saw major increases in the systematic and scholarly exploration of Shakespeare's life and works. Philological research established a more reliable chronology of the work than had been hitherto available. Edward Dowden, in his *Shakspere: A Critical Study of His Mind and Art* (1875), analyzed the shape of Shakespeare's career in a way that had not been possible earlier. A. C. Bradley's magisterial *Shakespearean Tragedy* (1904), a book that remains highly readable, showed how the achievements of scholarship could be applied to a humane and moving interpretation of Shakespeare's greatest work. As in earlier studies of the 19th century, Bradley's approach focused largely on character.

Historical Criticism

Increasingly in the 20th century, scholarship furthered an understanding of Shakespeare's social, political, economic, and theatrical milieu. Shakespeare's sources came under new and intense scrutiny. Elmer Edgar Stoll, in *Art and Artifice in Shakespeare* (1933), stressed the ways in which the plays could be seen as constructs intimately connected with their historical environment. Playacting depends on conventions, which must be understood in their historical context. Costuming signals meaning to the audience; so do the theater building, the props, the actors' gestures.

Accordingly, historical critics sought to know more about the history of London's theaters (as in John Cranford Adams's well-known model of the Globe playhouse or in C. Walter Hodges's *The Globe Restored* [1953]), about audiences (Alfred Harbage, *As They Liked It* [1947]; and Ann Jennalie Cook, *The Privileged Playgoers of Shakespeare's London, 1576–1642* [1981]), about staging methods (Bernard Beckerman, *Shakespeare at the Globe 1599–1609* [1962]), and much more. Other scholarly studies examined censorship, the religious controversies of the Elizabethan era and how they affected playwriting, and the heritage of native medieval English drama. Studies in the history of ideas have examined Elizabethan cosmology, astrology, philosophical ideas such as the Great Chain of Being, physiological theories about the four bodily humors, political theories of Machiavelli and others, the skepticism of Montaigne, and much more.

New Criticism

As valuable as it is, historical criticism has not been without its opponents. A major critical movement of the 1930s and 1940s was the so-called New Criticism of F. R. Leavis, L. C. Knights, Derek Traversi, Robert Heilman, and many others, urging a more formalist approach to the poetry. "Close reading" became the mantra of this movement. At its most extreme, it urged the ignoring of historical background in favor of an intense and personal engagement with Shakespeare's language: tone, speaker, image patterns, and verbal repetitions and rhythms. Studies of imagery, rhetorical patterns, wordplay, and still more gave support to the movement. At the commencement of the 21st century, close reading remained an acceptable approach to the Shakespearean text.

New Interpretive Approaches

Shakespeare criticism of the 20th and 21st centuries has seen an extraordinary flourishing of new schools of critical approach. Psychological and psychoanalytic critics such as Ernest Jones have explored questions of character in terms of Oedipal complexes, narcissism, and psychotic behavior or, more simply, in terms of the conflicting needs in any relationship for autonomy and dependence. Mythological and archetypal criticism, especially in the influential work of Northrop Frye, has examined myths of vegetation having to do with the death and rebirth of nature as a basis for great cycles in the creative process. Christian interpretation seeks to find in Shakespeare's plays a series of deep analogies to the Christian story of sacrifice and redemption.

Conversely, some criticism has pursued a vigorously iconoclastic line of interpretation. Jan Kott, writing in the disillusioning aftermath of World War II and from an eastern European perspective, reshaped Shakespeare as a dramatist of the absurd, skeptical, ridiculing, and antiauthoritarian. Kott's deeply ironic view of the political process impressed filmmakers and theater directors such as Peter Brook (*King Lear, A Midsummer Night's Dream*). He also caught the imagination of many academic critics who were chafing at a modern political world increasingly caught up in image making and the various other manipulations of the powerful new media of television and electronic communication.

A number of the so-called New Historicists (among them Stephen Greenblatt, Stephen Orgel, and Richard Helgerson) read avidly in cultural anthropology, learning from Clifford Geertz and others how to analyze literary production as a part of a cultural exchange through which a society fashions itself by means of its political ceremonials. Stephen Greenblatt's *Renaissance Self-Fashioning* (1980) provided an energizing model for the ways in which literary criticism could analyze the process. Mikhail Bakhtin was another dominant influence. In Britain the movement came to be known as Cultural Materialism; it was a first cousin to American New Historicism, though often with a more class-conscious and Marxist ideology. The chief proponents of this movement with regard to Shakespeare criticism are Jonathan Dollimore, Alan Sinfield, John Drakakis, and Terry Eagleton.

Feminist Criticism and Gender Studies

Feminist and gender-study approaches to Shakespeare criticism made significant gains after 1980. Feminists, like New Historicists, were interested in contextualizing Shakespeare's writings rather than subjecting them to ahistorical formalist analysis. Turning to anthropologists such as Claude Lévi-Strauss, feminist critics illuminated the extent to which Shakespeare inhabited a patriarchal world dominated by men and fathers, in which women were essentially the means of exchange in power relationships among those men. Feminist criticism is deeply interested in marriage and courtship customs, gender relations, and family structures. In *The Tempest*, for example, feminist interest tends to center on Prospero's dominating role as father and on the way in which Ferdinand and Miranda become engaged and, in effect, married when they pledge their love to one another in the presence of a witness—Miranda's father. Plays and poems dealing with domestic strife (such as Shakespeare's *The Rape of Lucrece*) take on a new centrality in this criticism. Diaries, marriage-counseling manuals, and other such documents become important to feminist study. Revealing patterns emerge in Shakespeare's plays as to male insecurities about women, men's need to dominate and possess women, their fears of growing old, and the like. *Much Ado about Nothing* can be seen as about men's fears of being cuckolded; *Othello* treats the same male weakness with deeply tragic consequences. The tragedy in *Romeo and Juliet* depends in part on Romeo's sensitivity to peer pressure, which seemingly obliges him to kill

Tybalt and thus choose macho male loyalties over the more gentle and forgiving model of behavior he has learned from Juliet. These are only a few examples. Feminist critics of the late 20th and early 21st centuries included, among many others, Lynda Boose, Lisa Jardine, Gail Paster, Jean Howard, Karen Newman, Carol Neely, Peter Erickson, and Madelon Sprengnether.

Gender studies such as those of Bruce R. Smith and Valerie Traub also dealt importantly with issues of gender as a social construction and with changing social attitudes toward "deviant" sexual behavior: cross-dressing, same-sex relationships, and bisexuality.

Deconstruction

The critical movement generally known as deconstruction centered on the instability and protean ambiguity of language. It owed its origins in part to the linguistic and other work of French philosophers and critics such as Ferdinand de Saussure, Michel Foucault, and Jacques Derrida. Some of the earliest practitioners and devotees of the method in the United States were Geoffrey Hartmann, J. Hillis Miller, and Paul de Man, all of Yale University. Deconstruction stressed the extent to which "meaning" and "authorial intention" are virtually impossible to fix precisely. Translation and paraphrase are exercises in approximation at best.

The implications of deconstruction for Shakespeare criticism have to do with language and its protean flexibility of meanings. Patricia Parker's *Shakespeare from the Margins: Language, Culture, Context* (1996), for example, offers many brilliant demonstrations of this, one of which is her study of the word *preposterous*, a word she finds throughout the plays. It means literally behind for before, back for front, second for first, end or sequel for beginning. It suggests the cart before the horse, the last first, and "arsie versie," with obscene overtones. It is thus a term for disorder in discourse, in sexual relationships, in rights of inheritance, and much more. Deconstruction as a philosophical and critical movement aroused a good deal of animosity because it questioned the fixity of meaning in language. At the same time, however, deconstruction attuned readers to verbal niceties, to layers of meaning, to nuance.

Late-20th-century and early-21st-century scholars were often revolutionary in their criticism of Shakespeare. To readers the result frequently appeared overly postmodern and trendy, presenting Shakespeare as a contemporary at the expense of more traditional values of tragic intensity, comic delight, and pure insight into the human condition. No doubt some of this criticism, as well as some older criticism, was too obscure and ideologically driven. Yet deconstructionists and feminists, for example, at their best portray a Shakespeare of enduring greatness. His durability is demonstrable in the very fact that so much modern criticism, despite its mistrust of canonical texts written by "dead white European males," turns to Shakespeare again and again. He is dead, white, European, and male, and yet he appeals irresistibly to readers and theater audiences all over the world. In the eyes of many feminist critics, he portrays women with the kind of fullness and depth found in authors such as Virginia Woolf and George Eliot.

Cymbeline

This comedy in five acts is one of Shakespeare's later plays, written in 1608–1610 and published in the First Folio of 1623 from a careful transcript of an authorial manuscript incorporating a theatrical playbook that had included many authorial stage directions. Set in the pre-Christian Roman world, *Cymbeline* draws its main theme, that of a wager by a husband on his wife's fidelity, from a story in Giovanni Boccaccio's *Decameron*.

In the play Cymbeline, the king of Britain, decides that his daughter, Imogen, must marry his horrid stepson Cloten. When Cymbeline learns that Imogen is secretly married to Posthumus, he banishes Posthumus, who heads for Rome. In a conversation with a villainous Italian, Iachimo, Posthumus finds himself drawn unwisely into betting Iachimo that Imogen's fidelity to her marriage is unassailable. Journeying to England, Iachimo furtively obtains from the sleeping Imogen a token that he uses to convince Posthumus of her infidelity. Posthumus sends a servant to kill Imogen, but the servant instead warns her of the plan. Disguising herself as a young boy (Fidele), she sets out for Rome but loses her way in Wales. There she encounters Belarius and her two brothers, whom she had believed dead (Belarius had kidnapped Cymbeline's sons in retribution for his unjust banishment). Posthumus (who has left Rome), Imogen, and her brothers are caught up in the advance of the Roman army, which has come to collect the tribute that Cymbeline has refused to pay to Rome. The forces clash, and Cymbeline's army is victorious, largely because of the valor of Posthumus, Cymbeline's sons, and Belarius. A lengthy series of revelations and explanations ensue. Posthumus and Imogen are reunited; Cymbeline's now-dead queen is revealed to have been thoroughly wicked; her son Cloten has died at the hands of one of Cymbeline's sons; and Cymbeline is reconciled to all his beleaguered family and to Belarius as well.

▌The Dark Lady

One of two individuals (the other was a young man, a "fair youth") who are the main subjects addressed in William Shakespeare's sonnets. In Sonnet 144 the poet refers explicitly to "a woman colour'd ill," and scholars have since referred to her as the Dark Lady. Most of the late sonnets (numbers 127 to 154) concern the poet's relationship to her. This series of poems—believed to have been written before the sonnets that precede them—suggests that this "worser spirit" was a mistress to both the poet and the young man.

A number of individuals have been proposed as the real-life

models for the Dark Lady. These include Emilia Bassano Lanier (proposed by A. L. Rowse), the engaging mistress of George Carey, 2nd Lord Hunsdon (later Lord Chamberlain); Mary Fitton, a maid of honor to Queen Elizabeth; and Lucy Morgan, a brothel owner and former maid to the queen. The true identity of the Dark Lady, if indeed there was a real-life model, is still unknown, and the subject has fueled intense and continuing scholarly debate.

The whole discussion is given a new twist by the arguments presented in Clare Asquith's 2005 work *Shadowplay: The Hidden Beliefs and Coded Politics of William Shakespeare*, which maintains that Shakespeare coded many references to hide his Roman Catholic beliefs. In this interpretation, "high" and "fair" stand for Catholicism, "low" and "dark" for Protestantism.

Davenant, William

William Davenant (1606–1668) was an English poet, playwright,

Sir William Davenant, engraving by William Faithorne after John Greenhill, 1672

and theater manager who was made poet laureate on the strength of such successes as *The Witts* (licensed 1634), a comedy; the masques *The Temple of Love, Britannia Triumphans*, and *Luminalia*; and a volume of poems, *Madagascar* (published 1638).

Shakespeare was apparently Davenant's godfather, and gossip held that the famous playwright may even have been his father. Davenant became a page in London in 1622 and later served a famous literary courtier, Fulke

Greville, Lord Brooke. Meanwhile he was writing his early revenge tragedies, such as *Albovine* (produced c. 1629), and tragicomedies, such as *The Colonel*. After he had served in continental wars, his engaging, reckless personality and his plays and occasional verses attracted the patronage of Queen Henrietta Maria. Davenant was appointed to the poet laureateship in 1638, after the death of Ben Jonson the previous year.

In 1641 Davenant risked his life in a bungled army plot, and the outbreak of the Civil War in 1642 nullified a royal patent he had secured to build a theater. A supporter of King Charles I during the Civil War, he was knighted by the king in 1643 for running supplies across the English Channel. Later, having joined the defeated and exiled Stuart court in Paris, he began his uncompleted verse epic *Gondibert* (1651), a tale of chivalry in 1,700 quatrains. After the execution of Charles I, his queen sent Davenant to aid the Royalist cause in America as lieutenant governor of Maryland. Davenant's ship was captured in the English Channel, however, and he was imprisoned in the Tower of London until 1654.

In 1656 Davenant made the first attempt to revive English drama, which had been banned under Cromwell, with *The First Day's Entertainment* (produced 1656), a work disguised under the title *Declamations and Musick*. This work led to his creating the first public opera in England, *The Siege of Rhodes Made a Representation by the Art of Prospective in Scenes, And the Story Sung in Recitative Musick* (produced 1656). In *The Siege* he introduced three innovations to the English public stage: an opera, painted stage sets, and a female actress-singer.

In 1660, after the Restoration, he was granted a royal patent to establish new acting companies, and he founded the new Duke of York's Playhouse in Lincoln's Inn Fields. As manager, director, and playwright, he continued to produce, write, and adapt plays. The charter was later transferred to Covent Garden. Together with the poet John Dryden, he adapted Shakespeare's *The Tempest* in 1667.

▌Dekker, Thomas

Thomas Dekker (c. 1572–1632), a contemporary of Shakespeare, was an English dramatist and writer of prose pamphlets who is particularly known for his lively depictions of London life.

Few facts of Dekker's life are certain. He may have been born into a family of Dutch immigrants living in London and is first mentioned as a playwright in 1598. He apparently wrote to support himself, and he had a hand in at least 42 plays written in the next 30 years. In the dispute known as "the poets' war," or "the war of the theaters," he was satirized in Ben Jonson's *Poetaster* (produced 1601) as Demetrius Fannius, "a very simple honest fellow, . . . a dresser of plays." This precipitated Dekker's own attack on Jonson in the play *Satiro-mastix* (produced 1601). Thirteen more plays survive in which Dekker collaborated with such figures as Thomas Middleton, John Webster, Philip Massinger, John Ford, and William Rowley.

Of the nine surviving plays that are entirely Dekker's work, probably the best known are *The Shoemakers Holiday* (1600) and *The Honest Whore, Part 2* (1630). These plays are typical of his work in their use of the moralistic tone of traditional drama, in the rush of their prose, in their boisterousness, and in their mixture of realistic detail with a romanticized plot. Dekker's ear for colloquial speech served him well in his vivid portrayals of daily life in London, and his work appealed strongly to a citizen audience eager for plays on middle-class, patriotic, and Protestant themes.

He exhibited a similar vigor in such prose pamphlets as *The Wonderfull Yeare* (1603), about the plague; *The Belman of London* (1608), about roguery and crime, with much material borrowed from Robert Greene and others; and *The Guls Horne-Booke* (1609), a valuable account of behavior in the London theaters.

Between 1613 and 1619 Dekker was in prison for debt. This firsthand experience may be behind his six prison scenes first included in the sixth edition (1616) of Sir Thomas Overbury's *Characters*. Dekker was partly responsible for devising the street entertainment to celebrate the entry of James I into London in 1603; he provided the lord mayor's pageant in 1612, 1627, 1628, and 1629. All this labor did not bring prosperity, however, for Dekker was likely in debt when he died.

Derby, William Stanley, 6th Earl of

William Stanley (1561–1642), an English writer and patron of the theater, has been offered by some theorists as the true author of the plays of William Shakespeare.

He succeeded his elder brother, Ferdinando, as the earl of Derby in 1594. Like Ferdinando (who was known as Lord Strange), he held an avid interest in the theater and maintained a company of actors known as Derby's Men. The troupe, which should not be confused with Lord Strange's Men (who were for a brief time known as Derby's Men), performed at court in 1599–1601. It is possible that the first performance of *A Midsummer Night's Dream* took place at his wedding banquet in 1595.

The case for the earl of Derby as the true author of Shakespeare's plays was first made by English archivist James Greenstreet in *The Genealogist* (1891–1892). His and subsequent arguments for the earl were based on his involvement in theater, his international travels, his intimacy with court life, and several poems authored by an unknown "W. S."

Early Plays

Shakespeare arrived in London probably sometime in the late 1580s. He was in his mid-20s. It is not known how he got started in the theater or for what acting companies he wrote his early plays, which are not easy to date. Indicating a time of apprenticeship, these plays show a more direct debt to London dramatists of the 1580s and to classical examples than do his later works. He learned a great deal about writing plays by imitating the successes of the London theater, as any young poet and budding dramatist might do.

Titus Andronicus (c. 1589–1592) is a case in point. As Shakespeare's first full-length tragedy, it owes much of its theme, structure, and language to Thomas Kyd's *The Spanish Tragedy*, which was a huge success in the late 1580s. Kyd had hit on the formula of adapting the dramaturgy of Seneca (the younger), the great Stoic philosopher and statesman, to the needs of a burgeoning new London theater. The result was the revenge tragedy, an astonishingly successful genre that was to be refigured in *Hamlet* and many other revenge plays. Shakespeare also borrowed a leaf from his great contemporary Christopher Marlowe. The evil protagonist of Marlowe's *The Jew of Malta*, Barabas, may have inspired Shakespeare in his depiction of the villainous Aaron the Moor in *Titus Andronicus*, though other personifications of corruption were available to him as well.

The Senecan model offered Kyd, and then Shakespeare, a story of bloody revenge, occasioned originally by the murder or rape of a person whose near relatives (fathers, sons, brothers) are bound by sacred oath to revenge the atrocity. The avenger must proceed with caution, since his opponent is canny, secretive, and ruthless. The avenger becomes mad or feigns madness to cover his intent. He becomes more and more ruthless himself as he moves toward his goal of vengeance. At the same time he is hesitant, being deeply distressed by ethical considerations. An ethos of revenge is opposed to one of Christian forbearance. The avenger may see the spirit of the person whose wrongful death he must avenge. He employs the device of a play within the play in order to accomplish his aims. The play ends in a bloodbath and a vindication of the avenger. Evident in this model is the story of Titus Andronicus, whose sons are butchered and whose daughter is raped and mutilated, as well as the story of Hamlet and still others.

The Early Romantic Comedies

Other than *Titus Andronicus*, Shakespeare did not experiment with formal tragedy in his early years. (Though his English history plays from this period portrayed tragic events, their theme was focused elsewhere.) The young playwright was drawn more quickly into comedy, and with more immediate success. For this his models include the dramatists Robert Greene and John Lyly, along with Thomas Nashe. The result is a genre recognizably and distinctively Shakespearean, even if he learned a lot from Greene and Lyly: the romantic comedy. As in the work of his models, Shakespeare's early comedies revel in stories of amorous courtship in which a plucky and admirable young woman (played by a boy actor) is paired off against her male wooer. Julia, one of two young heroines in *The Two Gentlemen of Verona* (c. 1590–1594), disguises herself as a man in order to follow her lover, Proteus, when he is sent from Verona to Milan. Proteus (appropriately named for the changeable Proteus of Greek myth), she discovers, is paying far too much attention to Sylvia, the beloved of Proteus's best friend, Valentine. Love and friendship thus do battle for the divided loyalties of the erring male until the generosity of his friend and, most of all, the enduring chaste loyalty of the two women bring Proteus to his senses. The motif of the young woman disguised as a male was to prove invaluable to Shakespeare in subsequent romantic comedies, including *The Merchant of Venice*, *As You Like It*, and *Twelfth Night*. As is generally true of Shakespeare, he derived the essentials of his plot from a narrative source, in this case a long Spanish prose romance, the *Diana* of Jorge de Montemayor.

Shakespeare's most classically inspired early comedy is *The Comedy of Errors* (c. 1589–1594). Here he turned particularly to Plautus's farcical play called *Menaechmi* (*Twins*). The story of one twin (Antipholus) looking for his lost brother, accompanied by a clever servant (Dromio) whose twin has also disappeared, results in a farce of mistaken identities that also thoughtfully explores issues of identity and self-knowing. The young women of the play, one the wife of Antipholus of Ephesus (Adriana) and the other her sister (Luciana), engage in meaningful dialogue on issues of wifely obedience and autonomy. Marriage resolves these difficulties at the end, as is routinely the case in Shakespearean romantic comedy, but not before the plot complications have tested the characters' needs to know who they are and what men and women ought to expect from one another.

Shakespeare's early romantic comedy most indebted to John Lyly is *Love's Labour's Lost* (c. 1588–1597), a confection set in the never-never land of Navarre, where the king and his companions are visited by the Princess of France and her ladies-in-waiting on a diplomatic mission that soon devolves into a game of courtship. As is often the case in Shakespearean romantic comedy, the young women are sure of who they are and whom they intend to marry; one cannot be certain that they ever really fall in love, since they begin by knowing what they want. The young men, conversely, fall all over themselves in their comically futile attempts to eschew romantic love in favor of more serious pursuits. They perjure themselves, are shamed and put down, and are finally forgiven their follies by the women. Shakespeare brilliantly portrays male discomfiture and female self-assurance as he explores the treacherous but desirable world of sexual attraction, while the verbal gymnastics of the play emphasize the wonder and the delicious foolishness of falling in love.

In *The Taming of the Shrew* (c. 1590–1594), Shakespeare employed a device of multiple plotting that would become a standard feature of his romantic comedies. In one plot, derived from Ludovico Ariosto's *I suppositi* (*Supposes*, as it had been translated into English by George Gascoigne), a young woman (Bianca) carries on a risky courtship with a young man who appears to be a tutor, much to the dismay of her father, who hopes to marry her to a wealthy suitor of his own choosing. Eventually the mistaken identities are straightened out, establishing the presumed tutor as Lucentio, wealthy and suitable enough. Simultaneously, Bianca's shrewish sister Kate denounces (and terrorizes) all men. Bianca's suitors commission the self-

assured Petruchio to pursue Kate so that Bianca, the younger
sister, will be free to wed. The wife-taming plot is itself based on
a folktale and ballad tradition in which men assure their ascendancy in the marriage relationship by beating their wives into
submission. Shakespeare transforms this raw, antifeminist material into a study of the struggle for dominance in the marriage
relationship. And, whereas he does opt in this play for male triumph over the female, he gives to Kate a sense of humor that
enables her to see how she is to play the game to her own advantage as well. She is, arguably, happy at the end with a relationship based on wit and companionship, whereas her sister Bianca
turns out to be simply spoiled.

The Early Histories

In Shakespeare's explorations of English history, as in romantic
comedy, he put his distinctive mark on a genre and made it his.
The genre was, moreover, an unusual one. There was as yet no
definition of an English history play, and there were no aesthetic rules regarding its shaping. The ancient classical world
had recognized two broad categories of genre, comedy and
tragedy. (This account leaves out more specialized genres like
the satyr play.) Aristotle and other critics, including Horace,
had evolved, over centuries, classical definitions. Tragedy dealt
with the disaster struck lives of great persons, was written in
elevated verse, and took as its setting a mythological and
ancient world of gods and heroes: Agamemnon, Theseus,
Oedipus, Medea, and the rest. Pity and terror were the prevailing emotional responses in plays that sought to understand,
however imperfectly, the will of the supreme gods. Classical
comedy, conversely, dramatized the everyday. Its chief figures
were citizens of Athens and Rome—householders, courtesans,
slaves, scoundrels, and so forth. The humor was immediate,
contemporary, topical; the lampooning was satirical, even savage. Members of the audience were invited to look at mimetic
representations of their own daily lives and to laugh at greed
and folly.

The English history play had no such ideal theoretical structure. It was an existential invention: the dramatic treatment of recent English history. It might be tragic or comic or, more commonly, a hybrid. Polonius's list of generic possibilities captures the ludicrous potential for endless hybridizations: "tragedy, comedy, history, pastoral, pastoral-comical, historical-pastoral, tragical-historical, tragical-comical-historical-pastoral," and so on (*Hamlet*, Act II, scene 2, lines 397–399). (By "pastoral," Polonius presumably means a play based on romances telling of shepherds and rural life, as contrasted with the corruptions of city and court.) Shakespeare's history plays were so successful in the 1590s' London theater that the editors of Shakespeare's complete works, in 1623, chose to group his dramatic output under three headings: comedies, histories, and tragedies. The genre established itself by the sheer force of its compelling popularity.

Shakespeare in 1590 or thereabouts had really only one viable model for the English history play, an anonymous and sprawling drama called *The Famous Victories of Henry the Fifth* (1583–1588) that told the saga of Henry IV's son, Prince Hal, from the days of his adolescent rebellion down through his victory over the French at the Battle of Agincourt in 1415— in other words, the material that Shakespeare would later use in writing three major plays, *1 Henry IV*, *2 Henry IV*, and *Henry V*. Shakespeare chose to start not with Prince Hal but with more recent history in the reign of Henry V's son Henry VI and with the civil wars that saw the overthrow of Henry VI by Edward IV and then the accession to power in 1483 of Richard III. This material proved to be so rich in themes and dramatic conflicts that he wrote four plays on it, a "tetralogy" extending from *Henry VI* in three parts (c. 1589–1593) to *Richard III* (c. 1592–1594).

These plays were immediately successful. Contemporary references indicate that audiences of the early 1590s thrilled to the story (in *1 Henry VI*) of the brave Lord Talbot doing battle in France against the witch Joan of Arc and her lover, the French Dauphin, but being undermined in his heroic effort by effeminacy and corruption at home. Henry VI himself is, as Shakespeare portrays him, a weak king, raised to the kingship by the early death of his father Henry V, incapable of controlling factionalism in his court and enervated personally by his infatuation with a dangerous Frenchwoman, Margaret of Anjou. Henry VI is cuckolded by his wife and her lover, the Duke of Suffolk, and (in 2 *Henry VI*) proves unable to defend his virtuous uncle, the Duke of Gloucester, against opportunistic enemies. The result is civil unrest, lower-class rebellion (led by Jack Cade), and eventually all-out civil war between the Lancastrian faction, nominally headed by Henry VI, and the Yorkist claimants under the leadership of Edward IV and his brothers. *Richard III* completes the saga with its account of the baleful rise of Richard of Gloucester through the murder of his brother the Duke of Clarence and of Edward IV's two sons, who were also Richard's nephews. Richard's tyrannical reign yields eventually and inevitably to the newest and most successful claimant of the throne, Henry Tudor, earl of Richmond. This is the man who becomes Henry VII, scion of the Tudor dynasty and grandfather of Queen Elizabeth I, who reigned from 1558 to 1603 and hence during the entire first decade and more of Shakespeare's productive career.

The Shakespearean English history play told of the country's history at a time when the English nation was struggling with its own sense of national identity and experiencing a new sense of power. Queen Elizabeth had brought stability and a relative freedom from war to her decades of rule. She had held at bay the Roman Catholic powers of the Continent, notably Philip II of Spain, and, with the help of a storm at sea, had fought off Philip's attempts to invade her kingdom with the great Spanish Armada of 1588. In England the triumph of the nation was viewed universally as a divine deliverance. The second edition of Holinshed's *Chronicles* was at hand as a vast source for Shakespeare's historical playwriting. It, too, celebrated the emergence of England as a major Protestant power, led by a popular and astute monarch.

From the perspective of the 1590s, the history of the 15th century also seemed newly relevant. England had emerged from a terrible civil war in 1485, with Henry Tudor's victory over Richard III at the Battle of Bosworth Field. The chief personages of these wars, known as the Wars of the Roses—Henry Tudor, Richard III, the duke of Buckingham, Hastings, Rivers, Gray, and many more—were very familiar to contemporary English readers.

Because these historical plays of Shakespeare in the early 1590s were so intent on telling the saga of emergent nationhood, they exhibit a strong tendency to identify villains and heroes. Shakespeare is writing dramas, not schoolbook texts, and he freely alters dates and facts and emphases. Lord Talbot in *1 Henry VI* is a hero because he dies defending English interests against the corrupt French. In *2 Henry VI*, Humphrey, Duke of Gloucester, is cut down by opportunists because he represents the best interests of the commoners and the nation as a whole. Most of all, Richard of Gloucester is made out to be a villain epitomizing the very worst features of a chaotic century of civil strife. He foments strife, lies, and murders and makes outrageous promises he has no intention of keeping. He is a brilliantly theatrical figure because he is so inventive and clever, but he is also deeply threatening. Shakespeare gives him every defect that popular tradition imagined: a hunchback, a baleful glittering eye, a conspiratorial genius. The real Richard was no such villain, it seems; at least, his politically inspired murders were no worse than the systematic elimination of all opposition by his successor, the historical Henry VII. The difference is that Henry VII lived to commission historians to tell the story his way, whereas Richard lost everything through defeat. As founder of the Tudor dynasty and grandfather of Queen Elizabeth, Henry VII could command a respect that even Shakespeare was bound to honor, and accordingly the Henry Tudor that he portrays at the end of *Richard III* is a God-fearing patriot and loving husband of the Yorkist princess who is to give birth to the next generation of Tudor monarchs.

Richard III is a tremendous play, both in length and in the bravura depiction of its titular protagonist. It is called a tragedy on its original title page, as are other of these early English history plays. Certainly they present us with brutal deaths and with instructive falls of great men from positions of high authority to degradation and misery. Yet these plays are not tragedies in the classical sense of the term. They contain so much else, and notably they end on a major key: the accession to power of the Tudor dynasty that will give England its great years under Elizabeth. The story line is one of suffering and of eventual salvation, of deliverance by mighty forces of history, and of divine oversight that will not allow England to continue to suffer once she has returned to the true path of duty and decency. In this important sense, the early history plays are like tragicomedies or romances.

Edward III

This play in five acts is sometimes attributed to William Shakespeare, though without much evidence other than the resemblances of this play to Shakespeare's early history plays and an occasional passage. It was not included in the First Folio of 1623. A quarto text was published in 1596; the play must have been written prior to that date, presumably in the early 1590s, when history plays of this sort were much in vogue. It was based largely on Raphael Holinshed's *Chronicles*.

The play depicts Edward III's great victories in France, especially at Crécy (1346) and Poitiers (1356), during the 14th century. Edward is portrayed as a heroic king, and his son Edward, the Black Prince, is even more stalwart than he. Much of the latter part of the play is devoted to military action in France, some of it near Calais. The play opens as Edward justifies his wars (historically, the Hundred Years' War, beginning in 1337) on the basis of genealogical claims that sound like those of Henry V to the French kingdom in *Henry V*. The play *Edward*

III patriotically defends the English claim. The French and their allies—King John, his sons Charles and Philip, the Duke of Lorraine, Lord Villiers, and others—are at times duplicitous and cowardly, though some of the Frenchmen do keep their word. The Scots are presented in an even more unattractive light: King David II and the Douglas cravenly take advantage of England's preoccupation with France to attack England from the rear. They prove no match for the English, however; Edward is able, at Halidon Hill, to avenge England's terrible loss to the Scots at the infamous Battle of Bannockburn in the time of Edward II (1314), which resulted in Scotland's independence.

An attractive sidelight in the play, unhistorical and so engaging that it is a sentimental favorite among critics to have been written by Shakespeare, is the wooing by Edward III of the Countess of Salisbury, daughter of the Earl of Warwick. Living in the north of England during her husband's absence, the Countess is especially vulnerable to Scottish depredations across the border, though she shows herself bravely able to fend them off without much help. Edward, coming north to encounter the Scottish invasion, is smitten with the Countess's charms and proposes a relationship that is plainly adulterous, since the Countess's husband is alive and well, even if necessarily absent from their home. Worse still, Edward falls so under the tyranny of his passion that he uses his great authority over the Earl of Warwick to suggest that he prevail upon his daughter to give in to royal importunity. Eventually the Countess's own fearless virtue, prompting her to threaten suicide if Edward persists, persuades the king that he has erred egregiously in his pursuit of a married woman, however attractive. He comes to his senses and goes on to become England's great warrior king against the French. The episode illustrates both how mighty men have their failings and how the best of them are able to control their own improper instincts. The political ramifications are telling: a king of England is an absolute monarch whom no one may correct except himself. Edward absorbs this useful lesson and is much the stronger for having done so.

▌ Elizabeth I

Elizabeth (1533–1603) was the queen of England during a period, often called the Elizabethan Age, when England asserted itself vigorously as a major European power in politics, commerce, and the arts. Her reign extended from 1558 until her death in 1603.

Although her small kingdom was threatened by grave internal divisions, Elizabeth's blend of shrewdness, courage, and majestic self-display inspired ardent expressions of loyalty and helped unify the nation against foreign enemies. The adulation bestowed upon her both in her lifetime and in the ensuing centuries was not altogether a spontaneous effusion; it was the result of a carefully crafted, brilliantly executed campaign in which the queen fashioned herself as the glittering symbol of the nation's destiny. This political symbolism, common to

Elizabeth I, the Armada portrait by Gower (d. 1596).

monarchies, had more substance than usual, for the queen was by no means a mere figurehead. While she did not wield the absolute power of which Renaissance rulers dreamed, she tenaciously upheld her authority to make critical decisions and to set the central policies of both state and church. The latter half of the 16th century in England is justly called the Elizabethan Age: rarely has the collective life of a whole era been given so distinctively personal a stamp.

Elizabeth's early years were not auspicious. She was born at Greenwich Palace, the daughter of the Tudor king Henry VIII and his second wife, Anne Boleyn. Henry had defied the pope and broken England from the authority of the Roman Catholic church in order to dissolve his marriage with his first wife, Catherine of Aragon, who had borne him a daughter, Mary. Since the king ardently hoped that Anne Boleyn would give birth to the male heir regarded as the key to stable dynastic succession, the birth of a second daughter was a bitter disappointment that dangerously weakened the new queen's position. Before Elizabeth reached her third birthday, her father had her mother beheaded on charges of adultery and treason. Moreover, at Henry's instigation, an act of Parliament declared his marriage with Anne Boleyn invalid from the beginning, thus making their daughter Elizabeth illegitimate, as Roman Catholics had all along claimed her to be. (Apparently the king was undeterred by the logical inconsistency of simultaneously invalidating the marriage and accusing his wife of adultery.) The emotional impact of these events on the little girl, who had been brought up from infancy in a separate household at Hatfield, is not known; presumably no one thought it worth recording. What was noted was her precocious seriousness; at six years old, it was admiringly observed, she had as much gravity as if she were 40.

When in 1537 Henry's third wife, Jane Seymour, gave birth to a son, Edward, Elizabeth receded still further into relative obscurity, but she was not neglected. Despite his capacity for monstrous cruelty, Henry VIII treated all his children with what contemporaries regarded as affection; Elizabeth was present at ceremonial occasions and was declared third in line to the throne. She spent much of the time with her half brother Edward and, from her 10th year onward, profited from the loving attention of her stepmother, Catherine Parr, the king's sixth and last wife. Under a series of distinguished tutors, of whom the best known is the Cambridge humanist Roger Ascham, Elizabeth received the rigorous education normally reserved for male heirs, consisting of a course of studies centering on classical languages, history, rhetoric, and moral philosophy. "Her mind has no womanly weakness," Ascham wrote with the unselfconscious sexism of the age, "her perseverance is equal to that of a man, and her memory long keeps what it quickly picks up." In addition to Greek and Latin, she became fluent in French and Italian, attainments of which she was proud and which were in later years to serve her well in the conduct of diplomacy. Thus steeped in the secular learning of the Renaissance, the quick-witted and intellectually serious princess also studied theology, imbibing the tenets of English Protestantism in its formative period. Her association with the Reformation is critically important, for it shaped the future course of the nation, but it does not appear to have been a personal passion: observers noted the young princess's fascination more with languages than with religious dogma.

With her father's death in 1547 and the accession to the throne of her frail 10-year-old brother, Edward, Elizabeth's life took a perilous turn. Her guardian, the dowager queen Catherine Parr, almost immediately married Thomas Seymour, the lord high admiral. Handsome, ambitious, and discontented, Seymour began to scheme against his powerful older brother, Edward Seymour, protector of the realm during Edward VI's minority. In January 1549, shortly after the death of Catherine Parr, Thomas Seymour was arrested for treason and accused of plotting to marry Elizabeth in order to rule the kingdom. Repeated interrogations of Elizabeth and her servants led to the charge that even when his wife was alive Seymour had on several occasions behaved in a flirtatious and overly familiar manner toward the young princess. Under humiliating close questioning and in some danger, Elizabeth was extraordinarily circumspect and poised. When she was told that Seymour had been beheaded, she betrayed no emotion.

The need for circumspection, self-control, and political acumen became even greater after the death of the Protestant Edward in 1553 and the accession of Elizabeth's older half sister, Mary, a religious zealot set on returning England, by force if necessary, to the Roman Catholic faith. This attempt, along with her unpopular marriage to the ardently Catholic king Philip II of Spain, aroused bitter Protestant opposition. In a charged atmosphere of treasonous rebellion and inquisitorial repression, Elizabeth's life was in grave danger. For though, as her sister demanded, she conformed outwardly to official Catholic observance, she inevitably became the focus and the obvious beneficiary of plots to overthrow the government and restore Protestantism. Arrested and sent to the Tower of London after Sir Thomas Wyatt's rebellion in January 1554, Elizabeth narrowly escaped her mother's fate. Two months later, after extensive interrogation and spying had revealed no conclusive evidence of treason on her part, she was released from the Tower and placed in close custody for a year at Woodstock. The difficulty of her situation eased somewhat, though she was never far from suspicious scrutiny. Throughout the unhappy years of Mary's childless reign, with its burning of Protestants and its military disasters, Elizabeth had continually to protest her innocence, affirm her unwavering loyalty, and proclaim her pious abhorrence of heresy. It was a sustained lesson in survival through self-discipline and the tactful manipulation of appearances.

Many Protestants and Roman Catholics alike assumed that her outward presentation was deceptive, but Elizabeth managed to keep her inward convictions to herself, and in religion as in much else they have remained something of a mystery. There is with Elizabeth a continual gap between a dazzling surface and an interior that she kept carefully concealed. Observers were repeatedly tantalized with what they thought was a glimpse of the interior, only to find that they had been shown another facet of the surface. Everything in Elizabeth's early life taught her to pay careful attention to how she represented herself and how she was represented by others. She learned her lesson well.

At the death of Mary on November 17, 1558, Elizabeth came to the throne amid bells, bonfires, patriotic demonstrations, and other signs of public jubilation. Her entry into London and the great coronation procession that followed were masterpieces of political courtship. "If ever any person," wrote one enthusiastic observer, "had either the gift or the style to win the hearts of people, it was this Queen, and if ever she did express the same it was at that present, in coupling mildness with majesty as she did, and in stately stooping to the meanest sort." Elizabeth's smallest gestures were scrutinized for signs of the policies and tone of the new regime: When an old man in the crowd turned his back on the new queen and wept, Elizabeth exclaimed confidently that he did so out of gladness; when a girl in an allegorical pageant presented her with a Bible in English translation—banned under Mary's reign—Elizabeth kissed the book, held it up reverently, and then laid it on her breast; and when the abbot and monks of Westminster Abbey came to greet her in broad daylight with candles in their hands, she briskly dismissed them with the words "Away with those torches! we can see well enough." Spectators were thus assured that under Elizabeth England had returned, cautiously but decisively, to the Reformation.

The first weeks of her reign were not entirely given over to symbolic gestures and public ceremonial. The queen began at once to form her government and issue proclamations. She reduced the size of the Privy Council, in part to purge some of its Catholic members and in part to make it more efficient as an advisory body; she began a restructuring of the enormous royal household; she carefully balanced the need for substantial administrative and judicial continuity with the desire for change; and she assembled a core of experienced and trustworthy advisers, including William Cecil, Nicholas Bacon, Francis Walsingham, and Nicholas Throckmorton. Chief among these was Cecil (afterward Lord Burghley), whom Elizabeth appointed her principal secretary of state on the morning of her accession and who was to serve her (first in this capacity and after 1571 as lord treasurer) with remarkable sagacity and skill for 40 years.

In the last year of Mary's reign, the Scottish Calvinist preacher John Knox wrote in *The First Blast of the Trumpet Against the Monstrous Regiment of Women* that "God hath revealed to some in this our age that it is more than a monster in nature that a woman should reign and bear empire above man." With the accession of the Protestant Elizabeth, Knox's trumpet was quickly muted, but there remained a widespread conviction, reinforced by both custom and teaching, that while men were naturally endowed with authority, women were temperamentally, intellectually, and morally unfit to govern. Men saw themselves as rational beings; they saw women as creatures likely to be dominated by impulse and passion. Gentlemen were trained in eloquence and the arts of war; gentlewomen were urged to keep silent and attend to their needlework. In men of the upper classes a will to dominate was admired or at least assumed; in women it was viewed as dangerous or grotesque.

Apologists for the queen countered that there had always been significant exceptions, such as the biblical Deborah, the prophetess who had judged Israel. Crown lawyers, moreover, elaborated a mystical legal theory known as "the king's two bodies." When she ascended the throne, according to this theory, the queen's whole being was profoundly altered: her mortal "body natural" was wedded to an immortal "body politic." "I am but one body, naturally considered," Elizabeth declared in her accession speech, "though by [God's] permission a Body Politic to govern." Her body of flesh was subject to the imperfections of all human beings (including those specific to womankind), but the body politic was timeless and perfect. Hence in theory the queen's gender was no threat to the stability and glory of the nation.

Elizabeth made it immediately clear that she intended to rule in more than name only and that she would not subordinate her judgment to that of any one individual or faction. Since her sister's reign did not provide a satisfactory model for female authority, Elizabeth had to improvise a new model, one that would overcome the considerable cultural liability of her sex. Moreover, quite apart from this liability, any English ruler's power to compel obedience had its limits. The monarch was at the pinnacle of the state, but that state was relatively impoverished and weak, without a standing army, an efficient police force, or a highly developed, effective bureaucracy. To obtain sufficient revenue to govern, the crown had to request subsidies and taxes from a potentially fractious and recalcitrant Parliament. Under these difficult circumstances, Elizabeth developed a strategy of rule that blended imperious command with an extravagant, histrionic cult of love.

The cult of Elizabeth as the Virgin Queen wedded to her kingdom was a gradual creation that unfolded over many years, but its roots may be glimpsed at least as early as 1555. At that time, according to a report that reached the French court, Queen Mary had proposed to marry her sister to the staunchly Catholic duke of Savoy; the usually cautious and impassive Elizabeth burst into tears, declaring that she had no wish for any husband. Other matches were proposed and summarily rejected. But in this vulnerable period of her life there were obvious reasons for Elizabeth to bide her time and keep her options open. No one—not even the princess herself—need have taken very seriously her professed desire to remain single. When she became queen, speculation about a suitable match immediately intensified, and the available options became a matter of grave national concern. Beyond the general conviction that the proper role for a woman was that of a wife, the dynastic and diplomatic stakes in the projected royal marriage were extremely high. If Elizabeth died childless, the Tudor line would come to an end. The nearest heir was Mary, Queen of Scots, the granddaughter of Henry VIII's sister Margaret. Mary, a Catholic whose claim was supported by France and other powerful Catholic states, was regarded by Protestants as a nightmarish threat that could best be averted if Elizabeth produced a Protestant heir.

The queen's marriage was critical not only for the question of succession but also for the tangled web of international diplomacy. England, isolated and militarily weak, was sorely in need of the major alliances that an advantageous marriage could forge. Important suitors eagerly came forward: Philip II of Spain, who hoped to renew the link between Catholic Spain and England; Archduke Charles of Austria; Erik XIV, king of Sweden; Henry, duke of Anjou and later king of France; François, duke of Alençon; and others. Many scholars think it unlikely that Elizabeth ever seriously intended to marry any of these aspirants to her hand, for the dangers always outweighed the possible benefits, but she skillfully played one off against another and kept the marriage negotiations going for months, even years, at one moment seeming on the brink of acceptance, at the next veering away toward vows of perpetual virginity. "She is a Princess," the French ambassador remarked, "who can act any part she pleases."

Elizabeth was courted by English suitors as well, most assiduously by her principal favorite, Robert Dudley, earl of Leicester. As master of the horse and a member of the Privy Council, Leicester was constantly in attendance on the queen, who displayed toward him all the signs of an ardent romantic attachment. When in September 1560 Leicester's wife, Amy Robsart, died in a suspicious fall, the favorite seemed poised to marry his royal mistress—so at least widespread rumors had it—but, though the queen's behavior toward him continued to generate scandalous gossip, the decisive step was never taken. Elizabeth's resistance to a marriage she herself seemed to desire may have been politically motivated, for Leicester had many enemies at court and an unsavory reputation in the country at large. But in October 1562 the queen nearly died of smallpox, and, faced with the real possibility of a contested succession and a civil war, even rival factions were likely to have countenanced the marriage.

Probably at the core of Elizabeth's decision to remain single was an unwillingness to compromise her power. Sir Robert Naunton recorded that the queen once said angrily to Leicester, when he tried to insist upon a favor, "I will have here but one mistress and no master." To her ministers she was steadfastly loyal, encouraging their frank counsel and weighing their advice, but she did not cede ultimate authority even to the most trusted. Though she patiently received petitions and listened to anxious advice, she zealously retained her power to make the final decision in all crucial affairs of state. Unsolicited advice could at times be dangerous: when in 1579 a pamphlet was published vehemently denouncing the queen's proposed marriage to the Catholic duke of Alençon, its author John Stubbs and his publisher William Page were arrested and had their right hands chopped off.

Elizabeth's performances—her displays of infatuation, her apparent inclination to marry the suitor of the moment—often convinced even close advisers, so that the level of intrigue and anxiety, always high in royal courts, often rose to a feverish pitch. Far from trying to allay the anxiety, the queen seemed to augment and use it, for she was skilled at manipulating factions. This skill extended beyond marriage negotiations and became one of the hallmarks of her regime. A powerful nobleman would be led to believe that he possessed unique influence over the queen, only to discover that a hated rival shared a similar belief. A golden shower of royal favor—apparent intimacies, public honors, the bestowal of such valuable perquisites as land grants and monopolies—would give way to royal aloofness or, still worse, to royal anger. The queen's anger was particularly aroused by challenges to what she regarded as her prerogative (whose scope she cannily left undefined) and indeed by any unwelcome signs of independence. The courtly atmosphere of vivacity, wit, and romance would then suddenly chill, and the queen's behavior, as her godson Sir John Harington put it, "left no doubtings whose daughter she was." This identification of Elizabeth with her father, and particularly with his capacity for wrath, is something that the queen herself—who never made mention of her mother—periodically invoked.

A similar blend of charm and imperiousness characterized the queen's relations with Parliament, on which she had to depend for revenue. Many sessions of Parliament, particularly in the early years of her rule, were more than cooperative with the queen; they had the rhetorical air of celebrations. But under the strain of the marriage-and-succession question, the celebratory tone, which masked serious policy differences, began over the years to wear thin, and the sessions involved complicated, often acrimonious negotiations between crown and commons. More radical members of Parliament wanted to include in debate broad areas of public policy; the queen's spokesmen struggled to restrict free discussion to government bills. Elizabeth had a rare gift for combining calculated displays of intransigence with equally calculated displays of graciousness and, on rare occasions, a prudent willingness to concede. Whenever possible, she transformed the language of politics into the language of love, likening herself to the spouse or the mother of her kingdom. Characteristic of this rhetorical strategy was her famous "Golden Speech" of 1601, when, in the face of bitter parliamentary opposition to royal monopolies, she promised reforms:

> I do assure you, there is no prince that loveth his subjects better, or whose love can countervail our love. There is no jewel, be it of never so rich a price, which I set before this jewel; I mean, your love: for I do more esteem of it, than of any treasure or riches.

A discourse of rights or interests thus became a discourse of mutual gratitude, obligation, and love. "We all loved her," Harington wrote with just a trace of irony, "for she said she loved us." In her dealings with parliamentary delegations, as with suitors and courtiers, the queen contrived to turn her gender from a serious liability into a distinct advantage.

Elizabeth restored England to Protantism. The Act of

Supremacy, passed by Parliament and approved in 1559, revived the antipapal statutes of Henry VIII and declared the queen supreme governor of the church, while the Act of Uniformity established a slightly revised version of the second Edwardian prayer book as the official order of worship. Elizabeth's government moved cautiously but steadily to transfer these structural and liturgical reforms from the statute books to the local parishes throughout the kingdom. Priests, temporal officers, and men proceeding to university degrees were required to swear an oath to the royal supremacy or lose their positions; absence from Sunday church service was punishable by a fine; royal commissioners sought to ensure doctrinal and liturgical conformity. Many of the nobles and gentry, along with a majority of the common people, remained loyal to the old faith, but all the key positions in the government and church were held by Protestants who employed patronage, pressure, and propaganda, as well as threats, to secure an outward observance of the religious settlement.

But to militant Protestants, including exiles from the reign of Queen Mary newly returned to England from Calvinist Geneva and other centers of continental reform, these measures seemed hopelessly pusillanimous and inadequate. They pressed for a drastic reform of the church hierarchy and church courts, a purging of residual Catholic elements in the prayer book and ritual, and a vigorous searching out and persecution of recusants. Each of these demands was repugnant to the queen. She felt that the reforms had gone far enough and that any further agitation would provoke public disorder, a dangerous itch for novelty, and an erosion of loyalty to established authority. Elizabeth, moreover, had no interest in probing the inward convictions of her subjects; provided that she could obtain public uniformity and obedience, she was willing to let the private beliefs of the heart remain hidden. This policy was consistent with her own survival strategy, her deep conservatism, and her personal dislike of evangelical fervor. When in 1576 the archbishop of Canterbury, Edmund Grindal, refused the queen's orders to suppress certain reformist educational exercises, called "propheseyings," Grindal was suspended from his functions and never restored to them. Upon Grindal's death, Elizabeth appointed a successor, Archbishop Whitgift, who vigorously pursued her policy of an authoritarian ecclesiastical regime and a relentless hostility to Puritan reformers.

If Elizabeth's religious settlement was threatened by Protestant dissidents, it was equally threatened by the recalcitrance and opposition of English Catholics. At first this opposition seemed relatively passive, but a series of crises in the late 1560s and early 1570s disclosed its potential for serious, even fatal, menace. In 1569 a rebellion of feudal aristocrats and their followers in the staunchly Catholic north of England was put down by savage military force, while in 1571 the queen's informers and spies uncovered an international conspiracy against her life, known as the Ridolfi Plot. Both threats were linked at least indirectly to Mary, Queen of Scots, who had been driven from her own kingdom in 1568 and had taken refuge in England. The presence, more as prisoner than as guest, of the woman whom the Roman Catholic church regarded as the rightful queen of England posed a serious political and diplomatic problem for Elizabeth, a problem greatly exacerbated by Mary's restless ambition and penchant for conspiracy. Elizabeth judged that it was too dangerous to let Mary leave the country, but at the same time she firmly rejected the advice of Parliament and many of her councilors that Mary should be executed. So a captive, at once ominous, malevolent, and pathetic, Mary remained.

The alarming increase in religious tension, political intrigue, and violence was not only an internal, English concern. In 1570 Pope Pius V excommunicated Elizabeth and absolved her subjects from any oath of allegiance that they might have taken to her. The immediate effect was to make life more difficult for English Catholics, who were the objects of a suspicion that greatly intensified in 1572 after word reached England of the St. Bartholomew's Day massacre of Protestants (Huguenots) in France. Tension and official persecution of recusants increased in the wake of the daring clandestine missionary activities of English Jesuits, trained on the Continent and smuggled back to England. Elizabeth was under great pressure to become more involved in the continental struggle between Roman Catholics and Protestants, in particular to aid the rebels fighting the Spanish armies in the Netherlands. But she was very reluctant to become involved, in part because she detested rebellion, even rebellion undertaken in the name of Protestantism, and in part because she detested expenditures. Eventually, after vacillations that drove her councilors to despair, she agreed first to provide some limited funds and then, in 1585, to send a small expeditionary force to the Netherlands.

Fears of an assassination attempt against Elizabeth increased after Pope Gregory XIII proclaimed in 1580 that it would be no sin to rid the world of such a miserable heretic. In 1584 Europe's other major Protestant leader, William of Orange, was assassinated. Elizabeth herself showed few signs of concern — throughout her life she was a person of remarkable personal courage—but the anxiety of the ruling elite was intense. In an ugly atmosphere of intrigue, torture and execution of Jesuits, and rumors of foreign plots to kill the queen and invade England, Elizabeth's Privy Council drew up a Bond of Association, pledging its signers, in the event of an attempt on Elizabeth's life, to kill not only the assassins but also the claimant to the throne in whose interest the attempt had been made. The Association was clearly aimed at Mary, whom government spies, under the direction of Sir Francis Walsingham, had by this time discovered to be thoroughly implicated in plots against the queen's life. When Walsingham's men in 1586 uncovered the Babington Plot, another conspiracy to murder Elizabeth, the wretched Queen of Scots, her secret correspondence intercepted and her involvement clearly proved, was doomed. Mary was tried and sentenced to death. Parliament petitioned that the sentence be carried out without delay. For three months the queen hesitated and then with every sign of extreme reluctance signed the death warrant. When the news was brought to her that on February 8, 1587,

Mary had been beheaded, Elizabeth responded with an impressive show of grief and rage. She had not, she wrote to Mary's son, James VI of Scotland, ever intended that the execution actually take place, and she imprisoned the man who had delivered the signed warrant. It is impossible to know how many people believed Elizabeth's professions of grief; Catholics on the Continent wrote bitter denunciations of the queen, while Protestants throughout the kingdom enthusiastically celebrated the death of a woman they had feared and hated.

For years Elizabeth had cannily played a complex diplomatic game with the rival interests of France and Spain, a game comparable to her domestic manipulation of rival factions. State-sanctioned privateering raids, led by Sir Francis Drake and others, on Spanish shipping and ports alternated with conciliatory gestures and peace talks. But by the mid-1580s it became increasingly clear that England could not avoid a direct military confrontation with Spain. Word reached London that the Spanish king, Philip II, had begun to assemble an enormous fleet that would sail to the Netherlands, join forces with a waiting Spanish army led by the duke of Parma, and then proceed to an invasion and conquest of Protestant England. Always reluctant to spend money, the queen had nonetheless authorized sufficient funds during her reign to maintain a fleet of maneuverable, well-armed fighting ships, to which could be added other vessels from the merchant fleet. When in July 1588 the Invincible Armada reached English waters, the queen's ships, in one of the most famous naval encounters in history, defeated the enemy fleet, which then, in an attempt to return to Spain, was all but destroyed by terrible storms.

At the moment when the Spanish invasion was imminently expected, Elizabeth resolved to review in person a detachment of soldiers assembled at Tilbury. Dressed in a white gown and a silver breastplate, she rode through the camp and proceeded to deliver a celebrated speech. Some of her councilors, she said, had cautioned her against appearing before a large, armed crowd, but she did not and would not distrust her faithful and loving people. Nor was she afraid of Parma's army: "I know I have the body of a weak and feeble woman," Elizabeth declared, "but I have the heart and stomach of a king, and of a king of England too." She then promised, "in the word of a Prince," richly to reward her loyal troops, a promise that she characteristically proved reluctant to keep. The scene exemplifies many of the queen's qualities: her courage, her histrionic command of grand public occasions, her rhetorical blending of magniloquence and the language of love, her strategic identification with martial virtues considered male, and even her princely parsimony.

Elizabeth's parsimony did not extend to personal adornments. She possessed a vast repertory of fantastically elaborate dresses and rich jewels. Her passion for dress was bound up with political calculation and an acute self-consciousness about her image. She tried to control the royal portraits that circulated widely in England and abroad, and her appearances in public were dazzling displays of wealth and magnificence. Throughout her reign she moved restlessly from one of her palaces to another—Whitehall, Nonsuch, Greenwich, Windsor, Richmond, Hampton Court, and Oatlands—and availed herself of the hospitality of her wealthy subjects. On her journeys, known as royal progresses, she wooed her people and was received with lavish entertainments. Artists, including poets like Edmund Spenser and painters like Nicholas Hilliard, celebrated her in a variety of mythological guises—as Diana, the chaste goddess of the moon; Astraea, the goddess of justice; Gloriana, the queen of the fairies—and Elizabeth, in addition to adopting these fanciful roles, appropriated to herself some of the veneration that pious Englishmen had directed to the Virgin Mary.

"She imagined," wrote Francis Bacon a few years after the queen's death, "that the people, who are much influenced by externals, would be diverted by the glitter of her jewels, from noticing the decay of her personal attractions." Bacon's cynicism reflects the darkening tone of the last decade of Elizabeth's reign, when her control over her country's political, religious, and economic forces and over her representation of herself began to show severe strains. Bad harvests, persistent inflation, and unemployment caused hardship and a loss of public morale. Charges of corruption and greed led to widespread popular hatred of many of the queen's favorites to whom she had given lucrative and much-resented monopolies. A series of disastrous military attempts to subjugate the Irish culminated in a crisis of authority with her last great favorite, Robert Devereux, the proud earl of Essex, who had undertaken to defeat rebel forces led by Hugh O'Neill, earl of Tyrone. Essex returned from Ireland against the queen's orders, insulted her in her presence, and then made a desperate, foolhardy attempt to raise an insurrection. He was tried for treason and executed on February 25, 1601.

Elizabeth continued to make brilliant speeches, to exercise her authority, and to receive the extravagant compliments of her admirers, but she was, as Sir Walter Raleigh remarked, "a lady surprised by time," and her long reign was drawing to a close. She suffered from bouts of melancholy and ill health and showed signs of increasing debility. Her more astute advisers—among them Lord Burghley's son, Sir Robert Cecil, who had succeeded his father as her principal counselor—secretly entered into correspondence with the likeliest claimant to the throne, James VI of Scotland. Having reportedly indicated James as her successor, Elizabeth died quietly. The nation enthusiastically welcomed its new king. But in a very few years the English began to express nostalgia for the rule of "Good Queen Bess." Long before her death she had transformed herself into a powerful image of female authority, regal magnificence, and national pride, and that image has endured to the present.

Elizabethan Poetry and Prose

English poetry and prose burst into sudden glory in the late 1570s. A decisive shift of taste toward a fluent artistry self-consciously displaying its own grace and sophistication was announced in the works of Edmund Spenser and Sir Philip Sidney. It was accompanied by an upsurge in literary production that came to fruition in the 1590s and 1600s, two decades of astonishing productivity by writers of every persuasion and caliber.

The groundwork was laid in the 30-year period beginning in 1550, a time of slowly increasing confidence in the literary competence of the language and tremendous advances in education, which for the first time produced a substantial English readership, keen for literature and possessing cultivated tastes. This development was underpinned by the technological maturity and accelerating output (mainly in pious or technical subjects) of Elizabethan printing. The Stationers' Company, which controlled the publication of books, was incorporated in 1557, and Richard Tottel's *Miscellany* (1557) revolutionized the relationship of poet and audience by making publicly available lyric poetry, which hitherto had circulated only among a courtly coterie. Spenser was the first major English poet deliberately to use print for the advertisement of his talents.

The Development of the English Language

The prevailing opinion of the language's inadequacy, its lack of "terms" and innate inferiority to the eloquent classical tongues, was combated in the work of the humanists Thomas Wilson, Roger Ascham, and Sir John Cheke, whose treatises on rhetoric, education, and even archery argued in favor of an unaffected vernacular prose and a judicious attitude toward linguistic borrowings. Their stylistic ideals are attractively embodied in Ascham's educational tract *The Scholemaster* (1570), and their tonic effect on that particularly Elizabethan art, translation, can be felt in the earliest important examples, Sir Thomas Hoby's Castiglione (1561) and Sir Thomas North's Plutarch (1579). A further stimulus was the religious upheaval that took place in the middle of the century. The desire of Reformers to address as comprehensive an audience as possible—the bishop and the boy who follows the plough, as Tyndale put it—produced the first true classics of English prose: the reformed Anglican Book of Common Prayer (1549, 1552, 1559); John Foxe's *Actes and Monuments* (1563), which celebrates the martyrs, great and small, of English Protestantism; and the various English versions of Scripture, including translations by William Tyndale (1525) and Miles Coverdale (1535), the Geneva Bible (1560), and the syncretic Authorized Version (or King James Version, 1611). The latter's combination of grandeur and plainness is justly celebrated, even if it represents an idiom never spoken in heaven or on earth. Nationalism inspired by the Reformation motivated the historical chronicles of the capable and stylish Edward Hall (1548), who bequeathed to Shakespeare the tendentious Tudor interpretation of the 15th century, and of the rather less capable Raphael Holinshed (1577). John Ponet's remarkable *Short Treatise of Politic Power* (1556) is a vigorous polemic against Mary Tudor, whom he saw as a papist tyrant.

In verse, Tottel's much reprinted *Miscellany* generated a series of imitations and, by popularizing the lyrics of Sir Thomas Wyatt and Henry Howard, earl of Surrey, carried into the 1570s the tastes of the early Tudor court. The newer poets collected by Tottel and other anthologists include Nicholas Grimald, Richard Edwardes, George Turberville, Barnabe Googe, George Gascoigne, Sir John Harington, and many others, of whom Gascoigne is the most prominent. The modern preference for the ornamental manner of the next generation has eclipsed these poets, who continued the tradition of plain, weighty verse, addressing themselves to ethical and didactic themes and favoring the meditative lyric, satire, and epigram. But their taste for economy, restraint, and aphoristic density was, in the verse of Ben Jonson and John Donne, to outlive the cult of elegance. The period's major project was *A Mirror for Magistrates* (1559; enlarged editions 1563, 1578, 1587), a collection of verse laments by several hands, purporting to be spoken by participants in the Wars of the Roses and preaching the Tudor doctrine of obedience. The quality is uneven, but Thomas Sackville's "Induction" and Thomas Churchyard's *Legend of Shore's Wife* are distinguished, and the intermingling of history, tragedy, and political morality would be influential on the drama.

Sidney and Spenser

With the work of Sidney and Spenser, Tottel's contributors suddenly began to look old-fashioned. Sidney epitomized the new Renaissance "universal man": a courtier, diplomat, soldier, and poet whose *Defence of Poesie* included the first considered account of the state of English letters. Sidney's treatise defends literature on the ground of its unique power to teach, but his real emphasis is on its delight, its ability to depict the world not as it is but as it ought to be. This quality of "forcefulness or *energia*" he himself demonstrated in his sonnet sequence of unrequited desire, *Astrophel and Stella* (written c. 1582, published 1591). His *Arcadia*, in its first version (written c. 1577–1580), is a pastoral romance in which courtiers disguised as Amazons and shepherds make love and sing delicate experimental verses. The revised version (written c. 1580–1584, published 1590, now lacking the last three books of the first version, which were added in 1593), vastly expanded but abandoned in midsentence, added sprawling plots of heroism in love and war, philosophical and political discourses, and set pieces of aristocratic etiquette. Sidney was a dazzling and assured innovator whose pioneering of new forms and stylistic melody was seminal for his generation. His public fame was as an aristocratic champion of an aggressively Protestant foreign policy, but Elizabeth had no time for idealistic warmongering, and the unresolved conflicts in his fiction—desire against restraint, heroism against patience, rebellion against submission—mirror his own discomfort with his situation as an unsuccessful courtier.

Protestantism also loomed large in the life of Spenser. He enjoyed the patronage of the earl of Leicester, who sought to advance militant Protestantism at court, and his poetic manifesto, *The Shepheardes Calender* (1579), covertly praised Archbishop Edmund Grindal, who had been suspended by Elizabeth for his Puritan sympathies. Spenser's masterpiece, *The Faerie Queene* (1590–1609), is an epic of Protestant nationalism in which the villains are infidels or papists, the hero is King Arthur, and the central value is married chastity.

Spenser was one of the humanistically trained breed of public servants, and the *Calender,* an expertly crafted collection of pastoral eclogues, both advertised his talents and announced his epic ambitions, the exquisite lyric gift that it reveals being voiced again in the marriage poems *Epithalamion* (1595) and *Prothalamion* (1596). With *The Faerie Queene* he achieved the central poem of the Elizabethan period. Its form fuses the medieval allegory with the Italian romantic epic; its purpose was "to fashion a gentleman or noble person in virtuous and gentle discipline." The plan was for 12 books (six were completed), focusing on 12 virtues exemplified in the quests of 12 knights from the court of Gloriana, the Faerie Queene, a symbol for Elizabeth herself. Arthur, in quest of Gloriana's love, would appear in each book and come to exemplify Magnificence, the complete man. Spenser took the decorative chivalry of the Elizabethan court festivals and reworked it through a constantly shifting veil of allegory, so that the knight's adventures and loves build into a complex, multileveled portrayal of the moral life. The verse, a spacious and slow-moving, nine-lined stanza, and archaic language frequently rise to an unrivaled sensuousness.

The Faerie Queene was a public poem, addressed to the queen, and politically it echoed the hopes of the Leicester circle for government motivated by godliness and militancy. Spenser's increasing disillusion with the court and with the active life, a disillusion noticeable in the later books and in his bitter satire *Colin Clouts Come Home Againe* of 1591, voiced the fading of these expectations in the last decade of Elizabeth's reign, the beginning of that remarkable failure of political and cultural confidence in the monarchy. In the "Mutabilitie Cantos," melancholy fragments of a projected seventh book (published posthumously in 1609), Spenser turned away from the public world altogether, toward the ambiguous consolations of eternity.

The lessons taught by Sidney and Spenser in the cultivation of melodic smoothness and graceful refinement appear to good effect in the subsequent virtuoso outpouring of lyrics and sonnets. These are among the most engaging achievements of the age, though the outpouring was itself partly a product of frustration, as a generation trained to expect office or preferment but faced with courtly parsimony channeled its energies in new directions in search of patronage. For Sidney's fellow courtiers, pastoral and love lyric were also a means of obliquely expressing one's relationship with the queen, of advancing a proposal or an appeal.

The Elizabethan Lyric

Virtually every Elizabethan poet tried his hand at the lyric; few, if any, failed to write one that is not still anthologized today. The fashion for interspersing prose fiction with lyric interludes, begun in the *Arcadia*, was continued by Robert Greene and Thomas Lodge (notably in the latter's *Rosalynde*, 1590, the source for Shakespeare's *As You Like It*), and in the theaters plays of every kind were enlivened by songs both popular and courtly. Fine examples are in the plays of John Lyly, George Peele, Thomas Nashe, Ben Jonson, and Thomas Dekker (though all, of course, are outshone by Shakespeare). The most important influence, though, was the outstanding richness of late Tudor music, in both the native tradition of expressive lute song, represented by John Dowland, and the complex Italianate madrigal newly imported by William Byrd and Thomas Morley. The foremost talent among lyricists, Thomas Campion, was composer as well as poet; his songs (four *Bookes of Ayres*, 1601–1617) are unsurpassed for their clarity, harmoniousness, and rhythmic subtlety. Even the work of a lesser talent, however, such as Nicholas Breton, is remarkable for the suggestion of depth and poise in the slightest performances; the smoothness and apparent spontaneity of Elizabethan lyric conceals a consciously ordered and labored artifice, attentive to decorum and rhetorical fitness. These are not personal but public pieces, intended for singing and governed by a Neoplatonic aesthetic in which delight is a means of addressing the moral sense and harmonizing and attuning the auditor's mind to the discipline of reason and virtue. This necessitates a deliberate narrowing of scope—to the readily comprehensible situations of pastoral or Petrarchan hope and despair—and makes for a certain uniformity of effect, albeit an agreeable one. The lesser talents are well displayed in the miscellanies *The Phoenix Nest* (1593), *Englands Helicon* (1600), and *A Poetical Rhapsody* (1602).

The Sonnet Sequence

The publication of Sidney's *Astrophel and Stella* in 1591 generated an equally extraordinary vogue for the sonnet sequence; Sidney's principal imitators being Samuel Daniel, Michael Drayton, Fulke Greville, Spenser, and Shakespeare, and his lesser, Henry Constable, Barnabe Barnes, Giles Fletcher, Thomas Lodge, Richard Barnfield, and many more. *Astrophel* had recreated the Petrarchan world of proud beauty and despairing lover in a single, brilliant stroke, though in English hands the preferred division of the sonnet into three quatrains and a couplet gave Petrarch's contemplative form a more forensic turn, investing it with an argumentative terseness and epigrammatic sting. Within the common ground shared by the sequences there is much diversity. Only Sidney's sonnet sequences endeavor to tell a story, the others being more loosely organized as variations focusing on a central (usually fictional) relationship. Daniel's *Delia* (1592) is eloquent and elegant, dignified and high-minded; Drayton's *Ideas Mirrour* (1594; much revised by 1619) rises to a strongly imagined, passionate intensity; Spenser's *Amoretti* (1595) celebrates, unusually, fulfilled sexual love achieved within marriage. Shakespeare's sonnets (published 1609) present a different world altogether, the conventions upside down, the lady no beauty but dark and treacherous, the loved one genuinely beyond considerations of sexual possession because he is a boy. The sonnet tended to gravitate toward correctness or politeness, and for most readers its chief pleasure must have been rhetorical, in its forceful pleading and consciously exhibited artifice, but under the pressure of Shakespeare's urgent metaphysical concerns, dramatic toughness, and shifting and highly charged ironies, the form's conventional limits were exploded.

Other Poetic Styles

Sonnet and lyric represent one tradition of verse within the period, that most conventionally delineated as Elizabethan, but the picture is complicated by the coexistence of other poetic styles in which ornament was distrusted or turned to different purposes; the sonnet was even parodied by Sir John Davies in his *Gulling Sonnets* (c. 1594) and by the Jesuit poet Robert Southwell. A particular stimulus to experiment was the variety of new possibilities made available by verse translation, from Richard Stanyhurst's extraordinary *Aeneid* (1582), in quantitative hexameter and littered with obscure or invented diction, and Sir John Harington's version of Ariosto's *Orlando Furioso* (1591), with its Byronic ease and narrative fluency, to Christopher Marlowe's blank verse rendering of *Lucan's First Book* (published 1600), probably the finest Elizabethan translation.

The genre to benefit most from translation was the epyllion, or little epic. This short narrative in verse was usually on a mythological subject, taking most of its material from Ovid, either his *Metamorphoses* (English version by Arthur Golding, 1565–1567) or his *Heroides* (English version by George Turberville, 1567). This form flourished from Thomas Lodge's *Scillaes Metamorphosis* (1589) to Francis Beaumont's *Salmacis and Hermaphroditus* (1602) and is best represented by Marlowe's *Hero and Leander* (published 1598) and Shakespeare's *Venus and*

Adonis (1593). Ovid's reputation as an esoteric philosopher left its mark on George Chapman's *Ovid's Banquet of Sense* (1595) and Drayton's *Endimion and Phoebe* (1595), in which the love of mortal for goddess becomes a parable of wisdom. But Ovid's real attraction was as an authority on the erotic, and most epyllia treat physical love with sophistication and sympathy, unrelieved by the gloss of allegory—a tendency culminating in John Marston's *The Metamorphosis of Pigmalion's Image* (1598), a poem that has shocked tender sensibilities. Inevitably, the shift of attitude had an effect on style: for Marlowe the experience of translating (inaccurately) Ovid's *Amores* meant a gain for *Hero and Leander* in terms of urbanity and, more important, wit.

With the epyllion comes a hint of the tastes of the following reign, and a similar shift of taste can be felt among those poets of the 1590s who began to modify the ornamental style in the direction of native plainness or classical restraint. An astute courtier like Sir John Davies might, in his *Orchestra* (1596) and *Hymns of Astraea* (1599), write confident panegyrics to the aging Elizabeth, but in Sir Walter Raleigh's "Eleventh Book of the Ocean to Cynthia," a kind of broken pastoral eclogue, praise of the queen is undermined by an obscure but eloquent sense of hopelessness and disillusionment. For Raleigh the complimental manner seems to be disintegrating under the weight of disgrace and isolation at court; his scattered lyrics, notably that contemptuous dismissal of the court, "The Lie," often draw their resonance from the resources of the plain style. Another courtier whose writing suggests similar pressures is Fulke Greville, Lord Brooke. Greville's *Caelica* (published 1633) begins as a conventional sonnet sequence but gradually abandons Neoplatonism for pessimistic reflections on religion and politics. Other works in his sinewy and demanding verse include philosophical treatises and unperformed melodramas (*Alaham* and *Mustapha*) that have a somber Calvinist tone, presenting humanity as vulnerable creatures inhabiting a world of unresolved contradictions:

Oh wearisome condition of humanity!
Born under one law, to another bound;
Vainly begot, and yet forbidden vanity,
Created sick, commanded to be sound.

(*Mustapha*, chorus)

Greville was a friend of the earl of Essex, whose revolt against Elizabeth ended in 1601 on the scaffold, and other poets on the edge of the Essex circle fueled the taste for aristocratic heroism and individualist ethics. George Chapman's masterpiece, his translation of Homer (1598), is dedicated to Essex, and his original poems are intellectual and recondite, often deliberately difficult and obscure; his abstruseness is a means of restricting his audience to a worthy, understanding elite. Samuel Daniel, in his verse *Epistles* (1603), written to various noblemen, strikes a mean between plainness and compliment; his *Musophilus* (1599), dedicated to Greville, defends the worth of poetry but says there are too many frivolous wits writing. The cast of Daniel's mind is stoical, and his language is classically precise. His major project was a verse history of *The Civil Wars between the Two Houses of Lancaster and York* (1595–1609), and versified history is also strongly represented in the *Legends* (1593–1607), *Barons' Wars* (1596, 1603), and *Englands Heroicall Epistles* (1597) of Michael Drayton.

The form that really set its face against Elizabethan politeness was the satire. Satire was related to the complaint, of which there were notable examples by Daniel (*The Complaint of Rosamond*, 1592) and Shakespeare (*The Rape of Lucrece*, 1594), and these are dignified and tragic laments in supple verse, but the Elizabethans mistakenly held the term *satire* to derive from the Greek *satyros* ("satyr") and so set out to match their manner to their matter and make their verses snarl. In the works of the principal satirists, John Donne (five satires, 1593–1598), Joseph Hall (*Virgidemiarum*, 1597–1598), and John Marston (*Certaine Satyres* and *The Scourge of Villainy*, 1598), the denunciation of vice and folly repeatedly tips into invective, raillery, and sheer abuse. The versification of Donne's satires is frequently so rough as barely to be verse at all; Hall apologized for not being harsh enough, and Marston was himself pilloried in Ben Jonson's play *Poetaster* (1601) for using ridiculously difficult language. "Vex all the world," wrote Marston to himself, "so that thyself be pleased." The satirists popularized a new persona, that of the malcontent who denounces his society not from above but from within, and their continuing attraction resides in their self-contradictory delight in the world they profess to abhor and their evident fascination with the minutiae of life in court and city. They were enthusiastically followed by Everard Guilpin, Samuel Rowlands, Thomas Middleton, and Cyril Tourneur, and so scandalous was the flood of satires that in 1599 their printing was banned. Thereafter the form survived in Jonson's classically balanced epigrams and poems of the good life, but its more immediate impact was on the drama, in helping to create the vigorously skeptical voices that people *The Revenger's Tragedy* and *Hamlet.*

Prose Styles

Delineation of the development of Elizabethan prose begins with the 1570s. Prose was easily the principal medium in the Elizabethan period, and despite the mid-century uncertainties over the language's weaknesses and strengths—whether coined and imported words should be admitted; whether the structural modeling of English prose on Latin writing was beneficial or, as Bacon would complain, a pursuit of "choiceness of phrase" at the expense of "soundness of argument"—the general attainment of prose writing was uniformly high, as is often manifested in contexts not conventionally imaginative or "literary," such as tracts, pamphlets, and treatises. The obvious instance of such casual success is Richard Hakluyt's *Principall Navigations, Voiages, and Discoveries of the English Nation* (1589; expanded 1598–1600), a massive collection of travelers' tales, of which some are highly accomplished narratives. William Harrison's gossipy, entertaining *Description of England* (1577), Philip Stubbes's excitable and humane social critique *The Anatomy of Abuses* (1583), Reginald Scot's anecdotal *Discovery of Witchcraft* (1584), and John Stow's invaluable *Survey of London* (1598) also deserve passing mention. William Kempe's account of his morris dance from London to Norwich, *Kempe's Nine Days' Wonder* (1600), has great charm.

The writers listed above all use an unpretentious style, enlivened with a vivid vocabulary; the early prose fiction, on the other hand, delights in ingenious formal embellishment at the expense of narrative economy. This runs up against preferences ingrained in the modern reader by the novel, but Elizabethan fiction is not at all novelistic and finds room for debate, song, and the conscious elaboration of style. The unique exception is George Gascoigne's "Adventures of Master F. J." (1573), a tale of thwarted love set in an English great house, which is the first success in English imaginative prose. Gascoigne's story has a surprising authenticity and almost psychological realism (it may be autobiographical), but even so it is heavily imbued with the influence of Castiglione.

The existence of an audience for polite fiction was signaled in the collections of stories imported from France and Italy by William Painter (1566), Geoffrey Fenton (1577), and George Pettie (1576). Pettie, who claimed not to care "to displease twenty men to please one woman," believed his readership was substantially female. There were later collections by Barnaby Rich (1581) and George Whetstone (1583); historically, their importance was as sources of plots for many Elizabethan plays. The direction fiction was to take was established by John Lyly's *Euphues: The Anatomy of Wit* (1578), which, with its sequel *Euphues and His England* (1580), set a fashion for an extreme rhetorical mannerism that came to be known as "euphuism." The priggish plot of *Euphues*—a rake's fall from virtue and his recovery—is but an excuse for a series of debates, letters, and speechifyings, thick with assonance, antithesis, parallelism, and balance and displaying a pseudoscientific learning. Lyly's style was to be successful on the stage, but in fiction its density and monotony are wearing. The other major prose work of the 1570s, Sidney's *Arcadia,* is no less rhetorical (Abraham Fraunce illustrated his handbook of style, *The Arcadian Rhetoric*, 1588, almost entirely with examples from the *Arcadia*), but with Sidney rhetoric is in the service of psychological insight and an exciting plot. Dozens of imitations of *Arcadia* and *Euphues* followed from the pens of Robert Greene, Thomas Lodge, Anthony Munday, Emanuel Forde, and others; none has much distinction.

Prose was to be decisively transformed through its involvement in the bitter and learned controversies of the 1570s and 1580s over the reform of the English church and the problems the controversies raised in matters of authority, obedience, and conscience. The fragile ecclesiastical compromise threatened to collapse under the demands for further reformation made by Elizabeth's more godly subjects, and its defense culminated in Richard Hooker's *Of the Laws of Ecclesiastical Polity* (eight books, 1593–1662), the first English classic of serious prose. Hooker's is a monumental work, structured in massive and complex paragraphs brilliantly recreating the orotund style of Cicero. His air of maturity and detachment has recommended him to modern tastes, but no more than his opponents was he above the cut and thrust of controversy. On the contrary, his magisterial rhetoric was designed all the more effectively to fix blame onto his enemies, and even his account (in books 6 to 8) of the relationship of church and state was deemed too sensitive for publication in the 1590s.

More decisive for English fiction was the appearance of the "Martin Marprelate" tracts of 1588–1590. These seven pamphlets argued the Puritan case but with an unpuritanical scurrility and created great scandal by hurling invective and abuse at Elizabeth's bishops with comical gusto. The bishops employed Lyly and Thomas Nashe to reply to Marprelate, and the consequence may be read in Nashe's prose satires of the following decade, especially *Piers Penniless His Supplication to the Devil* (1592), *The Unfortunate Traveller* (1594), and *Lenten Stuffe*

(1599), the latter a mock encomium on red herring. Nashe's "extemporal vein" makes fullest use of the flexibility of colloquial speech and delights in nonsense, redundancy, and disconcerting shifts of tone, which demand an answering agility from the reader. His language is probably the most profusely inventive of all Elizabethan writers', and he even makes the low-life pamphlets of Robert Greene (1591–1592), with their sensational tales from the underworld, look conventional. His only rival is Thomas Deloney, whose *Jack of Newbury* (1597), *The Gentle Craft* (1597–1598), and *Thomas of Reading* (1600) are enduringly attractive for their depiction of the lives of ordinary citizens, interspersed with elements of romance, jest book, and folktale. Deloney's entirely convincing dialogue indicates how important for the development of a flexible prose must have been the example of a flourishing theater in Elizabethan London. In this respect, as in so many others, the role of the drama was crucial.

Elizabethan Theater

In the Elizabethan and early Stuart period the theater was the focal point of the age. Public life was shot through with theatricality—monarchs ruled with ostentatious pageantry, rank and status were defined in a rigid code of dress—while on the stages the tensions and contradictions working to change the nation were embodied and played out. More than any other form, the drama addressed itself to the total experience of its society. Playgoing was inexpensive, and the playhouse yards were thronged with apprentices, fishwives, laborers, and the like, but the same play that was performed to citizen spectators in the afternoon would often be restaged at court by night. The drama's power to activate complex, multiple perspectives on a single issue or event resides in its sensitivity to the competing prejudices and sympathies of this diverse audience.

Moreover, the theater was fully responsive to the developing technical sophistication of nondramatic literature. In the hands of Shakespeare the blank verse employed for translation by the earl of Surrey became a medium infinitely mobile between extremes of formality and intimacy, while prose encompassed both the control of theologian Richard Hooker and the immediacy of pamphleteer, poet, playwright, and novelist Thomas Nashe. This was above all a spoken drama, glorying in the theatrical energies of language. And the stage was able to attract the most technically accomplished writers of its day because it offered, uniquely, a literary career with some realistic prospect of financial return. The decisive event was the opening of the first purpose-built London playhouse in 1576, and during the next 70 years some 20 theaters more are known to have operated. The quantity and diversity of plays they commissioned is little short of astonishing.

So the London theaters were a meeting ground of humanism and popular taste. They inherited, on the one hand, a tradition of humanistic drama current at court, the universities, and the Inns of Court (collegiate institutions responsible for legal education). This tradition involved the revival of classical plays and attempts to adapt Latin conventions to English, particularly to reproduce the type of tragedy, with its choruses, ghosts, and sententiously formal verse, associated with Seneca (10 tragedies by Seneca in English translation appeared in 1581). A fine example of the type is *Gorboduc* (1561), by Thomas Sackville and Thomas Norton, a tragedy based on British chronicle history that draws for Elizabeth's benefit a grave political moral about irresponsible government. It is also the first English play in blank verse. On the other hand, all the professional companies performing in London continued also to tour in the provinces, and the stage was never allowed to lose contact with its roots in country show, pastime, and festival. The simple moral scheme that pitted virtues against vices in the mid-Tudor interlude was never entirely submerged in more sophisticated drama, and the character "Vice," the tricksy villain of the morality play, survives, in infinitely more amusing and terrifying form, in Shakespeare's *Richard III*. Another survival was the clown or fool, apt at any moment to step beyond the play's illusion and share jokes directly with the spectators. The intermingling of traditions is clear in two farces, Nicholas Udall's *Ralph Roister Doister* (1553) and the anonymous *Gammer Gurton's Needle* (1559), in which academic pastiche is overlaid with country game; and what the popular tradition did for tragedy is indicated in Thomas Preston's *Cambises, King of Persia* (c. 1560), a blood-and-thunder tyrant play with plenty of energetic spectacle and comedy. A third tradition was that of revelry and masques, practiced at the princely courts across Europe and preserved in England in the witty and impudent productions of the schoolboy troupes of choristers who sometimes played in London alongside the professionals. An early play related to this kind is the first English prose comedy, George Gascoigne's *Supposes* (1566), translated from a reveling play in Italian. Courtly revel reached its apogee in England in the ruinously expensive court masques staged for James I and Charles I, magnificent displays of song, dance, and changing scenery performed before a tiny aristocratic audience and glorifying the king. The principal masque writer was Ben Jonson, the scene designer Inigo Jones.

The first generation of professional playwrights in England was known collectively as the "university wits." Their nickname identifies their social pretensions, but their drama was primarily middle-class, patriotic, and romantic. Their preferred subjects were historical or pseudo-historical, mixed with clowning, music, and love interest. At times plot virtually evaporated; George Peele's *Old Wives' Tale* (c. 1595) and Nashe's *Summer's Last Will and Testament* (1600) are simply popular shows, charming medleys of comic turns, spectacle, and song. Peele was a civic poet, and his serious plays are bold and pageant-like; *The Arraignment of Paris* (1584) is a pastoral entertainment, designed to compliment Elizabeth. Robert Greene's specialty was comical histories, interweaving a serious plot set among kings with comic action involving clowns. In his *Friar Bacon and Friar Bungay* (1594) and *James IV* (1598) the antics of vulgar characters complement but also criticize the follies of their betters. Only John Lyly, writing for the choristers, endeavored to achieve a courtly refinement. His *Gallathea* (1584) and *Endimion* (1591) are fantastic comedies in which courtiers, nymphs, and goddesses make rarefied love in intricate, artificial patterns, the very stuff of courtly dreaming.

Shakespeare's perception of a crisis in public norms and private belief became the overriding concern of the drama until the closing of the theaters in 1642. The prevailing manner of the playwrights who succeeded him was realistic, satirical, and antiromantic, and their comedies and tragedies focused predominantly on those two symbolic locations, the city and the court, with their typical activities, the pursuit of wealth and power. "Riches and glory," wrote Sir Walter Raleigh, "Machiavel's two marks to shoot at" had become the universal aims, and this situation was addressed by both "city comedy" and "tragedy of state." Increasingly, it was on the stages that the rethinking of early Stuart assumptions took place.

On the one hand, in the works of Thomas Heywood, Thomas Dekker, John Day, Samuel Rowley, and others, the old tradition of festive comedy was reoriented toward the celebration of confidence in the dynamically expanding commercial metropolis. Heywood claimed to have been involved in some 200 plays, and they include fantastic adventures starring citizen heroes, spirited, patriotic, and inclined to a leveling attitude in social matters. His masterpiece, *A Woman Killed with Kindness* (1603), is a middle-class tragedy. Dekker was a kindred spirit, best seen in his *Shoemakers' Holiday* (1599), a celebration of citizen brotherliness and Dick Whittington–like success, which nevertheless faces squarely up to the hardships of work, thrift, and the contempt of the great. On the other hand, the very industriousness that the likes of Heywood viewed with civic pride became in the hands of Ben Jonson, George Chapman,

John Marston, and Thomas Middleton a sign of aggression, avarice, and anarchy, symptomatic of the sicknesses in society at large.

A CLOSER LOOK
Shakespeare on Theater
by Alvin B. Kernan

A hundred yards or so southeast of the new Globe Theatre is a vacant lot surrounded by a corrugated-iron fence marked with a bronze plaque as the site of the original Globe Theatre of 1599. A little closer to the new Globe, one can peer through dirty slit windows into a dimly lit space in the basement of a new office building, next to London Bridge, where about two-thirds of the foundations of the Elizabethan Rose Theatre can barely be made out. A little farther to the west, the new Globe rises up on the Bankside, asserting definite knowledge of William Shakespeare's theater and deserving praise for doing so; but the difficulty of seeing the earlier theaters in the shadows of the past better represents our understanding of performance in Shakespeare's theater.

Acting style—realistic or melodramatic—stage settings, props and machinery, swordplay, costumes, the speed with which the lines were delivered, length of performance, entrances and exits, boys playing the female roles, and other performance details remain problematic. Even the audience—rowdy, middle-class, or intellectual—is difficult to see clearly. Scholars have determined something of the mise-en-scène, but not nearly enough, and while the historians continue their painstaking researches, the best general sense of Shakespeare in his theater still comes from the little plays within his plays that across the centuries still give us something of the feel of performance in the Elizabethan theater.

The internal play appears frequently in the early plays *The*

Taming of the Shrew, *Love's Labour's Lost*, and *A Midsummer Night's Dream*. The *Taming of the Shrew*, for example, is a theatrical tour de force, consisting of plays set within plays and actors watching other actors acting, seemingly extending into infinity. All the world is a stage in Padua, where the theater is the true image of life. In the outermost frame-play, the drunken tinker Christopher Sly is picked out of the mud by a rich lord and transported to his house. A little pretense is arranged, purely for amusement, and when Sly awakes he finds himself in rich surroundings, addressed as a nobleman, obeyed in every wish, and waited on by a beautiful wife. At this point professional players appear, to provide entertainment. They are warmly welcomed and fed, and then they put on a play before Sly about the taming of Kate the shrew.

Shakespeare records the problems of playing and of audiences in more detail in *A Midsummer Night's Dream*. No players could be more hopeless than Nick Bottom, the weaver, and his amateur friends, who, in the hope of winning a small pension, perform the internal play, *Pyramus and Thisbe*, to celebrate the triple marriage of Duke Theseus and two of his courtiers. Bottom's company is so literal-minded as to require that the moon actually shine, that the wall through which Pyramus and Thisbe speak be solidly there, and that the actor who plays the lion assure the ladies in the audience that he is only a make-believe lion. The literalness that lies behind such a materialistic conception of theater is at odds with Shakespeare's poetic drama, which created most of its illusion with words, rich costumes, and a few props. In other respects too, the actors' stumbling rants, missed cues, mispronounced words and lines, willingness to converse directly with the audience, doggerel verse, and general ineptitude constitute a playwright's nightmare of dramatic illusion trampled into nonsense.

The courtly audience at *Pyramus and Thisbe* is socially superior to the actors but little more sophisticated about what makes a play work. The duke does understand that though this play may be, as his betrothed, Hippolyta, says, "the silliest stuff" he ever heard, it lies within the power of a gracious audience to improve it, for the best of actors "are but shadows; and the worst are no worse, if imagination amend them." But the nobles in the audience have little of the necessary audience imagination. They mock the actors and talk loudly among themselves during the performance. They are as literal-minded in their own way as the actors, and, as if unaware that they too are actors sitting on a stage, they laugh at what unrealistic and trivial things all plays and players are.

The necessity for "symbolic performance," which is indirectly defended in these early plays by showing a too-realistic opposite, is explained and directly apologized for in *Henry V*, written about 1599, where a Chorus speaks for the "bending author" and his actors who "force a play" on the "unworthy scaffold," the stage of the Globe's "wooden O." Here "time, . . . numbers, and due course of things, / . . . cannot in their huge and proper life / Be . . . presented" by players and a playwright who unavoidably must "in little room [confine] mighty men."

In *Hamlet* (c. 1599–1601) Shakespeare offers his most detailed image of theatrical performance. Here a professional repertory troupe, similar to Shakespeare's own Lord Chamberlain's Men, comes to Elsinore and performs *The Murder of Gonzago* before the Danish court. Once arrived at the Danish palace, the players are servants, and their low social status determines their treatment by the king's councilor, Polonius; but Hamlet greets them warmly: "You are welcome, masters; welcome, all. I am glad to see thee well. Welcome, good friends." He jokes familiarly with the boy who plays female parts about his voice deepening, which will end his ability to play these roles, and twits one of the younger players about his new beard: "O, old friend! Why, thy face is valanced since I saw thee last. Com'st thou to beard me in Denmark?" Hamlet is a theater buff, like one of the young lords or lawyers from the Inns of Court who sat on the stage or in the gallery boxes above the stage in the London theaters and commented loudly and wittily on the action. Like them too he knows the latest Neoclassical aesthetic standards and looks down on what he considers the crudity of the popular theater: its ranting tragedians, melodramatic acting styles, parts "to tear a cat in," bombastic blank verse, "inexplicable dumb shows," vulgar clowns who improvise too much, and the crude audience of "groundlings" who watch the play from the pit. The prince has elevated views of acting—"Suit the action to the word, the word to the action, . . . o'erstep not the modesty of nature"—and of play construction—"well digested in the scenes, set down with as much modesty as cunning."

The players fail to meet Hamlet's Neoclassical standards in both their acting style and their plays. *The Murder of Gonzago* is an old-fashioned, rhetorical, bombastic tragedy, structured like a morality play, beginning with a dumb show and filled with stiff formal speeches. But the play does "hold as 'twere the mirror up to nature, to show virtue her feature, scorn her own image, and the very age and body of the time his form and pressure." *The Murder of Gonzago*, for all its artistic crudity, reveals the hidden disease of Denmark, the murder of the old king by his brother.

But the effect on the audience of this theatrical truth is not what either Hamlet or Shakespeare might hope for. Gertrude fails to see, or ignores, the mirror of her own unfaithfulness held up to her by the player queen: "The lady doth protest too much, methinks." Claudius, realizing his crime is known, immediately plots to murder Hamlet. Even Hamlet the critic is a bad audience. During the performance he makes loud remarks to other members of the audience, baits the actors, criticizes the play, and misses its main point about the necessity of accepting the imperfections of the world and of oneself.

Performance in these internal plays is always unsatisfactory in some respect, and the audience must for the most part read Shakespeare's own views on theatrical matters in the reverse of these mirror stages. Only near the end of his career does Shakespeare present an idealized theater of absolute illusion, perfect actors, and a receptive audience. In *The Tempest* (c. 1611), Prospero, living on a mysterious ocean island, is a magician whose art consists of staging redemptive illusions: storm and shipwreck, an allegorical banquet, "living drolleries," a marriage masque, moral tableaux, mysterious songs, and emblematic set pieces. All of these "playlets" have for once the desired effect on most of their audiences, bringing them to an admission of former crimes, repentance, and forgiveness. In Ariel, the spirit of fancy and playfulness, and his "rabble" of "meaner fellows," the playwright at last finds perfect actors who execute his commands with lightning swiftness, taking any shape desired in an instant. Prospero's greatest play is his "masque of Juno and Ceres," which he stages as an engagement celebration for his daughter and Prince Ferdinand. The masque tells the young lovers of the endless variety, energy, and fruitfulness of the world and reassures them that these things will be theirs to enjoy in their marriage.

But Shakespeare's old doubts about plays, theaters, players, and audiences still are not silenced. Prospero's masque is broken off by a crowd of drunken rowdies, and he, like some medieval poet writing his palinode, abjures his "rough magic," breaks and buries his staff, and drowns his book "deeper than did ever plummet sound." The great masque is spoken of slightingly only as "some vanity of mine art," and when the performance is over, the actors and the play, however extraordinary they may have been for a moment, are gone forever, "melted into air, into thin air."

To look at the Elizabethan theater through Shakespeare's internal plays is to, as Polonius advises, "by indirections find directions out." Seldom to be taken straight, these internal plays nonetheless reveal the aspects of presentation that regularly attracted Shakespeare's attention. His own professional actors were probably not as crude as Bottom's amateur players, nor were his plays by any means so old-fashioned as *The Murder of Gonzago*. And he probably never found actors as pliable and accommodating as Ariel and his company of spirits. But as he portrays his players, his stage, and his audience ironically, he always returns to the same performance issues. Do the players perform badly? How realistic is the stage setting? Does the audience hear and see the play in the right imaginative spirit, and does it move them toward some kind of moral reformation? Is the play put together in an effective manner? Sometimes the poet apologizes for the necessity of illusion on his bare stage, as does the Chorus in *Henry V*; sometimes he laughs at excessive realism, as in *Pyramus and Thisbe*; sometimes he laments the transience of theatrical illusion, as Prospero does; and sometimes he mocks his audiences for failing to enter into the artificial reality of the creative imagination. But all his oblique comments on performance in his theater show a relatively crude and limited performance on the actual stage contrasted with the powers of imagination, in the playwright's words and the audience's reception, to create understanding and moral regeneration through illusion.

Alvin B. Kernan is emeritus professor of humanities at Princeton University. He is the author of Shakespeare, the King's Playwright *and many other books.*

The First Folio

Acting companies in London during the Renaissance were perennially in search of new plays. They usually paid on a piece-work basis, to freelance writers. Shakespeare was an important exception; as a member of the Lord Chamberlain's Men and then the King's Men, he wrote for his company as a sharer in their capitalist enterprise.

The companies were not eager to sell their plays to publishers, especially when the plays were still popular and in the repertory. At certain times, however, the companies might be impelled to do so: when a company disbanded or when it was put into enforced inactivity by visitations of the plague or when the plays were no longer current. (The companies owned the plays; the individual authors had no intellectual property rights once the plays had been sold to the actors.)

Such plays were usually published in quarto form—that is, printed on both sides of large sheets of paper with four printed pages on each side. When the sheet was folded twice and bound, it yielded eight printed pages to each "gathering." A few plays were printed in octavo, with the sheet being folded thrice and yielding 16 smaller printed pages to each gathering.

Half of Shakespeare's plays were printed in quarto (at least one in octavo) during his lifetime. Occasionally a play was issued in a seemingly unauthorized volume—that is, not having been regularly sold by the company to the publisher. The acting company might then commission its own authorized version. The quarto title page of *Romeo and Juliet* (1599), known today as the second quarto, declares on its title page that it is "Newly corrected, augmented, and amended, as it hath been sundry times publicly acted by the Right Honorable the Lord Chamberlain His Servants." The second quarto of *Hamlet* (1604–1605) similarly advertises itself as "Newly imprinted and enlarged to almost as much again as it was, according to the true and perfect copy." Indeed, the first quarto of *Hamlet* (1603) is considerably shorter than the second, and the first quarto of *Romeo and Juliet* lacks some 800 lines found in its successor. Both contain what appear to be misprints or other errors that are then corrected in the second quarto. The first quarto of *Love's Labour's Lost* (1598) presents itself as "Newly corrected and augmented," implying perhaps that it, too, corrects an earlier, unauthorized version of the play, though none today is known to exist.

The status of these and other seemingly unauthorized editions is much debated today. The older view of A. W. Pollard, W. W. Greg, Fredson Bowers, and other practitioners of the so-called New Bibliography generally regards these texts as suspect and perhaps pirated, either by unscrupulous visitors to the theater or by minor actors who took part in performance and who then were paid to reconstruct the plays from memory.

The unauthorized texts do contain elements that sound like the work of eyewitnesses or actors (and are valuable for that reason). In some instances, the unauthorized text is notably closer to the authorized text when certain minor actors are on stage than at other times, suggesting that these actors may have been involved in a memorial reconstruction. The plays *2 Henry VI* and *3 Henry VI* originally appeared in shorter versions that may have been reconstructed from memory by actors.

A revisionary school of textual criticism that gained favor in the latter part of the 20th century argued that these texts might have been earlier versions with their own theatrical rationale and that they should be regarded as part of a theatrical process by which the plays evolved onstage. Certainly the situation varies from quarto to quarto, and unquestionably the unauthorized quartos are valuable to the understanding of stage history.

Several years after Shakespeare died in 1616, two of his colleagues in the King's Men, John Heminge and Henry Condell, undertook the assembling of a collected edition. Usually called the First Folio, it appeared in 1623 as *Mr. William Shakespeare's Comedies, Histories, and Tragedies, Published According to the True Original Copies*. It did not contain the poems and left out *Pericles* as perhaps of uncertain authorship; nor did it include *The Two Noble Kinsmen*, *Edward III*, or the portion of *The Book of Sir Thomas More* that Shakespeare may have contributed. It did nonetheless include 36 plays, half of them appearing in print for the first time.

Heminge and Condell had the burdensome task of choosing which materials to present to the printer, for they had on hand a number of authorial manuscripts, other documents that had served as promptbooks for performance (these were especially valuable since they bore the license for performance), and some 18 plays that had appeared in print. Fourteen of these had been published in what the editors regarded as more or less reliable texts (though only two were used unaltered): *Titus Andronicus*, *Romeo and Juliet* (the second quarto), *Richard II*, *Richard III*,

Love's Labour's Lost, 1 Henry IV, 2 Henry IV, A Midsummer Night's Dream, The Merchant of Venice, Much Ado about Nothing, Hamlet, King Lear, Troilus and Cressida, and *Othello. 1 Henry VI* and *2 Henry VI* had been published in quarto in shortened form and under different titles (*The First Part of the Contention Betwixt the Two Famous Houses of York and Lancaster* and *The True Tragedy of Richard Duke of York*) but were not used in this form by Heminge and Condell for the 1623 Folio.

Much was discovered by textual scholarship after Heminge and Condell did their original work, and the result was a considerable revision in what came to be regarded as the best choice of original text from which an editor ought to work. In plays published both in folio and quarto (or octavo) format, the task of choosing was immensely complicated. *King Lear* especially became a critical battleground in which editors argued for the superiority of various features of the 1608 quarto or the folio text. The two differ substantially and must indeed represent different stages of composition and of staging, so that both are germane to an understanding of the play's textual and theatrical history. The same is true of *Hamlet*, with its unauthorized quarto of 1603, its corrected quarto of 1604–1605, and the folio text, all significantly at variance with one another. Other plays in which the textual relationship of quarto to folio is highly problematic include *Troilus and Cressida, Othello, 2 Henry IV, 1 Henry VI* and *2 Henry VI, The Merry Wives of Windsor, Henry V,* and *A Midsummer Night's Dream.* Most of the cases where there are both quarto and folio originals are problematic in some interesting way. Individual situations are too complex to be described here, but information is readily available in critical editions of Shakespeare's plays and poems, especially in *The Oxford Shakespeare,* in a collected edition and in individual critical editions; *The New Cambridge Shakespeare;* and the third series of *The Arden Shakespeare.*

Fletcher, John

A contemporary of Shakespeare, John Fletcher (1579–1625) was an English Jacobean dramatist who collaborated with Francis Beaumont and other dramatists on comedies and tragedies between about 1606 and 1625.

His father, Richard Fletcher, was minister of the parish in which John was born and became afterward queen's chaplain, dean of Peterborough, and bishop successively of Bristol, Worcester, and London, gaining a measure of fame as an accuser in the trial of Mary, Queen of Scots, and as the chaplain sternly officiating at her execution. When not quite 12, John was apparently admitted pensioner of Corpus Christi College, Cambridge, and two years later became a Bible clerk. From the time of his father's death (1596) until 1607, nothing is known of him. His name is first linked with Beaumont's in Ben Jonson's *Volpone* (1607), to which both men contributed encomiums.

Fletcher began to work with Beaumont probably about 1607, at first for the Children of the Queen's Revels and its successor and then (from c. 1609 until Beaumont's retirement in 1613) mainly for the King's Men at the Globe and Blackfriars theaters. After 1613 he often collaborated with or had his plays revised by Philip Massinger, who actually succeeded him in 1625 as chief playwright of the King's Men; other collaborators included Nathan Field and William Rowley. Throughout his career he also wrote plays unaided. He died in the London plague of 1625, which killed some 40,000 others; the antiquarian John Aubrey claimed that he had lingered in the city to be measured for a suit of clothes instead of making his escape to the country.

John Fletcher, engraving by George Vertue, 1729.

The canon of the Beaumont and Fletcher plays is approximately represented by the 52 plays in the folio *Fifty Comedies and Tragedies . . .* (1679); but any consideration of the canon must omit one play from the 1679 folio (James Shirley's *Coronation*) and add three not to be found in it (*Henry VIII, Sir John van Olden Barnavelt, A Very Woman*). Of these 54 plays not more than 12 are by Beaumont or by Beaumont and Fletcher in collaboration. Another three were probably collaborations with Beaumont and Massinger. The others represent Fletcher either unaided or in collaboration with dramatists other than Beaumont, principally Massinger.

The masterpieces of the Beaumont and Fletcher collaboration—*Philaster, The Maides Tragedy*, and *A King and No King*—show, most clearly in the last, the emergence of most of the features that distinguish the Fletcherian mode from that of Shakespeare, George Chapman, or John Webster: the remote, often pseudohistorical, fairy-tale setting; the clear, smooth speech rising to great emotional arias of declamatory rhetoric; the basically sensational or bizarre plot that faces the characters with wild "either-or" choices between extremes and that can be manipulated toward a sad or a happy ending as the playwrights choose; the sacrifice of consistency and plausibility in characterization so that patterns can be made out of constantly shifting emotional states and piquant situations can be prolonged.

Of Fletcher's unaided plays, *The Faithfull Shepheardesse, The Mad Lover, The Loyall Subject, The Humorous Lieutenant, Women Pleas'd, The Island Princesse*, and *A Wife for a Moneth* (all between c. 1608 and c. 1624) are perhaps the best. Each of these is a series of extraordinary situations and extreme attitudes, displayed through intense declamations. The best of these are perhaps *The Loyall Subject* and *A Wife for a Moneth*, the latter a florid and loquacious play in which a bizarre sexual situation is handled with cunning piquancy, and the personages illustrate clearly Fletcher's tendency to make his men and women personifications of vices and virtues rather than individuals. The best of Fletcher's comedies, for urbanity and consistency of tone, is probably *The Wild-Goose Chase*, a play of episodes rather than of intricate intrigue, but alive with irony and easy wit.

Lastly, there are the Fletcherian plays in which others besides Beaumont had a hand. *Wit at Several Weapons* is a comedy that might have been written wholly by Thomas Middleton; and *The Captaine* (to which Beaumont may, however, have contributed) is a lively, complex play of sexual intrigue, with tragic dilemmas too. Notable among the numerous plays in this group are *The False One* and *The Beggars Bush*. The former is an original, incisive, and moderately subtle treatment of the story of Caesar and Cleopatra, which may well have helped John Dryden to compose *All for Love* and for which the greater credit goes to Massinger. The latter is worth reading for its "version of pastoral," which genially persuades the audience that it is better to be a country beggar than a tyrannical king.

▌Folger Shakespeare Library

This research center in Washington, D.C., is dedicated to the study of William Shakespeare, his contemporaries, Elizabethan society and culture, and 15th- through 18th-century British drama, literature, and history. The library, with approximately 280,000 books and manuscripts, possesses an unrivaled collection of Shakespeare's work—79 copies of the First Folio (1623), 118 copies of the later folios, and about 7,000 other Shakespeare editions—and constitutes the second-largest collection of English books printed prior to 1641. It also possesses world-famous collections of 18th- and 19th-century book illustrations and theatrical materials (such as theater playbills, theater programs, promptbooks, and costumes); 16th- and 17th-century French political pamphlets; tracts by various Reformation leaders, including Martin Luther; and materials associated with

Desiderius Erasmus and John Dryden. The library also contains musical instruments, costumes, and films.

Completed in 1932 and administered by the trustees of Amherst College, the library is named after Henry Clay Folger, a Standard Oil Company of New York executive whose will bequeathed his Shakespeare collection to the American people and provided the necessary funds to house, maintain, and expand it. The reading room is open to advanced scholars; it is open to the public only one day each year, on Shakespeare's birthday, which the library celebrates with Renaissance music, song, and dance. An exhibition gallery and a model Elizabethan theater are open to the public. Publications include a Folger Facsimile series, a series of booklets for the general reader, and the *Shakespeare Quarterly*. The Folger Institute, founded in 1970 by the Folger Shakespeare Library and a consortium of universities, is a multidisciplinary center for advanced study in the humanities.

The Globe Theatre

Early in 1599 Shakespeare, who had been acting with the Lord Chamberlain's Men since 1594, paid into the coffers of the company a sum of money amounting to 12.5 percent of the cost of building the Globe. He did so as a chief shareholder in the company, and by doing so he helped to establish a uniquely successful form of commercial operation for the actors of the time. This investment gave Shakespeare and the other leading actors both a share in the company's profits and a share in their playhouse.

At this time, officially approved playhouses and officially approved acting companies had been in existence in London for only five years. The Lord Chamberlain's Men was one of only two companies licensed to perform within the London city limits. The other company used the Rose playhouse, owned by an impresario and his ex-actor son-in-law.

Globe Theatre, from a 1612 engraving.

Shakespeare's company built the Globe only because it could not use the special roofed facility, Blackfriars Theatre, that James Burbage (the father of their leading actor, Richard Burbage) had built in 1596 for it inside the city. The elder Burbage had a long history as a theatrical entrepreneur. In 1576 he had built the first successful amphitheater, known as the Theatre, in a London suburb. Twenty years later, when the lease on the Theatre's land was about to expire, he built the theater in Blackfriars as its replacement. But the wealthy residents of Blackfriars persuaded the government to block its use for plays, so Burbage's capital was locked up. He died early in 1597, his plans for the future of theater in London frustrated.

Thus, the members of the Lord Chamberlain's Men were forced to rent a playhouse. At the end of 1598, they decided to build one for themselves. Because the inheritance of Burbage's sons, Cuthbert and Richard, was tied up in the Blackfriars, they formed a consortium with Shakespeare and four other actors, who became co-owners of the new Globe. The same shortage of cash made the consortium reluctant traditionalists; they gave up the idea of an indoor theater in the city. The old playhouse was one of their few remaining resources, but they could not use it in situ because the lease had expired, so they dismantled it, took the timbers (illegally) to make the skeleton of their new amphitheater, and kept the basic auditorium shape of the Theatre for the new building.

For all its hurried construction in 1599, the Globe proved a triumph. Its first decade of use made it a favorite not just with subsequent generations of theatergoers but with the company itself. In later years the troupe paid a lot to keep it going. At least two circumstances provide evidence for this statement. In 1608, when the company could finally fulfill James Burbage's original plan for the Blackfriars, the members chose, extravagantly, to operate the two theaters together, using the open-air Globe in the summer and the roofed Blackfriars in the winter. Had they chosen to, they easily could have rented one of the buildings to another company, since there was a shortage of playhouses in London in this period. But they kept both for themselves. They were given a second chance to transfer full-time to the Blackfriars in 1613, when the Globe burned to the ground, its thatch accidentally set alight by a cannon during a performance of *Henry VIII*. By then the Blackfriars was already beginning to bring better profits than the Globe, since the smaller house size was more than compensated by its higher prices. Instead, bearing the cost out of sentiment and traditional loyalty, the company members dug deep into their own pockets and rebuilt the Globe more splendidly than before.

Technically, the 1599 Globe and its 1614 replacement span an era in the history of theater design. The first Globe, based on the skeleton of the original Theatre of 1576, was unique not just as the most famous example of that peculiar and short-lived form of theater design but because it was actually the first to be built specifically for an existing acting company and financed by the company itself. Shakespeare designed *As You Like It*, *Hamlet*, *Twelfth Night*, *Othello*, *All's Well That Ends Well*, *Measure for Measure*, *King Lear*, *Macbeth*, *Antony and Cleopatra*, *Coriolanus*, *Pericles*, and *The Winter's Tale*, not to mention *Troilus and Cressida* and *Timon of Athens*, for performance there.

The Design of the Globe

The design of the original Theatre responded to a mix of traditions. Its name, which up to then had been used for atlases (such as Mercator's) rather than for playhouses, drew attention to the Roman theater tradition. Its circular shape, though, reflected not the D-shape of a Roman amphitheater but the gatherings of crowds in a circle around the actors in town marketplaces, where all the players of 1576 got their training. The concept of building a scaffold with three levels of galleries surrounding a circular yard mimicked the arrangement for audiences of existing bearbaiting and bullbaiting houses. The stage, a platform mounted in the yard, was the kind of thing that traveling companies set up in inn yards.

The old Theatre was a 20-sided structure, as near to a circle as Elizabethan carpentry could make it. It stood more than 30 feet (9 meters) high, with three levels of seating in its galleries. Audience access was either through two narrow passageways under the galleries into the standing room of the yard around the stage or up two external stair towers into the rear of the galleries. Five of the 20 bays of the galleries were cut off by the *frons scenae*, or tiring-house wall, behind which the actors kept their store of props, costumes, and playbooks and prepared themselves for their performances. The stage was a 5-foot- (1.5-meter-) high platform protruding from the tiring-house into the middle of the yard. Two posts supported a cover

over the stage that protected the players and their expensive costumes from rain. The audience standing in the yard had no cover, though when it rained they could pay more and take shelter in the lowest gallery.

The Globe reproduced this old shape, with a few innovations mainly in the fresh painting and decoration of the stage area. Each of the four London amphitheaters that scholars know most about, the Rose, the Swan, the Globe, and the Fortune, had auditorium bays of a certain size, about 10 feet 6 inches (roughly 3 meters) from front to back and an average width of 14 feet (about 4 meters). The Globe and the Fortune, and probably the Swan, had 20 bays in all, while the smaller Rose had 14. Seating in the form of degrees (wooden benches raked upward to the rear), along with the roofing over the topmost gallery, provided all the comfort short of a cushion that Elizabethans expected. A few rooms were reserved for the most privileged on the stage balcony itself. Including the space for nearly a thousand customers to stand in the yard around the stage, the small Rose had a total capacity of about 2,400 people, while contemporary estimates of total audience capacity at the Swan and the Globe claimed 3,000.

The stage was large, 43 or 44 feet (about 13 meters) across and 27 or more feet (some 8 meters) deep. The two stage posts were substantial, since they had to uphold the large cover, or heavens, which had a trapdoor in it with a windlass for winding boys playing gods down onto the stage. Below the heavens trapdoor was one in the stage, which served as the entry point for King Hamlet's ghost and the grave for Ophelia. The tiring-house wall had two doors on its flanks for entrances and exits and a central opening, normally covered by a set of hangings (Polonius's arras), which concealed the caskets in *The Merchant of Venice* and Hermione's statue in *The Winter's Tale*. Above the three openings, a balcony ran the width of the stage wall, the central room of which was used for scenes that required an upper window or balcony or the walls of a town.

Playing at the Globe

The experience of watching a performance at the Globe was radically different from that of viewing modern Shakespeare on-screen. The plays were staged in the afternoons, using the light of day, and the audience surrounded the stage on all sides. No scenery was used, except for occasional emblematic devices such as a throne or a bed. It was almost impossible not to see the other half of the audience standing behind the players. Consequently, much of the staging was metatheatrical, conceding the illusory nature of the game of playing and making little pretense of stage realism.

Rebuilding the Globe

The Globe was pulled down in 1644, two years after the Puritans closed all theaters, to make way for tenement dwellings. In 1970 the American actor Sam Wanamaker, who was driven by the notion of reconstructing a replica of the Globe, established the Shakespeare Globe Playhouse Trust. Seventeen years later a groundbreaking ceremony was held on a Bankside site near that of the original Globe, and in 1989 the foundations of the original building were discovered buried beneath a historic 19th-century building. Although only a small percentage of the original theater could be examined, the discovery of these foundations enabled scholars to make certain design adjustments. They changed the planned 24 sides to 20, for instance, and using the angles revealed by the archaeologists, they made the whole polygon 99 feet (30 meters) in outside diameter. By referring to a number of extant Elizabethan buildings for clues to the structure, style, interior, and roofing, scholars and architects completed the design of the Globe Theatre reconstruction. Using traditional methods and materials, with only a few concessions to modern fire regulations and the like, builders completed work on the new theater in the mid-1990s. It is now part of a larger complex of buildings known as the International Shakespeare Globe Centre.

The new theater is not a perfect replica of the original building. It is made, for example, from new green oak, like the Fortune, not from the 23-year-old timbers of a dismantled building, like the original Globe. Its design is still speculative in key areas, such as its size, the shape of the stage, and the decorations. In addition, certain compromises had to be made to satisfy the constraints of fire-safety regulations. These entailed making the stairways and access doors wider, increasing the number of entrances to the yard, positioning sprinkler valves in the ridging of the thatched gallery roofing, and including conduits for electrical wiring. These provisos—and a restriction on the size of the audience at any performance to a maximum of 1,600, roughly half the number that attended the original Globe—have secured the right for the new Globe to be used once again as a theater.

The basic justification for attempting to reconstruct the Globe in a faithful version of the original is that it can be used to learn more about Shakespeare's plays. The Globe was Shakespeare's machine, financed and built by the company that intended to use it. How it worked and what it produced have a great deal to offer to students of Shakespeare's plays—those written pre-texts, as they have been called with some justice, that record all he thought his fellows needed to know when they staged his plays. Everything that has been wrung from these pre-texts in the last four centuries is enhanced by a better knowledge of Shakespeare's original concept.

Greene, Robert

One of the most popular English prose writers of the later 16th century, Robert Greene (c. 1558–1592) was Shakespeare's most successful predecessor in blank-verse romantic comedy. He was also one of the first professional writers and among the earliest English autobiographers.

Greene obtained degrees at both Cambridge and Oxford. He then went to London, where he became an intimate of its underworld. He wrote more than 35 works between 1580 and 1592. To be certain of supplying material attractive to the public, Greene at first slavishly followed literary fashions. His first model was John Lyly's *Euphues.*

In the later 1580s Greene wrote prose pastorals in the manner of Sir Philip Sidney's *Arcadia,* interspersed with charming, often irrelevant lyrics that have given Greene a reputation as a poet. The best of his pastorals is *Pandosto* (1588), the direct source of Shakespeare's *The Winter's Tale.*

About 1590 Greene began to compose serious didactic works. Beginning with *Greenes never too late* (1590), he related prodigal son stories. That Greene drew on his own experience is evident from the tract *Greenes groats-worth of witte, bought with a million of repentance,* printed posthumously in 1592 with Greene's admission that Roberto's experiences were essentially his own. In *Groats-worth* appears the first printed reference to Shakespeare, assailed as "an upstart Crow, beautified with our feathers, that with his *Tygers heart wrapt in a Players hide,* supposes he is as well able to bumbast out a blanke verse as the best of you . . . in his owne conceit the onely Shake-scene in a countrie." (The words in italics are from Shakespeare's *1 Henry VI.*) Greene is thought to be criticizing Shakespeare the actor.

Greene's writings for the theater present numerous problems; the dating of his plays is conjectural, and his role as collaborator has produced much inconclusive discussion. With *The Honorable Historie of Friar Bacon, and Friar Bungay* (written c. 1591, published 1594), the first successful romantic comedy in English, Greene realized his comic talent in drama. In *The Scottish Historie of James the fourth, slaine at Flodden* (written c. 1590, published 1598), he used an Italian tale but drew on fairy lore for the characters of Oberon and Bohan. It was a forerunner of *As You Like It* and *A Midsummer Night's Dream.* As Marlowe anticipated the tragedies of Shakespeare, so, in a lesser way, Greene furnished him a model for dramatic comedy and romance.

In his last year Greene wrote exposés of the Elizabethan underworld, such as *A Notable Discovery of Coosnage* (1591) and the successful and amusing *A disputation betweene a hee conny-catcher and a shee conny-catcher* (1592).

Hamlet

This tragedy in five acts was written about 1599–1601 and published in a quarto edition in 1603 from an unauthorized text, with reference to an earlier play. The First Folio version was taken from a second quarto of 1604 that was based on Shakespeare's own papers with some annotations by the bookkeeper.

Shakespeare's telling of the story of Prince Hamlet was derived from several sources, notably from Books III and IV of Saxo Grammaticus's 12th century *Gesta Danorum* and from volume 5 (1570) of *Histoires tragiques*, a free translation of Saxo by François de Belleforest. The play was evidently preceded by another play of Hamlet (now lost), usually referred to as the *Ur-Hamlet*, of which Thomas Kyd is a conjectural author.

As Shakespeare's play opens, Hamlet is mourning his father, who has been killed, and lamenting the behavior of his mother, Gertrude, who married his uncle Claudius within a month of his father's death. The ghost of his father appears to Hamlet, informs him that he was poisoned by Claudius, and commands Hamlet to avenge his death. Though instantly galvanized by the ghost's command, Hamlet decides, on further reflection, to seek evidence in corroboration of the ghostly visitation, since, he knows, the Devil can assume a pleasing shape and can easily mislead a person whose mind is perturbed by intense grief. Hamlet adopts a guise of melancholic and mad behavior as a way of deceiving Claudius and others at court—a guise made all the easier by the fact that Hamlet is genuinely melancholic.

Driven by a guilty conscience, Claudius attempts to ascertain the cause of Hamlet's odd behavior by hiring Hamlet's one-time friends Rosencrantz and Guildenstern to spy on him. Hamlet quickly sees through the scheme and begins to act the part of a madman in front of them. To the pompous old courtier Polonius, it appears that Hamlet is lovesick over Polonius's daughter, Ophelia. Despite Ophelia's loyalty to him, Hamlet thinks that she, like everyone else, is turning against him; he feigns madness with her also and treats her cruelly as if she were representative, like his own mother, of her "treacherous" sex.

Hamlet contrives a plan to test the ghost's accusation. With a group of visiting actors, Hamlet arranges for the performance of a story representing circumstances similar to those described by the ghost, under which Claudius poisoned Hamlet's father. When the play is presented as planned, the performance clearly unnerves Claudius. Hamlet's dearest friend, Horatio, agrees with him that Claudius has unambiguously confirmed his guilt.

Moving swiftly in the wake of the actors' performance, Hamlet confronts his mother in her chambers with her culpable loyalty to Claudius. When he hears a man's voice behind the curtains, Hamlet stabs the person he understandably assumes to be Claudius. The victim, however, is Polonius, who has been eavesdropping in an attempt to find out more about Hamlet's erratic behavior. This act of violence persuades Claudius that his own life is in danger. He sends Hamlet to England escorted by Rosencrantz and Guildenstern, with secret orders that Hamlet be executed by the king of England. When Hamlet discovers the orders, he alters them to make his two friends the victims instead.

Upon his return to Denmark, Hamlet hears that Ophelia is dead of a suspected suicide (though more probably as a consequence of her having gone mad over her father's sudden death) and that her brother Laertes seeks to avenge Polonius's murder. Claudius is only too eager to arrange the duel. Carnage ensues. Hamlet dies of a wound inflicted by a sword that Claudius and Laertes have conspired to tip with poison; in the scuffle, Hamlet realizes what has happened and forces Laertes to exchange swords with him, so that Laertes too dies—as he admits, justly killed by his own treachery. Gertrude, also present at the duel, drinks from the cup of poison that Claudius has had placed near Hamlet to ensure his death. Before Hamlet himself dies, he manages to stab Claudius and to entrust the clearing of his honor to his friend Horatio.

Hathaway, Anne

Anne Hathaway (c. 1556–1623) was probably born at Shottery, near Stratford, the daughter of Richard Hathaway, a local landowner. She was married to Shakespeare in November 1582, when he was 18 and when she, according to the sole evidence of an inscription on her gravestone, was 26. Their daughter Susanna was born the following May.

After the birth (about 1585) of their twins, Hamnet and Judith, Shakespeare moved to London, probably leaving the family at Stratford. About 1596 Anne and the children were installed in New Place, Stratford, where Anne remained until her death in 1623. Shakespeare often visited his family there and lived there from his retirement in 1611 until his death.

Henry IV, Part 1

This chronicle play in five acts was written about 1596–1597 and published from a reliable authorial draft in a 1598 quarto edition. *Henry IV, Part 1* is the second in a sequence of four history plays (the others being *Richard II, Henry IV, Part 2*, and *Henry V*) known collectively as the "second tetralogy," treating major events of English history in the late 14th and early 15th centuries. The historical facts in the play were taken primarily from Raphael Holinshed's *Chronicles*, but Sir John Falstaff and his Eastcheap cronies are original creations (with some indebtedness to popular traditions about Prince Hal's prodigal youth that had been incorporated into a play of the 1580s called *The Famous Victories of Henry the Fifth*) who add an element of robust comedy to *Henry IV* that is missing in Shakespeare's earlier chronicles.

Set in a kingdom plagued with rebellion, treachery, and shifting alliances in the period following the deposition of King Richard II, the two parts of *Henry IV* focus especially on the development of Prince Hal (later Henry V) from wastrel to ruler rather than on the title character. Indeed, the king is often overshadowed not only by his son but also by Hotspur, the young rebel military leader, and by Hal's roguish companion Falstaff. Secondary characters (many of them comic) are numerous. The plot shifts rapidly between scenes of raucous comedy and the war against the alliance of the Welsh and the rebellious Percy family of Northumberland.

As *Part 1* begins, Henry IV, wearied from the strife that has accompanied his accession to the throne, is renewing his earlier vow to make a pilgrimage to the Holy Land. He learns that Owen Glendower, the Welsh chieftain, has captured Edmund Mortimer, the earl of March, and that Henry Percy, known as Hotspur, son of the Earl of Northumberland, has refused to release his Scottish prisoners until the king has ransomed Mortimer. Henry laments that his own son is not like the fearless Hotspur. As the war escalates, Glendower, Mortimer (now married to Glendower's daughter), and Hotspur (now allied with the Welsh) conspire to divide Henry's kingdom into three equal parts.

Meanwhile, Prince Hal and his cronies, including the fat, boisterous Falstaff and his red-nosed sidekick, Bardolph, have been drinking and playing childish pranks at Mistress Quickly's inn at Eastcheap. Hal, who admits in an aside that he is consorting with these thieving rogues only temporarily, nevertheless agrees to take part with them in an actual highway robbery. He does so under certain conditions: the money is to be taken away from Falstaff and his companions by Prince Hal and his comrade Poins in disguise, and the money is then to be returned to its rightful owners, so that the whole caper is a practical joke on Falstaff rather than a robbery. This merriment is interrupted by Hal's being called to his father's aid in the war against the Welsh and the Percys. Hal and his father manage to make up their differences, at least for a time, most of all when Hal saves the life of his father in combat. Hal further proves his valor in battle, where he chides Falstaff for malingering and drunkenness and then kills Hotspur in personal combat during the Battle of Shrewsbury. Hal laments the wasteful death of his noble opponent and of Falstaff, on the ground nearby. But Falstaff was only feigning death, and when he claims to have killed Hotspur, Hal agrees to support the lie. At the play's end, rebellion has been only temporarily suppressed.

▌*Henry IV, Part 2*

This chronicle play in five acts was written in 1597–1598 and published in a corrupt text based in part on reconstruction from memory in a quarto edition in 1600; a better text, printed in the main from an authorial manuscript, appeared in the First Folio of 1623 and is generally the more reliable version. *Henry IV, Part 2* is the third in a sequence of four history plays (the others being *Richard II, Henry IV, Part 1,* and *Henry V*) known collectively as the "second tetralogy," treating major events of English history in the late 14th and early 15th centuries. The historical facts of the play were taken primarily from Raphael Holinshed's *Chronicles,* but Sir John Falstaff and the other comic secondary characters are original. In *Henry IV, Part 2* these Eastcheap figures dominate the action even more than they do in *Part 1.*

Henry IV's son John of Lancaster is leading the ongoing war against the Welsh chieftain, Owen Glendower, and Hotspur's father, Henry Percy, Earl of Northumberland. The swaggering

Falstaff has become even more corpulent and outrageous, sponging off his hostess, Mistress Quickly, abusing the Lord Chief Justice, preening for the admiring Doll Tearsheet, and taking advantage of everyone, especially his ensign, Pistol, and his old friends Justice Shallow and Justice Silence.

Prince Hal, worried about his father's ill health but still curious about Falstaff's activities, goes to Eastcheap in disguise to spy on his old friends. When the king learns of Hal's whereabouts, he despairs for the future. News comes that Prince John has settled the war (through a perfidious betrayal of promises made to the enemy leaders as a condition of their disbanding their forces). Henry talks, yet again, about a pilgrimage so that he can die in the Holy Land. After a misunderstanding in which Hal—thinking his father has died—removes the crown from the king's pillow and leaves the sickroom, father and son are reconciled on the king's deathbed. The wily Henry advises Hal to avoid internal strife during his own reign by seeking foreign quarrels.

Hal prepares to become king, setting aside his previous frivolous image and reassuring his brothers of his loyalty to them and his genuine grief at their mutual loss. Falstaff arrives with his entourage, expecting a lively and generous welcome from his old friend. Instead, Hal, now King Henry V, denounces Falstaff, orders him and his cronies to repent their profligate ways, and has the Lord Chief Justice take them to the Fleet prison until they have reformed. As they are led away, Prince John prophesies war with France.

▮ *Henry V*

This chronicle play in five acts was first performed in 1599 and published in 1600 in a corrupt quarto edition; the text in the First Folio of 1623, printed seemingly from an authorial manuscript, is substantially longer and more reliable. *Henry V* is the last in a sequence of four plays (the others being *Richard II*,

Henry IV, Part 1, and *Henry IV, Part 2*) known collectively as the "second tetralogy," treating major events in English history of the late 14th and early 15th centuries. The main source of the play was Raphael Holinshed's *Chronicles*, but Shakespeare may also have been influenced by an earlier play about King Henry V called *The Famous Victories of Henry the Fifth*.

In keeping with his father's advice (*Henry IV, Part 2*) to seek foreign quarrels, Henry V, formerly Prince Hal, resolves to subjugate France and retake the lands in France previously held by England. His political and military advisers conclude that he has a rightful claim to the French crown and encourage him to follow the military exploits of his royal ancestors. The action of the play culminates in Henry's campaign in France with a ragtag army. The depiction of the character of Henry dominates the play throughout, from his nervous watch before the Battle of Agincourt, when he walks disguised among his fearful soldiers and prays for victory, to his courtship of Princess Katharine, which is romantic and tender despite the marriage's having been arranged by the Duke of Burgundy.

Although almost all the fighting occurs offstage, the recruits, professional soldiers, dukes, and princes are shown preparing for defeat or victory. Comic figures abound, notably the Welsh captain, Fluellen, and some of Henry's former companions, notably Nym, Bardolph, and Pistol, who is now married to Mistress Quickly. Falstaff, however, dies offstage, perhaps because Shakespeare felt his boisterous presence would detract from the more serious themes of the play.

Shakespeare hedges the patriotic fantasy of English greatness in *Henry V* with hesitations and qualifications about the validity of the myth of glorious nationhood offered by the Agincourt story. The king's speech to his troops before battle on St. Crispin's Day is particularly famous for its evocation of a brotherhood in arms, but Shakespeare has placed it in a context full of ironies and challenging contrasts. In the end the chorus reminds the audience that England was to be plunged into civil war during the reign of Henry V's son, Henry VI.

Henry VI, Part 1

This chronicle play in five acts was written sometime in 1589–1592 and published in the First Folio of 1623. *Henry VI, Part 1* is the first in a sequence of four history plays (the others being *Henry VI, Part 2*, *Henry VI, Part 3*, and *Richard III*) known collectively as the "first tetralogy," treating the Wars of the Roses between the houses of Lancaster and York. Shakespeare's primary sources for the historical events in the play were the chronicles of Edward Hall and Raphael Holinshed.

Part 1 begins at the funeral of Henry V, as political factions are forming around the boy king, Henry VI. The chief rivalry is between Henry's uncle Humphrey, duke of Gloucester, the Lord Protector, and his great-uncle, Henry Beaufort, bishop of Winchester. The peace Henry V had established in France is shattered as Joan la Pucelle (Joan of Arc) persuades the newly crowned French king, Charles VII, to reclaim French lands held by the English. Most of the play rapidly shifts between the power struggles at the English court and the war in France. The former spill into the latter when the feuding dukes of York and Somerset quarrel over who is responsible for sending reinforcements to save the noble Lord Talbot. As *Part 1* ends, the Earl (in *Part 2*, Duke) of Suffolk, who has persuaded Henry to marry Margaret of Anjou, plans to use the alliance to take power for himself: "Margaret shall now be Queen and rule the King; / But I will rule both her, the King, and realm."

Henry VI, Part 1 covers the early part of King Henry's reign and ends with events immediately preceding the opening of *Part 2*. It contains the entirely nonhistorical scene in which Richard Plantagenet, later duke of York, chooses a white rose and John Beaufort, earl (later duke) of Somerset, a red rose as emblems of their respective houses of York and Lancaster. It is uncertain whether *Part 1* was Shakespeare's first effort at a historical play, written before the other two parts, or a supplement that was written subsequently to provide an introduction to the events in

Part 2 and *Part 3*. With the Henry VI trilogy (leading up to the devastating portrayal of evil in *Richard III*), Shakespeare analyzes the harrowing process by which England suffered through decades of civil war until the victory of Henry Tudor (Henry VII) at the Battle of Bosworth Field in 1485.

Henry VI, Part 2

This chronicle play in five acts was written sometime in 1590–1592. It was first published in a corrupt quarto in 1594. The version published in the First Folio of 1623 is considerably longer and seems to have been based on an authorial manuscript. *Henry VI, Part 2* is the second in a sequence of four history plays (the others being *Henry VI, Part 1*, *Henry VI, Part 3*, and *Richard III*) known collectively as the "first tetralogy," treating the Wars of the Roses between the houses of Lancaster and York. Shakespeare's primary sources for the play were the chronicles of Edward Hall and Raphael Holinshed.

In *Part 2* the factional fighting at court is increased rather than lessened by the arrival of Margaret of Anjou, the new queen, who—together with her lover, the Duke of Suffolk—plots against Humphrey, duke of Gloucester, and his ambitious duchess, Eleanor. The power struggle swirls around the saintly, ineffectual King Henry until gradually the dynamic Richard Plantagenet, duke of York, who has pretended to support Margaret while secretly hatching his own plot, emerges as the chief contender for the throne. The commons grow increasingly restive, especially when Duke Humphrey appears to have been murdered by his political enemies. Anarchy reaches its zenith when a Kentishman named Jack Cade, encouraged by Richard Plantagenet, mounts an insurrection that plays havoc in the streets of London until it is finally put down. Open civil war between the Yorkists and the Lancastrians is now imminent.

▌ *Henry VI, Part 3*

This chronicle play in five acts was written in 1590–1593. Like *Henry IV, Part 2*, it was first published in a corrupt quarto, this time in 1595. The version published in the First Folio of 1623 is considerably longer and seems to have been based on an authorial manuscript. It is the third in a sequence of four history plays (the others being *Henry VI, Part 1*, *Henry VI, Part 2*, and *Richard III*) known collectively as the "first tetralogy," treating the Wars of the Roses between the houses of Lancaster and York. Shakespeare's primary sources for the historical events were the chronicles of Edward Hall and Raphael Holinshed.

Part 3 begins as the Yorkists seize power and inveigle the inept Henry VI to disinherit his son in favor of the Yorkist claim. Although this arrangement provides for Henry to reign until he dies, the Yorkists soon persuade themselves to violate that treaty and take the throne by force. Open war is the result. Queen Margaret focuses on gaining the throne for her disinherited son, Edward, prince of Wales. She elicits the aid of Lord Clifford and ultimately defeats York in battle, stabbing him to death while he curses her as "she-wolf of France" and "more inhuman, more inexorable, / Oh, ten times more, than tigers of Hyrcania." As Henry drifts wistfully through the action, lamenting his fate, York's sons consolidate their power. The Lancastrians briefly regain the ascendancy after Edward IV (the eldest of these sons and now king) ignores a proposed marriage to the French princess that has been arranged by the Earl of Warwick and King Lewis XI of France and instead marries the widowed Elizabeth, Lady Grey. Margaret's triumph is short-lived, however, and the Lancastrians are defeated at the Battle of Tewkesbury. Throughout this period of civil war, Richard, duke of Gloucester, the youngest brother of the new king Edward IV, emerges as a balefully ambitious schemer for power. He begins to reveal the accomplished villain who will emerge full-blown as the title figure in *Richard III*.

▌*Henry VIII*

This chronicle play in five acts was produced in 1613 and published in the First Folio of 1623 from a transcript of an authorial manuscript. The primary source of the play was Raphael Holinshed's *Chronicles*.

As the play opens, the Duke of Buckingham, having denounced Cardinal Wolsey, lord chancellor to King Henry VIII, for corruption and treason, is himself arrested, along with his son-in-law, Lord Abergavenny. Despite the king's reservations and Queen Katharine's entreaties for justice and truth, Buckingham is convicted as a traitor on the basis of the false testimony of a dismissed servant. As he is taken away for execution, Buckingham conveys a prophetic warning to beware of false friends.

Henry becomes enamored of the beautiful Anne Bullen (Boleyn) and, concerned over his lack of a male heir, expresses doubts about the validity of his marriage to Katharine, his brother's widow. Separately, Anne, though reluctant to supplant the queen, accepts the king's proposal. Wolsey tries to extend his power over the king by preventing this marriage, but the lord chancellor's machinations and longtime corruption are finally revealed to all. As he leaves the court, Wolsey encourages his servant Thomas Cromwell to offer his services to Henry, who soon promotes Cromwell to high office. Anne is married to Henry in secret and with great pomp is crowned queen. Although Katharine maintains her dignity throughout her divorce trial and subsequent exile from court, her goodness has no power in the face of political intrigues. She dies, soon after hearing that Wolsey has died a penitent.

The new lord chancellor and other court officials attempt to reassert control over the king by accusing Thomas Cranmer, Henry's loyal archbishop of Canterbury, of heresy. The king is no longer so easily manipulated, however, and Cranmer reveals to the plotters a ring he holds as a mark of the king's favor. Henry further asks Cranmer to baptize his newborn daughter, and the play ends with a final celebration and Cranmer's prophecy of England's glory under the future Queen Elizabeth I.

Henry VIII, which is widely thought to be Shakespeare's last completed play, has had a long and interesting stage history, but since the mid-19th century a number of critics have doubted that Shakespeare was its sole author. Many scenes and splendid speeches were written in a style very similar to that of John Fletcher.

Holinshed, Raphael

Raphael Holinshed (?–1580) is remembered chiefly because his *Chronicles* enjoyed great popularity and became a quarry for many Elizabethan dramatists, especially Shakespeare, who found, in the second edition, material for *Macbeth*, *King Lear*, *Cymbeline*, and many of his historical plays.

Holinshed probably belonged to a Cheshire family. From roughly 1560 he lived in London, where he was employed as a translator by Reginald Wolfe, who was preparing a universal history. After Wolfe's death in 1573 the scope of the work was abridged, and it appeared, with many illustrations, as the *Chronicles of England, Scotlande, and Irelande,* in two volumes (dated 1577).

The *Chronicles* was compiled largely uncritically from many sources of varying degrees of trustworthiness. The texts of the first and second (1587) editions were expurgated by order of the Privy Council, and the excisions from the second edition were published separately in 1723. An edition of the complete, unexpurgated text of 1587, edited by Henry Ellis and titled *Holinshed's Chronicles of England, Scotland, and Ireland,* was published in six volumes (1807–1808; reissued in six volumes, 1976). Several selections have also appeared, including *Holinshed's Chronicle as Used in Shakespeare's Plays,* edited by

Allardyce and Josephine Nicoll (1927); *Shakespeare's Holinshed*, compiled and edited by Richard Hosley (1968); and *The Peaceable and Prosperous Regiment of Blessed Queene Elisabeth* (2005).

▌Jonson, Ben

Ben Jonson (1572–1637) is generally regarded as the second-most-important English dramatist, after William Shakespeare, during the reign of James I. Among his major plays are the comedies *Every Man in His Humour* (1598), *Volpone* (1606), *The Alchemist* (1610), and *Bartholomew Fair* (1614).

Jonson was born two months after his father died. His stepfather was a bricklayer, but by good fortune the boy was able to attend Westminster School. His formal education, however, ended early, and he at first followed his stepfather's trade, then fought with some success with the English forces in the Netherlands. On returning to England, he became an actor and playwright, experiencing the life of a strolling player. He apparently played the leading role of Hieronimo in Thomas Kyd's *The Spanish Tragedie*. By 1597 he was writing plays for Philip Henslowe, the leading impresario for the public theater. With one exception (*The Case Is Altered*), these early plays are known, if at all, only by their titles. Jonson apparently wrote tragedies as well as comedies in these years, but his extant writings include only two tragedies, *Sejanus* (1603) and *Catiline* (1611).

Ben Jonson, oil painting by an unknown artist.

The year 1598 marked an abrupt change in Jonson's status, when *Every Man in His Humour* was successfully presented by the Lord Chamberlain's theatrical company (a legend has it that Shakespeare himself recommended it to them), and his reputation was established. In this play Jonson tried to bring the spirit and manner of Latin comedy to the English popular stage by presenting the story of a young man with an eye for a girl, who has difficulty with a phlegmatic father, is dependent on a clever servant, and is ultimately successful—in fact, the standard plot of the Latin dramatist Plautus. But at the same time Jonson sought to embody in four of the main characters the four "humors" of medieval and Renaissance medicine—choler, melancholy, phlegm, and blood—which were thought to determine human physical and mental makeup.

That same year Jonson killed a fellow actor in a duel, and though he escaped capital punishment by pleading "benefit of clergy" (the ability to read from the Latin Bible), he could not escape branding. During his brief imprisonment over the affair he became a Roman Catholic.

Following the success of *Every Man in His Humour*, the same theatrical company acted Jonson's *Every Man Out of His Humour* (1599), which was even more ambitious. It was the longest play ever written for the Elizabethan public theater, and it strove to provide an equivalent of the Greek comedy of Aristophanes; "induction," or "prelude," and regular between-act comment explicated the author's views on what the drama should be.

The play, however, proved a disaster, and Jonson had to look elsewhere for a theater in which to present his work. The obvious place was the "private" theaters, in which only young boys acted. The high price of admission they charged meant a select audience, and they were willing to try strong satire and formal experiment; for them Jonson wrote *Cynthia's Revels* (c. 1600) and *Poetaster* (1601). Even in these, however, there is the paradox of contempt for human behavior hand in hand with a longing for human order.

It appears that Jonson won royal attention by his *Entertainment at Althorpe*, given before James I's queen as she journeyed down from Scotland in 1603, and in 1605 *The Masque of Blackness* was presented at court. The "masque" was a quasi-dramatic entertainment, primarily providing a pretense for a group of strangers to dance and sing before an audience of guests and attendants in a royal court or nobleman's house. This elementary pattern was much elaborated during the reign of James I, when the architect Inigo Jones provided increasingly magnificent costumes and scenic effects for masques at court. The few spoken words that the masque had demanded in Elizabethan days expanded into a "text" of a few hundred lines and a number of set songs. Thus the author became important as well as the designer: he was to provide not only the necessary words but also a special "allegorical" meaning underlying the whole entertainment. It was Jonson, in collaboration with Jones, who gave the Jacobean masque its characteristic shape and style. He did this primarily by introducing the suggestion of a "dramatic" action. It was thus the poet who provided the informing idea and dictated the fashion of the whole night's assembly. Jonson's early masques were clearly successful, for during the following years he was repeatedly called upon to function as poet at court. Among his masques were *Hymenaei* (1606), *Hue and Cry after Cupid* (1608), *The Masque of Beauty* (1608), and *The Masque of Queens* (1609). In his masques Jonson was fertile in inventing new motives for the arrival of the strangers. But this was not enough: he also invented the "antimasque," which preceded the masque proper and which featured grotesques or comics who were primarily actors rather than dancers or musicians.

Important though Jonson was at the court in Whitehall, it was undoubtedly Jones's contributions that caused the most stir. That tension should arise between the two men was inevitable, and eventually friction led to a complete break: Jonson wrote the *Twelfth Night* masque for the court in 1625 but then had to wait five years before the court again asked for his services.

In 1606 Jonson and his wife (whom he had married in 1594) were brought before the consistory court in London to explain their lack of participation in the Anglican church. He denied that his wife was guilty but admitted that his own religious opinions held him aloof from attendance. The matter was patched up through his agreement to confer with learned men, who might persuade him if they could. Apparently it took six years for him to decide to conform. For some time before this he and his wife had lived apart, Jonson taking refuge in turn with his patrons Sir Robert Townshend and Esmé Stuart, Lord Aubigny.

During this period, nevertheless, he made a mark second only to Shakespeare's in the public theater. His comedies *Volpone; or, the Foxe* (1606) and *The Alchemist* (1610) were among the most popular and esteemed plays of the time. Each exhibited human folly in the pursuit of gold. Set respectively in Italy and London, they demonstrate Jonson's enthusiasm both for the typical Renaissance setting and for his own town on Europe's fringe. Both plays are eloquent and compact, sharptongued and controlled. The comedies *Epicoene* (1609) and *Bartholomew Fair* (1614) were also successful.

Jonson embarked on a walking tour in 1618–1619, which took him to Scotland. During the visit the city of Edinburgh made him an honorary burgess and guild brother. On his return to England he received an honorary Master of Arts degree from Oxford University, a most signal honor in his time. Jonson's life was a life of talk as well as of writing. He engaged in "wit-combats" with Shakespeare, and Jonson reigned supreme. It was a young man's ultimate honor to be regarded as a "son of Ben."

In 1623 his personal library was destroyed by fire. By this time his services were seldom called on for the entertainment of Charles I's court, and his last plays failed to please. In 1628 he suffered what was apparently a stroke and, as a result, was confined to his room and chair, ultimately to his bed. That same year he was made city chronologer (thus theoretically responsible for the city's pageants), though in 1634 his salary for the post was made into a pension. Jonson died in 1637 and was buried in Westminster Abbey.

The first folio edition of his works had appeared in 1616; posthumously, in a second Jonson folio (1640), appeared *Timber: or, Discoveries*, a series of observations on life and letters. Here Jonson held forth on the nature of poetry and drama and paid his final tribute to Shakespeare: in spite of acknowledging a belief that his great contemporary was, on occasion, "full of wind"—*sufflaminandus erat*—he declared that "I loved the man, and do honour his memory, on this side idolatry, as much as any."

Ben Jonson occupies by common consent the second place among English dramatists of the reigns of Elizabeth I and James I. He was a man of contraries. For "twelve years a papist," he was also—in fact though not in title—Protestant England's first poet laureate. His major comedies express a strong distaste for the world in which he lived and a delight in exposing its follies and vices. A gifted lyric poet, he wrote two of his most successful plays entirely in prose, an unusual mode of composition in his time. Though often an angry and stubborn man, no one had more disciples than he. He was easily the most learned dramatist of his time, and he was also a master of theatrical plot, language, and characterization. It is a measure of his reputation that his dramatic works were the first to be published in folio (the term, in effect, means the "collected works") and that his plays held their place on the stage until the period of the Restoration. Later they fell into neglect, though *The Alchemist* was revived during the 18th century, and in the mid-20th century several came back into favor: *Volpone, The Alchemist*, and *Bartholomew Fair* especially have been staged with striking success.

Jonson's chief plays are still very good theater. His insistence on putting classical theory into practice in them reinforced rather than weakened the effect of his gift of lively dialogue, robust characterization, and intricate, controlled plotting. In each of them he maneuvers a large cast of vital personages, all consistently differentiated from one another. Jonson's plots are skillfully put together; incident develops out of incident in a consistent chain of cause and effect, taking into account the respective natures of the personages involved and proceeding confidently through a twisting, turning action that is full of surprises without relying on coincidence or chance. Sometimes Jonson's comedy derives from the dialogue, especially when it is based on his observation of contemporary tricks of speech. But there are also superbly ludicrous situations, often hardly removed from practical joke.

Jonson is renowned for his method of concentrating on a selected side, or on selected sides, of a character, showing how they dominate the personality. This is to some extent a natural outcome of his classical conception of art, but it also stems from his clear, shrewd observation of people. In Jonson's plays both eccentricity and normal behavior are derived from a dominating characteristic, so that the result is a live, truthfully conceived personage in whom the ruling passion traces itself plainly. The later plays, for example, have characters whose behavior is dominated by one psychological idiosyncrasy. But Jonson did not deal exclusively in "humors." In some of his plays (notably *Every Man in His Humour*), the stock types of Latin comedy contributed as much as the humors theory did. What the theory provided for him and for his contemporaries was a convenient mode of distinguishing among human beings. The distinctions so made could be based on the "humors," on Latin comic types, or, as in *Volpone*, in the assimilation of humans to different members of the animal kingdom. The characters Volpone, Mosca, Sir Epicure Mammon, Face, Subtle, Dol Common, Overdo, and Ursula are not simply "humors"; they are glorious type figures, so vitally rendered as to take on a being that transcends the type. This method was one of simplification, of typification, and yet also of vitalization.

The Restoration dramatists' use of type names for their characters (Cockwood, Witwoud, Petulant, Pinchwife, and so on) was a harking back to Jonson, and similarly in the 18th century, with such characters as Peachum, Lumpkin, Candour, and Languish. And though, as the 18th century proceeded, comic dramatists increasingly used names quite arbitrarily, the idea of the Jonsonian "type" or "humor" was always at the root of their imagining. Jonson thus exerted a great influence on the playwrights who immediately followed him. In the late Jacobean and Caroline years, it was he, Shakespeare, and Francis Beaumont and John Fletcher who provided all the models. But it was he, and he alone, who gave the essential impulse to dramatic characterization in comedy of the Restoration and also in the 18th and 19th centuries.

▌*Julius Caesar*

This tragedy in five acts was produced in 1599–1600 and published in the First Folio of 1623 from a transcript of a promptbook.

Based on Sir Thomas North's 1579 translation (via a French version) of Plutarch's *Bioi paralleloi* (*Parallel Lives*), the drama takes place in 44 BC, after Caesar has returned to Rome. Fearing Caesar's ambition, Cassius forms a conspiracy among Roman republicans. He persuades the reluctant Brutus—Caesar's trusted friend—to join them. Brutus, troubled and sleepless, finds comfort in the companionship of his noble wife, Portia. Caesar's wife, Calpurnia, alarmed by prophetic dreams, warns her husband not to go to the Capitol the next day. Then, as planned, Caesar is slain in the Senate on March 15, "the ides of March." His friend Mark Antony, who has expediently shaken the bloodied hands of the conspirators, gives a stirring funeral oration that inspires the crowd to turn against them. Octavius, Caesar's nephew, forms a triumvirate with Antony and Lepidus; Brutus and Cassius are eventually defeated at the Battle of Philippi, where they kill themselves to avoid further dishonor.

King John

This chronicle play in five acts was written perhaps in 1594–1596 and published in the First Folio of 1623 from an authorial manuscript that may have been copied and supplied with some theatrical touches. The source of the play was a two-part drama generally known as *The Troublesome Raigne of John King of England*. This earlier play, first printed in 1591, was based on the chronicles of Raphael Holinshed and Edward Hall; Shakespeare also consulted some chronicle materials, as well as John Foxe's *Acts and Monuments* (1563), known as *The Book of Martyrs*. Shakespeare made few changes to the plot in his version, but the dialogue and insights about the characters are all his own.

The title figure provides the central focus of the play and is surrounded by many contrasting characters—each able to influence him, each bringing irresolvable and individual problems into dramatic focus. Chief among these characters are John's domineering mother, Queen Eleanor (formerly Eleanor of Aquitaine), and Philip the Bastard, who supports the king and yet mocks all political and moral pretensions.

As the play begins, King John, with the aid of his mother, has usurped the royal title of his nephew Arthur; the king of France, on threat of war, has demanded that Arthur be placed on the throne. Two brothers, Philip and Robert Faulconbridge, enter arguing over their inheritance. Eleanor recognizes the resemblance between Philip and her late son King Richard Coeur-de-lion. After Philip agrees to drop all claim to the Faulconbridge lands, his mother admits that he is indeed Richard's son. Thereafter, the Bastard, newly knighted as Sir Richard Plantagenet, becomes John's staunchest military commander in the war against France.

As the fighting rages on, a compromise is arranged in which Lewis, the dauphin, heir to the French throne, marries John's niece Blanche. This expediency fails to end the war, however, with armies led by Eleanor and by Arthur's combatant mother, Constance, at the forefront. An English victory delivers young Arthur into the hands of King John. This success soon turns against John, however, when he finds that Arthur is too dangerous a presence because he has become a rallying point for John's political enemies. John orders Hubert de Burgh to kill the captive Arthur. After Hubert finds that he cannot carry out such an inhumane command and allows the child to survive, Arthur dies in a tragic fall while trying to escape. Cardinal Pandulph, having urged the French to support the papacy against the rebellious John, does succeed in encouraging a French invasion of England only to discover, when John has reluctantly submitted to the papacy, that the French dauphin will not agree to call off his invading forces. The war thus becomes an exercise in futility on all sides. John, increasingly weak and uncertain, grows ill. Only the Bastard fights on, until news comes that John has been poisoned by a traitorous monk. After Prince Henry arrives to care for his dying father and accept his imminent accession to the throne, the Bastard at last accepts that peace is at hand and pledges fealty to the new king.

King Lear

This tragedy in five acts was written in 1605–1606 and published in a quarto edition in 1608, evidently based on Shakespeare's unrevised working papers. The text of the First Folio of 1623 often differs markedly from the quarto text and seemingly represents a theatrical revision done by the author with some cuts designed for shortened performance.

The aging King Lear decides to divide his kingdom among his three daughters, allotting each a portion in proportion to the eloquence of her declaration of love. The hypocritical Goneril and Regan make grand pronouncements and are rewarded;

Cordelia, the youngest daughter, who truly loves Lear, refuses to make an insincere speech to prove her love and is disinherited. The two older sisters mock Lear and renege on their promise to support him. Cast out, the king slips into madness and wanders about accompanied by his faithful Fool. He is aided by the Earl of Kent, who, though banished from the kingdom for having supported Cordelia, has remained in Britain disguised as a loyal follower of the king. Cordelia, having married the King of France, is obliged to invade her native country with a French army in order to rescue her neglected father. She is brought to Lear, cares for him, and helps him regain his reason. When her army is defeated, she and her father are taken into custody.

The subplot concerns the Earl of Gloucester, who gullibly believes the lies of his conniving illegitimate son, Edmund, and spurns his honest son, Edgar. Driven into exile disguised as a mad beggar, Edgar becomes a companion of the truly mad Lear and the Fool during a terrible storm. Edmund allies himself with Regan and Goneril to defend Britain against the French army mobilized by Cordelia. He turns his father over to Regan's brutal husband—the Duke of Cornwall, who gouges out Gloucester's eyes—and then imprisons Cordelia and Lear, but he is defeated in chivalric combat by Edgar. Jealous of Edmund's romantic attentions to Regan, Goneril poisons her and commits suicide. Cordelia is hanged on the orders of Edmund, who experiences a change of heart once he has been defeated and fatally wounded by Edgar but is too late in his attempt to reverse the death order. The Duke of Albany, Goneril's well-meaning husband, has attempted to remedy injustice in the kingdom but sees at last that events have overwhelmed his good intentions. Lear, broken, dies with Cordelia's body in his arms.

A CLOSER LOOK
Music in Shakespeare's Plays
by Mary Springfels

It was customary in Tudor and Stuart drama to include at least one song in every play. Only the most profound tragedies, in accordance with Senecan models, occasionally eschewed all music except for the sounds of trumpets and drums. In his later tragedies, William Shakespeare defied this orthodoxy and used songs startlingly and movingly, particularly in *Othello*, *King Lear*, and *Hamlet*.

Dramas produced at court were invariably much more lavish than those put on by the professional companies. Casts were larger, as were the instrumental ensembles used to accompany songs and provide incidental music. *Gorboduc* (1561) by Thomas Sackville and Thomas Norton, the first English five-act drama in blank verse, used a five part instrumental ensemble to accompany the dumb shows that introduced each act. *Wit and Science* (c. 1539) by John Redford provided as an interlude a composition played and sung by four allegorical characters. The sententious choirboy dramas presented at court throughout the second half of the 16th century were acted and sung by two companies, the Children of Paul's and the Gentlemen and Children of the Chapel Royal. Most of these plays included a lament to be sung by a treble voice and accompanied by a consort of viols. About eight of these pieces survive; several are sufficiently lovely to justify their dreary alliterative verse. Shakespeare parodies the genre mercilessly in the Pyramus and Thisbe interlude performed by the rustics in *A Midsummer Night's Dream*; the blissfully absurd lament "What dreadful dole is here?" is a send-up of "Gulchardo," a consort song that has survived into the 21st century.

The Vocal Music

The professional companies that put on plays in the public theaters worked with much-reduced musical resources. Normally, one boy actor could sing and perhaps play an instrument. Adult actors, especially those specializing in clown roles, sang as well. A special musical-comic genre, the jigg, was the particular domain of the great Shakespearean comedians Richard Tarlton and William Kempe. Jiggs (bawdy, half-improvised low-comedy burlesques) were put on at the conclusion of a history play or tragedy. They involved from two to five characters, were sung to popular melodies (such as "Walsingham" and "Rowland"), and were accompanied by the fiddle or cittern (a small wire-strung instrument strummed with a pick). Touring troupes created a vogue for jiggs on the Continent beginning in the 1590s. As a result, we have marvelous settings of jigg tunes by Jan Pieterszoon Sweelinck, Samuel Scheidt, and other important northern European composers. The most accomplished of the comedians was Robert Armin, who joined the Chamberlain's Men about 1598.

To what sorts of characters did Shakespeare assign most of the singing? They were generally servants (both children and adults), clowns, fools, rogues, or minor personalities. Major figures never sang, except when in disguise or in distracted mental states. Most songs, in fact, were addressed to the protagonists themselves.

It is thought that the boys' songs in commercial plays were often set pieces, drawn from a repertoire of music suitable to a variety of dramatic situations. Thus, in *Antony and Cleopatra* the boy musician of the company sings a generic drinking song, "Come, thou monarch of the vine" (for which there is no surviving melody). Another boy, who was sufficiently famous for his name to have been included in the stage directions of the First Folio of 1623—he was Jacke Wilson—sang "Sigh no more, ladies" in *Much Ado about Nothing*. There is some debate about whether "Take, O, take those lips away" from

Measure for Measure and "O mistress mine" from *Twelfth Night* predate these plays. The lyrics seem to most experts to be authentically Shakespearean, but there is the hint of an unperformed second verse to "Take, O, take," and instrumental settings of "O mistress" by William Byrd and Thomas Morley do indeed antedate the first production of *Twelfth Night*. It is reasonable to conclude that Shakespeare made use of songs that were established in the popular repertoire of the period and composed his own lyrics as well. In both cases, the songs in his plays never seem to be extraneous, though their reasons for being there can be complex.

Shakespeare used vocal music to evoke mood, as in "Come, thou monarch," and, while doing so, to provide ironic commentary on plot or character. "O mistress," sung by Robert Armin in the role of Feste, is directed toward the aging Sir Toby Belch and Sir Andrew Aguecheek; the lyrics touch on all the themes of the play and even hint at Viola's transgendered disguise in the phrase "that can sing both high and low." The incantatory, magical, and ritual uses of song are also central to such plays as *A Midsummer Night's Dream*, *The Tempest*, and *Macbeth*. In the first, the fairies use "You spotted snakes" as a sleep-inducing charm, while in *The Tempest*, Ariel's song "Come unto these yellow sands" reassures the shipwrecked arrivals in Prospero's magical realm. The heavily magical-musical Weird Sisters' (Three Witches') scenes in *Macbeth* were so popular that they were greatly expanded in Restoration revivals of the play. Songs of the ritual type usually occur near the conclusion of a play; at the end of *A Midsummer Night's Dream*, for example, Titania calls upon the fairies to "First, rehearse your song by rote, / To each word a warbling note. / Hand in hand, with fairy grace, / Will we sing, and bless this place." Juno's song "Honour, riches" in Act IV, scene 1, of *The Tempest* is clearly the ritual blessing of a marriage and a charm incanted to produce fruitfulness.

Shakespeare also used songs to establish the character or mental state of the singer. Ariel simply describes himself in

"Where the bee sucks." Iago uses songs to give himself the appearance of a rough soldier. Most significantly, Ophelia's snatches of folk song demonstrate the regressive breakdown of her personality. (The only other Shakespeare heroine who sings is Desdemona. To overwhelming effect, she sings a popular tune, "The Willow Song"—for which 16th-century words and music exist—just before she is murdered by Othello.) In *King Lear* Edgar feigns madness by singing snatches of folk song.

Other types of vocal music that appeared in the plays include serenades, part-songs, rounds, and catches, all used very much in imitation of real life in Renaissance England.

Instrumental Music

The instrumental forces available to Shakespeare were, for the most part, fairly sparse. Exceptions were the plays produced at court. *Twelfth Night* was first performed at Whitehall on Twelfth Night, 1601, as part of a traditional royal celebration of the holiday. *The Tempest* was given two court performances, the first in 1611 at Whitehall and the second in 1613 for the wedding festivities of the Princess Elizabeth and the elector palatine. Both plays contain nearly three times the amount of music normally present in the plays. For these special occasions, Shakespeare probably had access to court singers and instrumentalists. A more typical Globe Theatre production would have made do with a trumpeter, another wind player who doubtless doubled on shawm (a double-reed ancestor of the oboe, called "hoboy" in the First Folio stage directions), flute, and recorders. Textual evidence points to the availability of two string players who were competent at the violin, viol, and lute. A few plays, notably *Romeo and Juliet*, *The Two Gentlemen of Verona*, and *Cymbeline*, indicate specific consorts (ensembles) of instruments. More commonly, a stage direction will simply state that music is played. Small onstage bands accompanied serenades, dances, and masques. Offstage, they provided interludes between acts and "atmosphere" music to establish the emotional climate of a scene, very much as film music does today. "Solemn," "strange," or "still" music accompanied pageants and the magical actions in *The Tempest*.

Certain instruments had symbolic significance for Elizabethans. Hoboys (oboes) were ill winds that blew no good; their sounds presaged doom or disaster. They heralded the evil banquets in *Titus Andronicus* and *Macbeth* and accompanied the vision of the eight kings in the great witches' scene of the latter play. Hoboys provided a grim overture to the dumb show in *Hamlet*.

The sounds of the lute and viol were perceived by Elizabethans to act as benign forces over the human spirit; like musical homeopathy, they eased melancholy by transforming it into exquisite art. In *Much Ado*, as a prelude to Jacke Wilson's singing of "Sigh no more, ladies," Benedick observes: "Is it not strange that cheeps' guts [the strings of an instrument] should hale souls out of men's bodies?" The viol was becoming a very popular gentleman's instrument at the turn of the 17th century, challenging the primacy of the lute. Henry Peucham, in *The Compleat Gentleman* (1622), urges the young and socially ambitious to be able to "sing your part sure, and at first sight, withall, to play the same upon your viol, or the exercise of the lute, privately, to your self." It was probably the trendiness of the viol that attracted Sir Andrew Aguecheek to the instrument.

Not a single note of instrumental music from the Shakespeare plays has been preserved, with the possible exception of the witches' dances from *Macbeth*, which are thought to have been borrowed from a contemporary masque. Even descriptions of the kinds of music to be played are sparse. Trumpets sounded "flourishes," "sennets," and "tuckets." A flourish was a short blast of notes. The words *sennet* and *tucket* were English manglings of the Italian terms *sonata* and *toccata*. These were longer pieces, though still probably improvised. "Doleful dumps" were melancholy pieces (of which a few are still preserved) usually composed over a repeated bass line. "Measures" were dance steps of various sorts. The commonest court dances of the period were the pavane, a stately walking dance; the almain, a brisker walking dance; the galliard, a vigorous leaping dance in triple time, of which Queen Elizabeth was particularly fond; and the branle, or brawl, an easy circle dance.

The Authenticity of the Songs

The problem of authenticity plagues most of the vocal music as well. Barely a dozen of the songs exist in contemporary settings, and not all of them are known to have been used in Shakespeare's own productions. For example, the famous Thomas Morley version of "It was a lover and his lass" is a very ungratefully arranged lute song. In *As You Like It* the song was sung, rather badly it seems, by two pages, probably children. Some of the most important and beloved lyrics, such as "Sigh no more, ladies," "Who is Silvia?" and, saddest of all, "Come away, death," are no longer attached to their melodies. It is believed that, in addition to Morley, two other composers, Robert Johnson and John Wilson (probably the selfsame Jacke Wilson who sang "Sigh no more" in *Much Ado about Nothing* and "Take, O, take" in *Measure for Measure*), had some association with Shakespeare at the end of his career. As soon as public theater moved indoors, this frustrating state of preservation changed; there are examples of at least 50 intact songs from the plays of Francis Beaumont and John Fletcher and their contemporaries, many of them composed by Johnson and Wilson.

Musical Reference as a Dramatic Device

In addition to performed vocal music, Shakespeare used all kinds of music and musical instruments referentially. The folk song and ballad tunes he quoted so frequently were equally well known to the groundlings as to the more distinguished patrons. Scraps of these tunes were used to create in-jokes and to evoke other sentiments as well. The pathos of Ophelia's madness was increased with the knowledge, which probably went back to childhood, of the folk songs she croons in her distraction.

A favorite device of the playwright was to turn the lyrics of a popular song into a bantering dialogue between characters. A classic instance of this technique is the scene between the clown Peter and the household musicians in *Romeo and Juliet* (Act IV, scene 5). Peter first begs them to play "Heart's ease" and "My heart is full of woe," both well-loved popular tunes. Then Peter challenges the musicians Simon Catling, Hugh Rebeck, and James Soundpost to an interpretive debate over a fusty old lyric from *The Garden of Dainty Devices* (1576).

> When griping griefs the heart doth wound,
> And doleful dumps the mind oppress,
> Then music with her silver sound—

Peter then banters with the players, asking them whether "silver sound" refers to the sweet sound of silver—that is, money. The old lyric concludes

> Is wont with speed to give redress,
> Of troubled mind for every sore,
> Sweet music hath a salve therefore.

Shakespeare depended on the audience's prior knowledge of the verse to give meaning and pathos to this otherwise rather bizarre interchange.

Shakespeare used musical instruments and their playing techniques as the basis for sexual double entendre or extended metaphor. A fine example of the former can be found in Act II, scene 3, of *Cymbeline*, where Cloten reports: "I am advised to give her music o' mornings; they say it will penetrate." The musicians enter, and Cloten continues: "Come on, tune. If you can penetrate her with your fingering, so; we'll try with tongue too." The best-known instance of extended metaphor is Hamlet's warning to Rosencrantz and Guildenstern against trying to manipulate him, couched in the language of recorder technique (Act III, scene 2). He says:

> You would play upon me, you would seem to know my stops,
> you would pluck out the heart of my mystery, you would
> sound me from my lowest note to the top of my compass, and

there is much music, excellent voice, in this little organ, yet cannot you make it speak.

What can we learn from Shakespeare's use of music about his knowledge of and attitude toward that art? There is very little evidence to be found in the texts themselves to show that he had any particular knowledge of the art music of the period. He makes no allusions to the magnificent church polyphony being written at the time by William Byrd and his contemporaries or to the brilliantly witty madrigals of Thomas Weelkes and John Wilbye. The complexity of such music was perhaps inappropriate to outdoor theatrical performance and above the heads of most of Shakespeare's audience. Extant Elizabethan and Jacobean theater music is simple and vivid, almost Baroque in style. Shakespeare may even have had some antipathy for that most famous of melancholic musicians, John Dowland; his portrayal in *Twelfth Night* of Duke Orsino's rather superficial taste for the "dying fall" surely must refer to the opening strain of Dowland's "Flow My Tears." On the other hand, the playwright seems to have had a genuine fondness for honest English popular and traditional songs. He would never have taken the extraordinary step of giving "The Willow Song" to Desdemona in her hour of crisis if he did not believe in its emotional validity. Shakespeare certainly had a profound comprehension of the Renaissance Neoplatonic idea of the "music of the spheres" and the effect of both heavenly and earthly harmonies on the health of the human spirit. Perhaps his loveliest evocation of this concept comes from Act V, scene 1, of *The Merchant of Venice*, where Lorenzo speaks:

> Here will we sit and let the sounds of music
> Creep in our ears. Soft stillness and the night
> Become the touches of sweet harmony.
> Sit, Jessica. Look how the floor of heaven
> Is thick inlaid with patens of bright gold.
> There's not the smallest orb which thou behold'st
> But in his motion like an angel sings,

Still choiring to the young-eyed cherubins.
Such harmony is in immortal souls,
But whilst this muddy vesture of decay
Doth grossly close it in, we cannot hear it.

Lorenzo goes on to describe the calming effect of Orpheus's music on wild beasts:

Since naught so stockish, hard, and full of rage
But music for the time doth change his nature.
The man that hath no music in himself,
Nor is not moved with concord of sweet sounds,
Is fit for treasons, stratagems, and spoils;
The motions of his spirit are dull as night
And his affections dark as Erebus.
Let no such man be trusted. Mark the music.

Mary Springfels is musician-in-residence at the Newberry Library, Chicago. She is also director of the Early Music Ensemble at Northwestern University, Evanston, Illinois, and director of the Newberry Consort, an early music ensemble-in-residence at the Newberry Library, Northwestern University's School of Music, and the University of Chicago.

Kyd, Thomas

The English dramatist Thomas Kyd (1558–1594), with his *The Spanish Tragedie* (sometimes called *Hieronimo*, or *Jeronimo*, after its protagonist), initiated the revenge tragedy of his day. He anticipated the structure of many later plays, including the development of middle and final climaxes. In addition, he revealed an instinctive sense of tragic situation, while his characterization of Hieronimo in *The Spanish Tragedie* prepared the way for Shakespeare's psychological study of Hamlet.

The son of a scrivener, Kyd was educated at the Merchant

Taylors School in London. There is no evidence that he attended the university before turning to literature. He seems to have been in service for some years with a nobleman (possibly Ferdinando, Lord Strange, the patron of Lord Strange's Men). *The Spanish Tragedie* was entered in the Stationers' Register in October 1592, and the undated first quarto edition almost certainly appeared in that year. It is not known which company first played it, or when; but Strange's company played *Hieronimo* 16 times in 1592, and the Admiral's Men revived it in 1597, as apparently did the Lord Chamberlain's Men. It remained one of the most popular plays of the age and was often reprinted.

The only other play certainly by Kyd is *Cornelia* (1594), an essay in Senecan tragedy, translated from the French of Robert Garnier's academic *Cornélie*. He may also have written an earlier version of *Hamlet*, known to scholars as the *Ur-Hamlet*, and his hand has sometimes been detected in the anonymous *Arden of Feversham*, one of the first domestic tragedies, and in a number of other plays.

About 1591 Kyd was sharing lodgings with Christopher Marlowe, and on May 13, 1593, he was arrested and then tortured, being suspected of treasonable activity. His room had been searched and certain "atheistical" disputations denying the deity of Jesus Christ found there. He probably averred then and certainly confirmed later, in a letter, that these papers had belonged to Marlowe. That letter is the source for almost everything that is known about Kyd's life. He was dead by December 30, 1594, when his mother made a formal repudiation of her son's debt-ridden estate.

▌Life

Although the amount of factual knowledge available about Shakespeare is surprisingly large for one of his station in life, many find it a little disappointing, for it is mostly gleaned from documents of an official character. Dates of baptisms, marriages, deaths, and burials; wills, conveyances, legal processes, and payments by the court—these are the dusty details. There are, however, many contemporary allusions to him as a writer, and these add a reasonable amount of flesh and blood to the biographical skeleton.

The parish register of Holy Trinity Church in Stratford-upon-Avon, Warwickshire, shows that he was baptized there on April 26, 1564; his birthday is traditionally celebrated on April 23. His father, John Shakespeare, was a burgess of the borough, who in 1565 was chosen an alderman and in 1568 bailiff (the position corresponding to mayor, before the grant of a further charter to Stratford in 1664). He was engaged in various kinds of trade and appears to have suffered some fluctuations in prosperity. Shakespeare's mother, Mary Arden, of Wilmcote, Warwickshire, came from an ancient family and was the heiress to some land. (Given the somewhat rigid social distinctions of the 16th century, this marriage must have been a step up the social scale for John Shakespeare.)

Stratford enjoyed a grammar school of good quality, and the education there was free, the schoolmaster's salary being paid by the borough. No lists of the pupils who were at the school in the 16th century have survived, but it would be absurd to suppose the bailiff of the town did not send his son there. The boy's education would consist mostly of Latin studies—learning to read, write, and speak the language fairly well and studying some of the Classical historians, moralists, and poets. Shakespeare did not go on to the university, and indeed it is unlikely that the scholarly round of logic, rhetoric, and other studies then followed there would have interested him.

Instead, at age 18 he married. Where and exactly when are not known, but the episcopal registry at Worcester preserves a bond dated November 28, 1582, and executed by two yeomen of Stratford, named Sandells and Richardson, as a security to the bishop for the issue of a license for the marriage of William Shakespeare and "Anne Hathaway of Stratford," upon the consent of her friends and upon once asking of the banns. (Anne died in 1623, seven years after Shakespeare. There is good evidence to associate her with a family of Hathaways who inhabited a beautiful farmhouse, now much visited, 2 miles from Stratford.) The next date of interest is found in the records of the Stratford church, where a daughter, named Susanna, born to William Shakespeare, was baptized on May 26, 1583. On February 2, 1585, twins were baptized, Hamnet and Judith. (Hamnet, Shakespeare's only son, died 11 years later.)

How Shakespeare spent the next eight years or so, until his name begins to appear in London theater records, is not known. There are stories—given currency long after his death—of stealing deer and getting into trouble with a local magnate, Sir Thomas Lucy of Charlecote, near Stratford; of earning his living as a schoolmaster in the country; of going to London and gaining entry to the world of theater by minding the horses of theatergoers. It has also been conjectured that Shakespeare spent some time as a member of a great household and that he was a soldier, perhaps in the Low Countries. In lieu of external evidence, such extrapolations about Shakespeare's life have often been made from the internal "evidence" of his writings. But this method is unsatisfactory: one cannot conclude, for example, from his allusions to the law that Shakespeare was a lawyer, for he was clearly a writer who without difficulty could get whatever knowledge he needed for the composition of his plays.

The first reference to Shakespeare in the literary world of London comes in 1592, when a fellow dramatist, Robert Greene, declared in a pamphlet written on his deathbed:

> There is an upstart crow, beautified with our feathers, that with his Tygers heart wrapt in a Players hide supposes he is as well able to bombast out a blank verse as the best of you; and, being an absolute Johannes Factotum, is in his own conceit the only Shake-scene in a country.

What these words mean is difficult to determine, but clearly they are insulting, and clearly Shakespeare is the object of the sarcasms. When the book in which they appear (*Greenes groats-worth of witte, bought with a million of Repentance*, 1592) was published after Greene's death, a mutual acquaintance wrote a preface offering an apology to Shakespeare and testifying to his worth. This preface also indicates that Shakespeare was by then making important friends. For, although the puritanical city of London was generally hostile to the theater, many of the nobility were good patrons of the drama and friends of the actors. Shakespeare seems to have attracted the attention of the young Henry Wriothesley, the 3rd earl of Southampton, and to this nobleman were dedicated his first published poems, *Venus and Adonis* and *The Rape of Lucrece*.

One striking piece of evidence that Shakespeare began to prosper early and tried to retrieve the family's fortunes and establish its gentility is the fact that a coat of arms was granted to John Shakespeare in 1596. Rough drafts of this grant have been preserved in the College of Arms, London, though the final document, which must have been handed to the Shakespeares, has not survived. Almost certainly William himself took the initiative and paid the fees. The coat of arms appears on Shakespeare's monument (constructed before 1623) in the Stratford church. Equally interesting as evidence of Shakespeare's worldly success was his purchase in 1597 of New Place, a large house in Stratford, which he as a boy must have passed every day in walking to school.

How his career in the theater began is unclear, but from roughly 1594 onward he was an important member of the Lord Chamberlain's company of players (called the King's Men after the accession of James I in 1603). They had the best actor, Richard Burbage; they had the best theater, the Globe (finished by the autumn of 1599); they had the best dramatist, Shakespeare. It is no wonder that the company prospered. Shakespeare became a full-time professional man of his own theater, sharing in a cooperative enterprise and intimately concerned with the financial success of the plays he wrote.

Unfortunately, written records give little indication of the way in which Shakespeare's professional life molded his marvelous artistry. All that can be deduced is that for 20 years Shakespeare devoted himself assiduously to his art, writing more than a million words of poetic drama of the highest quality.

Shakespeare had little contact with officialdom, apart from walking in the procession—dressed in the royal livery as a member of the King's Men—at the coronation of King James I in 1604. He continued to look after his financial interests. He bought properties in London and in Stratford. In 1605 he purchased a share (about one-fifth) of the Stratford tithes—a fact that explains why he was eventually buried in the chancel of its parish church. For some time he lodged with a French Huguenot family called Mountjoy, who lived near St. Olave's Church in Cripplegate, London. The records of a lawsuit in May 1612, resulting from a Mountjoy family quarrel, show Shakespeare as giving evidence in a genial way (though unable to remember certain important facts that would have decided the case) and as interesting himself generally in the family's affairs.

No letters written by Shakespeare have survived, but a private letter to him happened to get caught up with some official transactions of the town of Stratford and so has been preserved in the borough archives. It was written by one Richard Quiney and addressed by him from the Bell Inn in Carter Lane, London, where he had gone from Stratford on business. On one side of the paper is inscribed: "To my loving good friend and countryman, Mr. Wm. Shakespeare, deliver these." Apparently Quiney thought his fellow Stratfordian a person to whom he could apply for the loan of £30—a large sum in Elizabethan times. Nothing further is known about the transaction, but, because so few opportunities of seeing into Shakespeare's private life present themselves, this begging letter becomes a touching document. It is of some interest, moreover, that 18 years later Quiney's son Thomas became the husband of Judith, Shakespeare's second daughter.

Shakespeare's will (made on March 25, 1616) is a long and detailed document. It entailed his quite ample property on the male heirs of his elder daughter, Susanna. (Both his daughters were then married, one to the aforementioned Thomas Quiney and the other to John Hall, a respected physician of Stratford.) As an afterthought, he bequeathed his "second-best bed" to his wife; no one can be certain what this legacy means. The testator's signatures to the will are apparently in a shaky hand. Perhaps Shakespeare was already ill. He died on April 23, 1616. No name was inscribed on his gravestone in the chancel of the parish church of Stratford-upon-Avon. Instead these lines, possibly his own, appeared:

> Good friend, for Jesus' sake forbear
> To dig the dust enclosed here.
> Blest be the man that spares these stones,
> And curst be he that moves my bones.

Shakespeare's family or friends, however, were not content with a simple gravestone, and within a few years, a monument was erected on the chancel wall. It seems to have existed by 1623. Its epitaph, written in Latin and inscribed immediately below the bust, attributes to Shakespeare the worldly wisdom of Nestor, the genius of Socrates, and the poetic art of Virgil. This apparently was how his contemporaries in Stratford-upon-Avon wished their fellow citizen to be remembered.

The memory of Shakespeare survived long in theatrical circles, for his plays remained a major part of the repertory of the King's Men until the closing of the theaters in 1642. The greatest of Shakespeare's great contemporaries in the theater, Ben Jonson, had a good deal to say about him. To William Drummond of Hawthornden in 1619 he said that Shakespeare "wanted art." But, when Jonson came to write his splendid poem prefixed to the Folio edition of Shakespeare's plays in 1623, he rose to the occasion with stirring words of praise:

> Triumph, my Britain, thou hast one to show
> To whom all scenes of Europe homage owe.
> He was not of an age, but for all time!

Besides almost retracting his earlier gibe about Shake-speare's lack of art, he gives testimony that Shakespeare's personality was to be felt, by those who knew him, in his poetry—that the style was the man. Jonson also reminded his readers of the strong impression the plays had made upon Queen Elizabeth I and King James I at court performances:

> Sweet Swan of Avon, what a sight it were
> To see thee in our waters yet appear,
> And make those flights upon the banks of Thames
> That so did take Eliza and our James!

Shakespeare seems to have been on affectionate terms with his theater colleagues. His fellow actors John Heminge and Henry Condell (who, with Burbage, were remembered in his will) dedicated the First Folio of 1623 to the earl of Pembroke and the earl of Montgomery, explaining that they had collected the plays "without ambition either of self-profit or fame; only to keep the memory of so worthy a friend and fellow alive as was our Shakespeare."

Seventeenth-century antiquaries began to collect anecdotes about Shakespeare, but no serious life was written until 1709, when Nicholas Rowe tried to assemble information from all available sources with the aim of producing a connected narrative. There were local traditions at Stratford: witticisms and lampoons of local characters; scandalous stories of drunkenness and sexual escapades. About 1661 the vicar of Stratford wrote in his diary: "Shakespeare, Drayton, and Ben Jonson had a merry meeting, and it seems drank too hard; for Shakespeare died of a fever there contracted." On the other hand, the antiquary John Aubrey wrote in some notes about Shakespeare: "He was not a company keeper; lived in Shoreditch; wouldn't be debauched, and, if invited to, writ he was in pain." Richard Davies, archdeacon of Lichfield, reported, "He died a papist." How much trust can be put in such a story is uncertain. In the early 18th century a story appeared that Queen Elizabeth had obliged Shakespeare "to write a play of Sir John Falstaff in love" and that he had performed the task (*The Merry Wives of Windsor*) in a fortnight. There are other stories, all of uncertain authenticity and some mere fabrications.

When serious scholarship began in the 18th century, it was too late to gain anything from traditions. But documents began to be discovered. Shakespeare's will was found in 1747 and his marriage license in 1836. The documents relating to the Mountjoy lawsuit already mentioned were found and published in 1910. It is conceivable that further documents of a legal nature may yet be discovered, but as time passes the hope becomes more remote. Modern scholarship is more concerned with studying Shakespeare in relation to his social environment, both in Stratford and in London. This is not easy, because the author and actor lived a somewhat detached life: a respected tithe-owning country gentleman in Stratford, perhaps, but a rather rootless artist in London.

▌ The Lord Chamberlain's Men

Shakespeare was intimately connected with this theatrical company for most of his professional career as a dramatist. It was the most important company of players in Elizabethan and Jacobean England.

The troupe's early history is somewhat complicated. A company known as Hunsdon's Men, whose patron was Henry Carey, 1st Lord Hunsdon, is traceable to 1564–1567. Hunsdon took office as Lord Chamberlain in 1585, and another company (the Lord Chamberlain's Men) under his patronage is traceable to 1590. Two years later the theaters closed because of plague; when they reopened in 1594, a good deal of reorganization and amalgamation between various theater companies took place. A strong Lord Chamberlain's company emerged. After their patron's death in 1596, the company came under the protection of his son, George Carey, 2nd Lord Hunsdon. Once more it was known as Hunsdon's Men, until their new patron himself took office as Lord Chamberlain in 1597. Thereafter, it was known as the Lord Chamberlain's Men, until the accession of James I in March 1603, when, by letters patent, it was taken under royal patronage and henceforth known as the King's Men.

The records of performances given at court show that they were by far the most favored of the theatrical companies. Their only rival was a company known during Elizabeth I's reign as the Admiral's Men and after that as Prince Henry's Men. From the summer of 1594 to March 1603 the Lord Chamberlain's Men seem to have played almost continuously in London. They undertook a provincial tour during the autumn of 1597, however, and traveled again in 1603 when the plague was in London. The company went on tour during part of the summers or autumns in most years thereafter.

In 1594 their London home was for a time a theater in Newington Butts (an archery range not far south of London Bridge) and after that most probably at the Cross Keys Inn in the city itself. Later, they presumably used the Theatre, situated in Shoreditch, which was owned by actor Richard Burbage's father. In the autumn of 1599, the company was rehoused in the Globe Theatre, built by Richard and Cuthbert Burbage on the south bank of the Thames, due west of London Bridge at Southwark. This was the company's most famous home. Profits there were shared between members of the company as such and the owners of the theater (called "housekeepers"), who included the two Burbages and five others, one of them Shakespeare. Shakespeare was the company's principal dramatist (he also acted with them), but in addition to his plays, works by Ben Jonson, Thomas Dekker, and the partnership of Francis Beaumont and John Fletcher were also presented. About 1608 another theater, in the converted monastery of the Blackfriars, became the winter headquarters of the King's Men. This was also managed by the Burbages, and profits were shared in a manner similar to that followed at the Globe.

Shakespeare, who had retired to his home town of Stratford-upon-Avon, died in 1616. Richard Burbage died in 1619. The longest-surviving member of the original company was John Heminge, who died in 1630. The company itself ceased to exist when, at the outbreak of the English Civil Wars in 1642, the theaters were closed and remained so until the Restoration 18 years later.

Love's Labour's Lost

This early comedy in five acts by was written sometime between 1588 and 1597, more likely in the early 1590s, and published in a quarto edition in 1598, with a title page suggesting that an earlier quarto had been lost. The 1598 quarto was printed seemingly from an authorial working draft showing signs of revision. The play's central comic device is that four young men, dedicated to study and the renunciation of women, meet four young women and inevitably abandon their unrealistic ideals.

The play opens as Ferdinand, the king of Navarre, and three of his noblemen—Berowne (Biron), Longaville, and Dumaine (Dumain)—debate their intellectual intentions. Their plans are thrown into disarray, however, when the Princess of France, attended by three ladies (Rosaline, Maria, and Katharine), arrives on a diplomatic mission from the king of France and must therefore be admitted into Navarre's park. The gentlemen soon discover that they are irresistibly attracted to the ladies. Their attempts at concealing their infatuations from one another are quickly exploded. Their next and more considerable problem, however, is to cope with the young ladies' devastating wit, through means of which the gentlemen are thoroughly put down. Adding to this romantic landscape, Shakespeare provides a group of entertaining eccentrics: Nathaniel (the curate), Holofernes (a schoolmaster), Dull (the constable), Costard (the clown), Mote (or Moth, a page), and Jaquenetta (a country girl). Linking both groups is Don Adriano de Armado, a Spanish grandee whose absurd pretensions to poetic eloquence and love melancholy are squandered on the wench Jaquenetta. The play ends with a brilliant coup de théâtre in the arrival of Marcade: his news of the death of the French king introduces into the never-never land of Navarre a note of somber reality that reminds both the young ladies and the gentlemen that wooing and marriage entail serious responsibilities. Shakespeare's deliberate abstention from the customary "and they all lived happily ever after" conclusion of the genre is remarkable: "Jack hath not Jill." To be sure, the audience is given a promise that the marriages will ultimately take place, after the gentlemen have had a year to think about themselves and come to maturity. Thus, the play ends with hope—perhaps the best kind of happy ending.

▌*Macbeth*

This tragedy in five acts was written sometime in 1606–1607 and published in the First Folio of 1623 from a playbook or a transcript of one. Some portions of the original text are corrupted or missing from the published edition. The play is the shortest of Shakespeare's tragedies, without diversions or subplots. It chronicles Macbeth's seizing of power and subsequent destruction, both his rise and his fall the result of blind ambition.

Macbeth and Banquo, who are generals serving King Duncan of Scotland, meet the Weird Sisters, three witches who prophesy that Macbeth will become thane of Cawdor, then king, and that Banquo will beget kings. Soon thereafter Macbeth discovers that he has indeed been made thane of Cawdor, which leads him to believe the rest of the prophecy. When King Duncan chooses this moment to honor Macbeth by visiting his castle of Dunsinane at Inverness, both Macbeth and his ambitious wife realize that the moment has arrived for them to carry out a plan of regicide that they have long contemplated. Spurred by his wife, Macbeth kills Duncan, and the murder is discovered when Macduff, the thane of Fife, arrives to call on the king. Duncan's sons Malcolm and Donalbain flee the country, fearing for their lives. Their speedy departure seems to implicate them in the crime, and Macbeth becomes king.

Worried by the witches' prophecy that Banquo's heirs instead of Macbeth's own progeny will be kings, Macbeth arranges the death of Banquo, though Banquo's son Fleance escapes. Banquo's ghost haunts Macbeth, and Lady Macbeth is driven to madness by her guilt. The witches assure Macbeth that he will be safe until Birnam Wood comes to Dunsinane and that no one "of woman born" shall harm him. Learning that Macduff is joining Malcolm's army, Macbeth orders the slaughter of Macduff's wife and children. When the army, using branches from Birnam Wood as camouflage, advances on Dunsinane, Macbeth sees the prophecy being fulfilled: Birnam Wood has indeed come to Dunsinane. Lady Macbeth dies; Macbeth is killed in battle by Macduff, who was "from his mother's womb untimely ripped" by cesarean section and in that quibbling sense was not "of woman born." Malcolm becomes the rightful king.

Marlowe, Christopher

An Elizabethan poet and Shakespeare's most important predecessor in English drama, Christopher Marlowe (1564–1593) is noted especially for his establishment of dramatic blank verse.

He was the second child and eldest son of John Marlowe, a Canterbury shoemaker. Nothing is known of his first schooling, but on January 14, 1579, he entered the King's School, Canterbury, as a scholar. A year later he went to Corpus Christi College, Cambridge. Obtaining his bachelor of arts degree in 1584, he continued in residence at Cambridge—which may imply that he

Detail of a portrait thought to be of Christopher Marlowe, dated 1585, artist unknown.

was intending to take Anglican orders. In 1587, however, the university hesitated about granting him the master's degree; its doubts (arising from his frequent absences from the university) were apparently set at rest when the Privy Council sent a letter declaring that he had been employed "on matters touching the benefit of his country"— apparently in Elizabeth I's secret service.

After 1587 Marlowe was in London, writing for the theaters, occasionally getting into trouble with the authorities because of his violent and disreputable behavior, and probably also engaging himself from time to time in government service. Marlowe won a dangerous reputation for "atheism," but this could, in Elizabeth I's time, indicate merely unorthodox religious opinions. In Robert Greene's deathbed tract, *Greenes groats-worth of witte,* Marlowe is referred to as a "famous gracer of Tragedians" and is reproved for having said, like Greene himself, "There is no god" and for having studied "pestilent Machiuilian pollicie." There is further evidence of his unorthodoxy, notably in the denunciation of him written by the spy Richard Baines and in the letter of Thomas Kyd to the lord keeper in 1593 after Marlowe's death. Kyd alleged that certain papers "denying the deity of Jesus Christ" that were found in his room belonged to Marlowe, who had shared the room two years before. Both Baines and Kyd suggested on Marlowe's part atheism in the stricter sense and a persistent delight in blasphemy. Whatever the case may be, on May 18, 1593, the Privy Council issued an order for Marlowe's arrest; two days later the poet was ordered to give daily attendance on their lordships "until he shall be licensed to the contrary." On May 30, however, Marlowe was killed by Ingram Frizer, in the dubious company of Nicholas Skeres and Robert Poley, at a lodging house in Deptford, where they had spent most of the day and where, it was alleged, a fight broke out between them over the bill.

In a playwriting career that spanned little more than six years, Marlowe's achievements were diverse and splendid. Perhaps before leaving Cambridge he had already written *Tamburlaine the Great* (in two parts, both performed by the end of 1587; published 1590). Almost certainly during his later Cambridge years, Marlowe had translated Ovid's *Amores* (*The Loves*) and the first book of Lucan's *Pharsalia* from the Latin. About this time he also wrote the play *Dido, Queen of Carthage* (published in 1594 as the joint work of Marlowe and Thomas Nashe). With the production of *Tamburlaine* he received recognition and acclaim, and playwriting became his major concern in the few years that lay ahead. Both parts of *Tamburlaine* were published anonymously in 1590, and the publisher omitted certain passages that he found incongruous with the play's serious concern with history; even so, the extant *Tamburlaine* text can be regarded as substantially Marlowe's. No other of his plays or poems or translations was published during his life. His unfinished but splendid poem *Hero and Leander*—which is almost certainly the finest nondramatic Elizabethan poem apart from those produced by Edmund Spenser—appeared in 1598.

There is argument among scholars concerning the order in which the plays subsequent to *Tamburlaine* were written. It is not uncommonly held that *Faustus* quickly followed *Tamburlaine* and that then Marlowe turned to a more neutral, more "social" kind of writing in *Edward II* and *The Massacre at Paris*. His last play may have been *The Jew of Malta*, in which he signally broke new ground. It is known that *Tamburlaine, Faustus*, and *The Jew of Malta* were performed by the Admiral's Men, a company whose outstanding actor was Edward Alleyn, who most certainly played Tamburlaine, Faustus, and Barabas the Jew.

In the earliest of Marlowe's plays, the two-part *Tamburlaine the Great* (c. 1587; published 1590), Marlowe's characteristic "mighty line" (as Ben Jonson called it) established blank verse as the staple medium for later Elizabethan and Jacobean dramatic writing. It appears that originally Marlowe intended to write only the first part, concluding with Tamburlaine's marriage to Zenocrate and his making "truce with all the world." But the popularity of the first part encouraged Marlowe to continue the story to Tamburlaine's death. This gave him some difficulty, as he had almost exhausted his historical sources in Part 1; consequently the sequel has, at first glance, an appearance of padding. Yet the effort demanded in writing the continuation made the young playwright look more coldly and searchingly at the hero he had chosen, and thus Part 2 makes explicit certain notions that were below the surface and insufficiently recognized by the dramatist in Part 1.

The play is based on the life and achievements of Timur (Timurlenk), the bloody 14th-century conqueror of Central Asia and India. Tamburlaine is a man avid for power and luxury and the possession of beauty: at the beginning of Part 1 he is only an obscure Scythian shepherd, but he wins the crown of Persia by eloquence and bravery and a readiness to discard loyalty. He then conquers Bajazeth, emperor of Turkey, he puts the town of Damascus to the sword, and he conquers the sultan of Egypt; but, at the pleas of the sultan's daughter Zenocrate, the captive whom he loves, he spares him and makes truce. In Part 2 Tamburlaine's conquests are further extended; whenever he fights a battle, he must win, even when his last illness is upon him. But Zenocrate dies, and their three sons provide a manifestly imperfect means for ensuring the preservation of his wide dominions; he kills Calyphas, one of these sons, when he refuses to follow his father into battle. Always, too, there are more battles to fight: when for a moment he has no immediate opponent on earth, he dreams of leading his army against the powers of heaven, though at other times he glories in seeing himself as "the scourge of God"; he burns the Qur'an, for he will have no intermediary between God and himself, and there is a hint of doubt whether even God is to be granted recognition. Certainly Marlowe feels sympathy with his hero, giving him magnificent verse to speak, delighting in his dreams of power and of the possession of beauty, as seen in the following of Tamburlaine's lines:

> Nature, that fram'd us of four elements
> Warring within our breasts for regiment,
> Doth teach us all to have aspiring minds:
> Our souls, whose faculties can comprehend
> The wondrous architecture of the world,
> And measure every wandering planet's course,
> Still climbing after knowledge infinite,
> And always moving as the restless spheres,
> Wills us to wear ourselves and never rest,
> Until we reach the ripest fruit of all,
> That perfect bliss and sole felicity,
> The sweet fruition of an earthly crown.

But, especially in Part 2, there are other strains: the hero can be absurd in his continual striving for more demonstrations of his power; his cruelty, which is extreme, becomes sickening; his human weakness is increasingly underlined, most notably in the onset of his fatal illness immediately after his arrogant burning of the Qur'an. In this early play Marlowe already shows the ability to view a tragic hero from more than one angle, achieving a simultaneous vision of grandeur and impotence.

Marlowe's most famous play is *The Tragicall History of Dr. Faustus*, but it has survived only in a corrupt form, and its date of composition has been much disputed. It was first published in 1604, and another version appeared in 1616. *Faustus* takes over the dramatic framework of the morality plays in its presentation of a story of temptation, fall, and damnation and its free use of morality figures such as the good angel and the bad angel and the seven deadly sins, along with the devils Lucifer and Mephistopheles. In *Faustus* Marlowe tells the story of the doctor-turned-necromancer Faustus, who sells his soul to the devil

in exchange for knowledge and power. The devil's intermediary
in the play, Mephistopheles, achieves tragic grandeur in his own
right as a fallen angel torn between satanic pride and dark
despair. The play gives eloquent expression to this idea of
damnation in the lament of Mephistopheles for a lost heaven
and in Faustus's final despairing entreaties to be saved by Christ
before his soul is claimed by the devil:

> The stars move still, time runs, the clock
>   will strike,
> The devil will come, and Faustus must
>   be damn'd.
> O, I'll leap up to my God!—Who pulls
>   me down?—
> See, see, where Christ's blood streams in
>   the firmament!
> One drop would save my soul, half a drop:
>   ah, my Christ!—
> Ah, rend not my heart for naming of my Christ!
> Yet will I call on him: O, spare me, Lucifer!—
> Where is it now? 'tis gone: and see, where God
> Stretcheth out his arm, and bends his
>   ireful brows!
> Mountains and hills, come, come, and fall
>   on me,
> And hide me from the heavy wrath of God!

Just as in *Tamburlaine* Marlowe had seen the cruelty and
absurdity of his hero as well as his magnificence, so here he can
enter into Faustus's grandiose intellectual ambition, simultaneously viewing those ambitions as futile, self-destructive, and
absurd. The text is problematic in the low comic scenes spuriously introduced by later hack writers, but its more sober and
consistent moments are certainly the uncorrupted work of
Marlowe.

In *The Famous Tragedy of the Rich Jew of Malta*, Marlowe
portrays another power-hungry figure in the Jew Barabas, who
in the villainous society of Christian Malta shows no scruple in

self-advancement. But this figure is more closely incorporated within his society than either Tamburlaine, the supreme conqueror, or Faustus, the lonely adventurer against God. In the end Barabas is overcome, not by a divine stroke but by the concerted action of his human enemies. There is a difficulty in deciding how fully the extant text of *The Jew of Malta* represents Marlowe's original play, for it was not published until 1633. But *The Jew* can be closely associated with *The Massacre at Paris* (1593), a dramatic presentation of incidents from contemporary French history, including the Massacre of St. Bartholomew's Day, and with *The Troublesome Raigne and Lamentable Death of Edward the Second* (published 1594), Marlowe's great contribution to the Elizabethan plays on historical themes.

As *The Massacre* introduces in the Duke of Guise a figure unscrupulously avid for power, so in the younger Mortimer of *Edward II* Marlowe shows a man developing an appetite for power and increasingly corrupted as power comes to him. In each instance the dramatist shares in the excitement of the pursuit of glory, but all three plays present such figures within a social framework: the notion of social responsibility, the notion of corruption through power, and the notion of the suffering that the exercise of power entails are all prominently the dramatist's concern. Apart from *Tamburlaine* and the minor work *Dido, Queen of Carthage* (of uncertain date, published 1594 and written in collaboration with Thomas Nashe), *Edward II* is the only one of Marlowe's plays whose extant text can be relied on as adequately representing the author's manuscript. And certainly *Edward II* is a major work, not merely one of the first Elizabethan plays on an English historical theme. The relationships linking the king, his neglected queen, the king's favorite, Gaveston, and the ambitious Mortimer are studied with detached sympathy and remarkable understanding: no character here is lightly disposed of, and the abdication and the brutal murder of Edward show the same dark and violent imagination as appeared in Marlowe's presentation of Faustus's last hour.

Though this play, along with *The Jew* and *The Massacre*, shows Marlowe's fascinated response to the distorted Elizabethan idea of Machiavelli, it more importantly shows Marlowe's deeply suggestive awareness of the nature of disaster, the power of society, and the dark extent of an individual's suffering.

In addition to translations (Ovid's *Amores* and the first book of Lucan's *Pharsalia*), Marlowe's nondramatic work includes the poem *Hero and Leander*. This work was incomplete at his death and was extended by George Chapman: the joint work of the two poets was published in 1598.

An authoritative edition of Marlowe's works was edited by Fredson Bowers, *The Complete Works of Christopher Marlowe*, 2nd ed., 2 vols. (1981).

▮ Mature Plays

In the second half of the 1590s, Shakespeare brought to perfection the genre of romantic comedy that he had helped to invent. *A Midsummer Night's Dream* (c. 1595–1596), one of the most successful of all his plays, displays the kind of multiple plotting he had practiced in *The Taming of the Shrew* and other earlier comedies. The overarching plot is of Duke Theseus of Athens and his impending marriage to an Amazonian warrior, Hippolyta, whom Theseus has recently conquered and brought back to Athens to be his bride. Their marriage ends the play. They share this concluding ceremony with the four young lovers Hermia and Lysander and Helena and Demetrius, who have fled into the forest nearby to escape the Athenian law and to pursue one another, whereupon they are subjected to a complicated series of mix-ups. Eventually all is righted by fairy magic, though the fairies are no less at strife. Oberon, king of the fairies, quarrels with his queen Titania over a changeling boy and punishes her by causing her to fall in love with an Athenian artisan who wears an ass's head. The artisans are in the forest to rehearse a play for the forthcoming marriage of Theseus and Hippolyta. Thus four separate strands or plots interact with one another. Despite the play's brevity, it is a masterpiece of artful construction.

The use of multiple plots encourages a varied treatment of the experiencing of love. For the two young human couples, falling in love is quite hazardous; the long-standing friendship between the two young women is threatened and almost destroyed by the rivalries of heterosexual encounter. The eventual transition to heterosexual marriage seems to them to have been a process of dreaming, indeed of nightmare, from which they emerge miraculously restored to their best selves. Meantime the marital strife of Oberon and Titania is, more disturbingly, one in which the female is humiliated until she submits to the will of her husband. Similarly, Hippolyta is an Amazon warrior queen who has had to submit to the authority of a husband. Fathers and daughters are no less at strife until, as in a dream, all is resolved by the magic of Puck and Oberon. Love is ambivalently both an enduring ideal relationship and a struggle for mastery in which the male has the upper hand.

The Merchant of Venice (c. 1596–1597) uses a double plot structure to contrast a tale of romantic wooing with one that comes close to tragedy. Portia is a fine example of a romantic heroine in Shakespeare's mature comedies; she is witty, rich, exacting in what she expects of men, and adept at putting herself in a male disguise to make her presence felt. She is loyally obedient to her father's will and yet determined that she shall have Bassanio. She triumphantly resolves the murky legal affairs of Venice when the men have all failed. Shylock, the Jewish moneylender, is at the point of exacting a pound of flesh from Bassanio's friend Antonio as payment for a forfeited loan. Portia foils him in his attempt in a way that is both clever and shystering. Sympathy is uneasily balanced in Shakespeare's portrayal of Shylock, who is both persecuted by his Christian opponents and all too ready to demand an eye for an eye according to ancient law. Ultimately Portia triumphs, not only with Shylock in the court of law but in her marriage with Bassanio.

Much Ado about Nothing (c. 1598–1599) revisits the issue of power struggles in courtship, again in a revealingly double plot. The young heroine of the more conventional story, derived from Italianate fiction, is wooed by a respectable young aristocrat named Claudio, who has won his spurs and now considers it his pleasant duty to take a wife. He knows so little about Hero (as she is named) that he gullibly credits the contrived evidence of the play's villain, Don John, that she has had many lovers, including one on the evening before the intended wedding. Other men as well, including Claudio's senior officer, Don Pedro, and Hero's father, Leonato, are all too ready to believe the slanderous accusation. Only comic circumstances rescue Hero from her accusers and reveal to the men that they have been fools. Meantime, Hero's cousin, Beatrice, finds it hard to overcome her skepticism about men, even when she is wooed by Benedick, who is also a skeptic about marriage. Here the barriers to romantic understanding are inner and psychological and must be defeated by the good-natured plotting of their friends, who see that Beatrice and Benedick are truly made for one another in their wit and candor if they can only overcome their fear of being outwitted by each other. In what could be regarded as a brilliant rewriting of *The Taming of the Shrew*, the witty battle of the sexes is no less amusing and complicated, but the eventual accommodation finds something much closer to mutual respect and equality between men and women.

Rosalind, in *As You Like It* (c. 1598–1600), makes use of the by now familiar device of disguise as a young man in order to pursue the ends of promoting a rich and substantial relationship between the sexes. As in other of these plays, Rosalind is more emotionally stable and mature than her young man, Orlando. He lacks formal education and is all rough edges, though fundamentally decent and attractive. She is the daughter of the banished Duke who finds herself obliged, in turn, to go into banishment with her dear cousin Celia and the court fool, Touchstone. Although Rosalind's male disguise is at first a means of survival in a seemingly inhospitable forest, it soon serves a more interesting function. As "Ganymede," Rosalind befriends Orlando, offering him counseling in the affairs of love. Orlando, much in need of such advice, readily accepts and proceeds to woo his "Rosalind" ("Ganymede" playing her own self) as though she were indeed a woman. Her wryly amusing perspectives on the follies of young love helpfully puncture Orlando's inflated and unrealistic "Petrarchan" stance as the young lover who writes poems to his mistress and sticks them up on trees. Once he has learned that love is not a fantasy of invented attitudes, Orlando is ready to be the husband of the real young woman (actually a boy actor, of course) who is presented to him as the transformed Ganymede-Rosalind. Other figures in the play further an understanding of love's glorious foolishness by their various attitudes: Silvius, the pale-faced wooer out of pastoral romance; Phoebe, the disdainful mistress whom he worships; William, the country bumpkin; and Audrey, the country wench; and, surveying and commenting on every imaginable kind of human folly, the clown Touchstone and the malcontent traveler Jaques.

Twelfth Night (c. 1600–1602) pursues a similar motif of female disguise. Viola, cast ashore in Illyria by a shipwreck and obliged to disguise herself as a young man in order to gain a place in the court of Duke Orsino, falls in love with the duke and uses her disguise as a cover for an educational process not unlike that given by Rosalind to Orlando. Orsino is as unrealistic a lover as one could hope to imagine; he pays fruitless court to the Countess Olivia and seems content with the unproductive love melancholy in which he wallows. Only Viola, as "Cesario," is able to awaken in him a genuine feeling for friendship and love. They become inseparable companions and then seeming rivals for the hand of Olivia until the presto change of Shakespeare's stage magic is able to restore "Cesario" to her woman's garments and thus present to Orsino the flesh-and-blood woman whom he has only distantly imagined. The transition from same-sex friendship to heterosexual union is a constant in Shakespearean comedy. The woman is the self-knowing, constant, loyal one; the man needs to learn a lot from the woman.

As in the other plays as well, *Twelfth Night* neatly plays off this courtship theme with a second plot, of Malvolio's self-deception that he is desired by Olivia—an illusion that can be addressed only by the satirical devices of exposure and humiliation.

The Merry Wives of Windsor (c. 1597–1601) is an interesting deviation from the usual Shakespearean romantic comedy in that it is set not in some imagined far-off place like Illyria or Belmont or the forest of Athens but in Windsor, a solidly bourgeois village near Windsor Castle in the heart of England. Uncertain tradition has it that Queen Elizabeth wanted to see Falstaff in love. There is little, however, in the way of romantic wooing (the story of Anne Page and her suitor Fenton is rather buried in the midst of so many other goings-on), but the play's portrayal of women, and especially of the two "merry wives," Mistress Alice Ford and Mistress Margaret Page, reaffirms what is so often true of women in these early plays, that they are good-hearted, chastely loyal, and wittily self-possessed. Falstaff, a suitable butt for their cleverness, is a scapegoat figure who must be publicly humiliated as a way of transferring onto him the human frailties that Windsor society wishes to expunge.

Completion of the Histories

Concurrent with his writing of these fine romantic comedies, Shakespeare also brought to completion (for the time being, at least) his project of writing 15th-century English history. After having finished in 1589–1594 the tetralogy about Henry VI, Edward IV, and Richard III, bringing the story down to 1485, and then a play about *King John* (c. 1594–1596) that deals with a chronological period (the 13th century) that sets it quite apart from his other history plays, Shakespeare returned to the late 14th and early 15th centuries and to the chronicle of Richard II, Henry IV, and Henry's legendary son, Henry V. This inversion of historical order in the two tetralogies allowed Shakespeare to finish his sweep of late medieval English history with Henry V, a hero king in a way that Richard III could never pretend to be.

Richard II (c. 1595–1596), written throughout in blank verse, is a somber play about political impasse. It contains almost no humor, other than a wry scene in which the new king, Henry IV, must adjudicate the competing claims of the Duke of York and the Duchess, the first of whom wishes to see his son Aumerle executed for treason and the second of whom begs for mercy. Henry is able to be merciful on this occasion, since he has now won the kingship, and thus gives to this scene an upbeat movement. Earlier, however, the mood is grim. Richard, installed at an early age into the kingship, proves irresponsible as a ruler. He unfairly banishes his own first cousin, Henry Bolingbroke (later to be Henry IV), whereas the king himself appears to be guilty of ordering the murder of an uncle. When Richard keeps the dukedom of Lancaster from Bolingbroke without proper legal authority, he manages to alienate many nobles and to encourage Bolingbroke's return from exile. That return, too, is illegal, but it is a fact, and when several of the nobles (including York) come over to Bolingbroke's side, Richard is forced to abdicate. The rights and wrongs of this power struggle are masterfully ambiguous. History proceeds without any sense of moral imperative. Henry IV is a more capable ruler, but his authority is tarnished by his crimes (including his seeming assent to the execution of Richard), and his own rebellion appears to teach the barons to rebel against him in turn. Henry eventually dies a disappointed man.

The dying king Henry IV must turn royal authority over to young Hal, or Henry, now Henry V. The prospect is dismal both to the dying king and to the members of his court, for Prince Hal has distinguished himself to this point mainly by his penchant for keeping company with the disreputable if engaging Falstaff. The son's attempts at reconciliation with the father succeed temporarily, especially when Hal saves his father's life at the battle of Shrewsbury, but (especially in *2 Henry IV*) his reputation as a wastrel will not leave him. Everyone expects from him a reign of irresponsible license, with Falstaff in an influential position. It is for these reasons that the young king must publicly repudiate his old companion of the tavern and the highway, however much that repudiation tugs at his heart and the audience's. Falstaff, for all his debauchery and irresponsibility, is infectiously amusing and delightful; he represents in Hal a spirit of youthful vitality that is left behind only with the greatest of regret as the young man assumes manhood and the role of crown prince. Hal manages all this with aplomb and goes on to defeat the French mightily at the Battle of Agincourt. Even his high jinks are a part of what is so attractive in him. Maturity and position come at a great personal cost: Hal becomes less a frail human being and more the figure of royal authority.

Thus, in his plays of the 1590s, the young Shakespeare concentrated to a remarkable extent on romantic comedies and English history plays. The two genres are nicely complementary: the one deals with courtship and marriage, while the other examines the career of a young man growing up to be a worthy king. Only at the end of the history plays does Henry V have any kind of romantic relationship with a woman, and this one instance is quite unlike courtships in the romantic comedies: Hal is given the Princess of France as his prize, his reward for sturdy manhood. He takes the lead in the wooing scene, in which he invites her to join him in a political marriage. In both romantic comedies and English history plays, a young man successfully negotiates the hazardous and potentially rewarding paths of sexual and social maturation.

Romeo and Juliet

Apart from the early *Titus Andronicus*, the only other play that Shakespeare wrote prior to 1599 that is classified as a tragedy is *Romeo and Juliet* (1594–1596), which is quite untypical of the tragedies that are to follow. Written more or less at the time when Shakespeare was writing *A Midsummer Night's Dream*, *Romeo and Juliet* shares many of the characteristics of romantic comedy. Romeo and Juliet are not persons of extraordinary social rank or position, like Hamlet, Othello, King Lear, and

Macbeth. They are the boy and girl next door, interesting not for their philosophical ideas but for their appealing love for each other. They are character types more suited to classical comedy in that they do not derive from the upper class. Their wealthy families are essentially bourgeois. The eagerness with which Capulet and his wife court Count Paris as their prospective son-in-law bespeaks their desire for social advancement.

Accordingly, the first half of *Romeo and Juliet* is very funny, while its delight in verse forms reminds us of *A Midsummer Night's Dream*. The bawdry of Mercutio and of the Nurse is richly suited to the comic texture of the opening scenes. Romeo, haplessly in love with a Rosaline whom we never meet, is a partly comic figure like Silvius in *As You Like It*. The plucky and self-knowing Juliet is much like the heroines of romantic comedies. She is able to instruct Romeo in the ways of speaking candidly and unaffectedly about their love rather than in the frayed cadences of the Petrarchan wooer.

The play is ultimately a tragedy, of course, and indeed warns its audience at the start that the lovers are "star-crossed." Yet the tragic vision is not remotely that of *Hamlet* or *King Lear*. Romeo and Juliet are unremarkable, nice young people doomed by a host of considerations outside themselves: the enmity of their two families, the misunderstandings that prevent Juliet from being able to tell her parents whom it is that she has married, and even unfortunate coincidence (such as the misdirection of the letter sent to Romeo to warn him of the Friar's plan for Juliet's recovery from a deathlike sleep). Yet there is the element of personal responsibility upon which most mature tragedy rests when Romeo chooses to avenge the death of Mercutio by killing Tybalt, knowing that this deed will undo the soft graces of forbearance that Juliet has taught him. Romeo succumbs to the macho peer pressure of his male companions, and tragedy results in part from this choice. Yet so much is at work that the reader ultimately sees *Romeo and Juliet* as a love tragedy—celebrating the exquisite brevity of young love, regretting an unfeeling world, and evoking an emotional response that differs from that produced by the other tragedies. Romeo and Juliet are, at last, "Poor sacrifices of our enmity" (Act V, scene 3, line 304). The emotional response the play evokes is a strong one, but it is not like the response called forth by the tragedies after 1599.

The "Problem" Plays

Whatever his reasons, about 1599–1600 Shakespeare turned with unsparing intensity to the exploration of darker issues such as revenge, sexual jealousy, aging, midlife crisis, and death. Perhaps he saw that his own life was moving into a new phase of more complex and vexing experiences. Perhaps he felt, or sensed, that he had worked through the romantic comedy and history play and the emotional trajectories of maturation that they encompassed. At any event, he began writing not only his great tragedies but a group of plays that are hard to classify in terms of genre. They are sometimes grouped today as "problem" plays or "problem" comedies. An examination of these plays is crucial to understanding this period of transition from 1599 to 1605.

The three problem plays dating from these years are *All's Well That Ends Well*, *Measure for Measure*, and *Troilus and Cressida*. *All's Well* is a comedy ending in acceptance of marriage, but in a way that poses thorny ethical issues. Count Bertram cannot initially accept his marriage to Helena, a woman of lower social station who has grown up in his noble household and has won Bertram as her husband by her seemingly miraculous cure of the French king. Bertram's reluctance to face the responsibilities of marriage is all the more dismaying when he turns his amorous intentions to a Florentine maiden, Diana, whom he wishes to seduce without marriage. Helena's stratagem to resolve this difficulty is the so-called bed trick, substituting herself in Bertram's bed for the arranged assignation and then calling her wayward husband to account when she is pregnant with his child. Her ends are achieved by such morally ambiguous means that marriage seems at best a precarious institution on which to base the presumed reassurances of romantic comedy. The pathway toward resolution and emotional maturity is not easy; Helena is a more ambiguous heroine than Rosalind or Viola.

Measure for Measure (c. 1603–1604) similarly employs the bed trick, and for a similar purpose, though in even murkier circumstances. Isabella, on the verge of becoming a nun, learns that she has attracted the sexual desire of Lord Angelo, the deputy ruler of Vienna serving in the mysterious absence of the Duke. Her plea to Angelo for her brother's life, when that brother (Claudio) has been sentenced to die for fornication with his fiancée, is met with a demand that she sleep with Angelo or forfeit Claudio's life. This ethical dilemma is resolved by a trick (devised by the Duke, in disguise) to substitute for Isabella a woman (Mariana) whom Angelo was supposed to marry but refused when she could produce no dowry. The Duke's motivations in manipulating these substitutions and false appearances are unclear, though arguably his wish is to see what the various characters of this play will do when faced with seemingly impossible choices. Angelo is revealed as a morally fallen man, a would-be seducer and murderer who is nonetheless remorseful and ultimately glad to have been prevented from carrying out his intended crimes; Claudio learns that he is coward enough to wish to live by any means, including the emotional and physical blackmail of his sister; and Isabella learns that she is capable of bitterness and hatred, even if, crucially, she finally discovers that she can and must forgive her enemy. Her charity, and the Duke's stratagems, make possible an ending in forgiveness and marriage, but in that process the nature and meaning of marriage are severely tested.

Troilus and Cressida (c. 1601–1602) is the most experimental and puzzling of these three plays. Simply in terms of genre, it is virtually unclassifiable. It can hardly be a comedy, ending as it does in the deaths of Patroclus and Hector and the looming defeat of the Trojans. Nor is the ending normative in terms of romantic comedy: the lovers, Troilus and Cressida, are separated from one another and embittered by the failure of their relationship. The play is a history play in a sense, dealing as it does with the great Trojan War celebrated in Homer's *Iliad*, and yet its purpose is hardly that of telling the story of the war. As a tragedy, it is perplexing in that the chief figures of the play (apart from Hector) do not die at the end, and the mood is one of desolation and even disgust rather than tragic catharsis. Perhaps the play should be thought of as a satire; the choric observations of Thersites and Pandarus serve throughout as a mordant commentary on the interconnectedness of war and lechery. With fitting ambiguity, the play was placed in the Folio of 1623 between the histories and the tragedies, in a category all by itself. Clearly, in these problem plays Shakespeare was opening up for himself a host of new problems in terms of genre and human sexuality.

Written in 1599 (the same year as *Henry V*) or 1600, probably for the opening of the Globe Theatre on the south bank of the Thames, *Julius Caesar* illustrates similarly the transition in Shakespeare's writing toward darker themes and tragedy. It, too, is a history play in a sense, dealing with a non-Christian civilization existing 16 centuries before Shakespeare wrote his plays. Roman history opened up for Shakespeare a world in which divine purpose could not be easily ascertained. The characters of *Julius Caesar* variously interpret the great event of the assassination of Caesar as one in which the gods are angry or disinterested or capricious or simply not there. The wise Cicero observes, "Men may construe things after their fashion, / Clean from the purpose of the things themselves" (Act I, scene 3, lines 34–35).

Human history in *Julius Caesar* seems to follow a pattern of rise and fall, in a way that is cyclical rather than divinely purposeful. Caesar enjoys his days of triumph, until he is cut down by the conspirators; Brutus and Cassius succeed to power, but not for long. Brutus's attempts to protect Roman republicanism and the freedom of the city's citizens to govern themselves through senatorial tradition end up in the destruction of the very liberties he most cherished. He and Cassius meet their destiny at the Battle of Philippi. They are truly tragic figures, especially Brutus, in that their essential characters are their fate; Brutus is a good man but also proud and stubborn, and these latter qualities ultimately bring about his death. Shakespeare's first major tragedy is Roman in spirit and classical in its notion of tragic character. It shows what Shakespeare had to learn from Classical precedent as he set about looking for workable models in tragedy.

The Tragedies

Hamlet (c. 1599–1601), on the other hand, chooses a tragic model closer to that of *Titus Andronicus* and Kyd's *The Spanish Tragedie*. In form, *Hamlet* is a revenge tragedy. It features characteristics found in *Titus* as well: a protagonist charged with the responsibility of avenging a heinous crime against the protagonist's family, a cunning antagonist, the appearance of the ghost of the murdered person, the feigning of madness to throw off the villain's suspicions, the play within the play as a means of testing the villain, and still more.

Yet to search out these comparisons is to highlight what is so extraordinary about *Hamlet*, for it refuses to be merely a revenge tragedy. Shakespeare's protagonist is unique in the genre in his moral qualms, and most of all in his finding a way to carry out his dread command without becoming a cold-blooded murderer. Hamlet does act bloodily, especially when he kills Polonius, thinking that the old man hidden in Gertrude's chambers must be Claudius, whom Hamlet is commissioned to kill. The act seems plausible and strongly motivated, and yet Hamlet sees at once that he has erred. He has killed the wrong man, even if Polonius has brought this on himself with his incessant spying. Hamlet sees that he has offended heaven and that he will have to pay for his act. When, at the play's end, Hamlet encounters his fate in a duel with Polonius's son, Laertes, Hamlet interprets his own tragic story as one that Providence has made meaningful. By placing himself in the hands of Providence and believing devoutly that "There's a divinity that shapes our ends, / Rough-hew them how we will" (Act V, scene 2, lines 10–11), Hamlet finds himself ready for a death that he has longed for. He also finds an opportunity for killing Claudius almost unpremeditatedly, spontaneously, as an act of reprisal for all that Claudius has done.

Hamlet thus finds tragic meaning in his own story. More broadly, too, he has searched for meaning in dilemmas of all sorts: his mother's overhasty marriage, Ophelia's weak-willed succumbing to the will of her father and brother, his being spied on by his erstwhile friends Rosencrantz and Guildenstern, and much more. His utterances are often despondent, relentlessly honest, and philosophically profound, as he ponders the nature of friendship, memory, romantic attachment, filial love, sensuous enslavement, corrupting habits (drinking, sexual lust), and almost every phase of human experience. One remarkable aspect about Shakespeare's great tragedies (*Hamlet, Othello, King Lear, Macbeth*, and *Antony and Cleopatra* most of all) is that they proceed through such a staggering range of human emotions, and especially the emotions that are appropriate to the mature years of the human cycle. Hamlet is 30, one learns— an age when a person is apt to perceive that the world around him is "an unweeded garden / That grows to seed. Things rank and gross in nature / Possess it merely" (Act I, scene 2, lines 135–137). Shakespeare was about 36 when he wrote this play. *Othello* (c. 1603–1604) centers on sexual jealousy in marriage. *King Lear* (c. 1605–1606) is about aging, generational conflict, and feelings of ingratitude. *Macbeth* (c. 1606–1607) explores ambition mad enough to kill a father figure who stands in the way. *Antony and Cleopatra*, written about 1606–1607 when Shakespeare was 42 or thereabouts, studies the exhilarating but ultimately dismaying phenomenon of midlife crisis. Shakespeare moves his readers vicariously through these life experiences while he himself struggles to capture, in tragic form, their terrors and challenges.

These plays are deeply concerned with domestic and family relationships. In *Othello* Desdemona is the only daughter of

Brabantio, an aging senator of Venice, who dies heartbroken because his daughter has eloped with a dark-skinned man who is her senior by many years and is of another culture. With Othello, Desdemona is briefly happy, despite her filial disobedience, until a terrible sexual jealousy is awakened in him, quite without cause other than his own fears and susceptibility to Iago's insinuations that it is only "natural" for Desdemona to seek erotic pleasure with a young man who shares her background. Driven by his own deeply irrational fear and hatred of women and seemingly mistrustful of his own masculinity, Iago can assuage his own inner torment only by persuading other men like Othello that their inevitable fate is to be cuckolded. As a tragedy, the play adroitly exemplifies the traditional classical model of a good man brought to misfortune by hamartia, or tragic flaw; as Othello grieves, he is one who has "loved not wisely, but too well" (Act V, scene 2, line 354). It bears remembering, however, that Shakespeare owed no loyalty to this classical model. Hamlet, for one, is a play that does not work well in Aristotelian terms. The search for an Aristotelian hamartia has led all too often to the trite argument that Hamlet suffers from melancholia and a tragic inability to act, whereas a more plausible reading of the play argues that finding the right course of action is highly problematic for him and for everyone. Hamlet sees examples on all sides of those whose forthright actions lead to fatal mistakes or absurd ironies (Laertes, Fortinbras), and indeed his own swift killing of the man he assumes to be Claudius hidden in his mother's chambers turns out to be a mistake for which he realizes heaven will hold him accountable.

Daughters and fathers are also at the heart of the major dilemma in *King Lear*. In this configuration, Shakespeare does what he often does in his late plays: erase the wife from the picture, so that father and daughter(s) are left to deal with one another. (Compare *Othello*, *The Winter's Tale*, *Cymbeline*, *The Tempest*, and perhaps the circumstances of Shakespeare's own life, in which his relations with his daughter Susanna especially seem to have meant more to him than his partly estranged marriage with Anne.) Lear's banishing of his favorite daughter, Cordelia, because of her laconic refusal to proclaim a love for him as the essence of her being brings upon this aging king the terrible punishment of being belittled and rejected by his ungrateful daughters, Goneril and Regan. Concurrently, in the play's second plot, the Earl of Gloucester makes a similar mistake with his good-hearted son, Edgar, and thereby delivers himself into the hands of his scheming bastard son, Edmund. Both these erring elderly fathers are ultimately nurtured by the loyal children they have banished, but not before the play has tested to its absolute limit the proposition that evil can flourish in a bad world.

The gods seem indifferent, perhaps absent entirely; pleas to them for assistance go unheeded while the storm of fortune rains down on the heads of those who have trusted in conventional pieties. Part of what is so great in this play is that its testing of the major characters requires them to seek out philosophical answers that can arm the resolute heart against ingratitude and misfortune by constantly pointing out that life owes one nothing. The consolations of philosophy painfully apprehended by Edgar and Cordelia are those that rely not on the suppositious gods but on an inner moral strength demanding that one be charitable and honest because life is otherwise monstrous and subhuman. The play exacts terrible prices of those who persevere in goodness, but it leaves them and the reader, or the audience, with the reassurance that it is simply better to be a Cordelia than to be a Goneril, to be an Edgar than to be an Edmund.

Macbeth is in some ways Shakespeare's most unsettling tragedy, because it invites the intense examination of the heart of a man who is well-intentioned in most ways but who discovers that he cannot resist the temptation to achieve power at any cost. Macbeth is a sensitive, even poetic person, and as such he understands with frightening clarity the stakes that are involved in his contemplated deed of murder. Duncan is a virtuous king and his guest. The deed is regicide and murder, a violation of the sacred obligations of hospitality. Macbeth knows that

Duncan's virtues, like angels, "trumpet-tongued," will plead against "the deep damnation of his taking-off" (Act I, scene 7, lines 19–20). The only factor weighing on the other side is personal ambition, which Macbeth understands to be a moral failing. The question of why he proceeds to murder is partly answered by the insidious temptations of the three Weird Sisters, who sense Macbeth's vulnerability to their prophecies, and the terrifying strength of his wife, who drives him on to the murder by describing his reluctance as unmanliness. Ultimately, though, the responsibility lies with Macbeth. His collapse of moral integrity confronts the audience and perhaps implicates it. The loyalty and decency of such characters as Macduff hardly offset what is so painfully weak in the play's protagonist.

Antony and Cleopatra approaches human frailty in terms that are less spiritually terrifying. The story of the lovers is certainly one of worldly failure. Plutarch's *Lives* gave to Shakespeare the object lesson of a brave general who lost his reputation and sense of self-worth through his infatuation with an admittedly attractive but nonetheless dangerous woman. Shakespeare changes none of the circumstances: Antony hates himself for dallying in Egypt with Cleopatra, agrees to marry Octavius Caesar's sister Octavia as a way of recovering his status in the Roman triumvirate, cheats on Octavia eventually, loses the battle of Actium because of his fatal attraction for Cleopatra, and dies in Egypt a defeated, aging warrior. Shakespeare adds to this narrative a compelling portrait of midlife crisis. Antony is deeply anxious about his loss of sexual potency and position in the world of affairs. His amorous life in Egypt is manifestly an attempt to affirm and recover his dwindling male power.

Yet the Roman model is not in Shakespeare's play the unassailably virtuous choice that it is in Plutarch. In *Antony and Cleopatra* Roman behavior does promote attentiveness to duty and worldly achievement, but as embodied in young Octavius, it is also obsessively male and cynical about women. Octavius is intent on capturing Cleopatra and leading her in triumph back to Rome—that is, on caging the unruly woman and placing her under male control. When Cleopatra perceives that aim, she chooses a noble suicide rather than humiliation by a patriarchal male. In her suicide, Cleopatra avers that she has called "great Caesar ass / Unpolicied" (Act V, scene 2, lines 307–308). Vastly to be preferred is the fleeting dream of greatness with Antony, both of them unfettered, godlike, like Isis and Osiris, immortalized as heroic lovers even if the actual circumstances of their lives were often disappointing and even tawdry. The vision in this tragedy is deliberately unstable, but at its most ethereal it encourages a vision of human greatness that is distant from the soul-corrupting evil of *Macbeth* or *King Lear*.

Two late tragedies also choose the ancient classical world as their setting but do so in a deeply dispiriting way. Shakespeare appears to have been much preoccupied with ingratitude and human greed in these years. *Timon of Athens* (c. 1605–1608), probably an unfinished play and possibly never produced, initially shows us a prosperous man fabled for his generosity. When he discovers that he has exceeded his means, he turns to his seeming friends for the kinds of assistance he has given them, only to discover that their memories are short. Retiring to a bitter isolation, Timon rails against all humanity and refuses every sort of consolation, even that of well-meant companionship and sympathy from a former servant. He dies in isolation. The unrelieved bitterness of this account is only partly ameliorated by the story of the military captain Alcibiades, who has also been the subject of Athenian ingratitude and forgetfulness but who manages to reassert his authority at the end. Alcibiades resolves to make some accommodation with the wretched condition of humanity; Timon will have none of it. Seldom has a more unrelievedly embittered play been written.

Coriolanus (c. 1608) similarly portrays the ungrateful responses of a city toward its military hero. The problem is complicated by the fact that Coriolanus, egged on by his mother and his conservative allies, undertakes a political role in Rome for which he is not temperamentally fitted. His friends urge him to hold off his intemperate speech until he is voted into office, but Coriolanus is too plainspoken to be tactful in this way. His contempt for the plebeians and their political leaders, the tribunes, is unsparing. His political philosophy, while relentlessly aristocratic and snobbish, is consistent and theoretically sophisticated; the citizens are, as he argues, incapable of governing themselves judiciously. Yet his fury only makes matters worse and leads to an exile from which he returns to conquer his own city, in league with his old enemy and friend, Aufidius. When his mother comes out on behalf of the city to plead for her life and that of other Romans, he relents and thereupon falls into defeat as a kind of mama's boy, unable to assert his own sense of self. As a tragedy, *Coriolanus* is again bitter, satirical, ending in defeat and humiliation. It is an immensely powerful play, and it captures a philosophical mood of nihilism and bitterness that hovers over Shakespeare's writings throughout these years in the first decade of the 1600s.

The Romances

Concurrently, nonetheless, and then in the years that followed, Shakespeare turned again to the writing of comedy. The late comedies are usually called romances or tragicomedies because they tell stories of wandering and separation leading eventually to tearful and joyous reunion. They are suffused with a bittersweet mood that seems eloquently appropriate to a writer who has explored with such unsparing honesty the depths of human suffering and degradation in the great tragedies.

Pericles, written perhaps in 1606–1608 and based on the familiar tale of Apollonius of Tyre, may involve some collaboration of authorship; the text is unusually imperfect, and it did not appear in the Folio of 1623. It employs a chorus figure, John Gower (author of an earlier version of this story), to guide the reader or viewer around the Mediterranean on

Pericles's various travels, as he avoids marriage with the daughter of the incestuous King Antiochus of Antioch; marries Thaisa, the daughter of King Simonides of Pentapolis; has a child by her; believes his wife to have died in childbirth during a storm at sea and has her body thrown overboard to quiet the superstitious fears of the sailors; puts his daughter Marina in the care of Cleon of Tarsus and his wicked wife, Dionyza; and is eventually restored to his wife and child after many years. The story is typical romance. Shakespeare adds touching scenes of reunion and a perception that beneath the naive account of travel lies a subtle dramatization of separation, loss, and recovery. Pericles is deeply burdened by his loss and perhaps, too, a sense of guilt for having consented to consign his wife's body to the sea. He is recovered from his despair only by the ministrations of a loving daughter, who is able to give him a reason to live again and then to be reunited with his wife.

The Winter's Tale (c. 1609–1611) is in some ways a replaying of this same story, in that King Leontes of Sicilia, smitten by an irrational jealousy of his wife, Hermione, brings about the seeming death of that wife and the real death of their son. The resulting guilt is unbearable for Leontes and yet ultimately curative over a period of many years that are required for his only daughter, Perdita (whom he has nearly killed also), to grow to maturity in distant Bohemia. This story, too, is based on a prose romance, in this case Robert Greene's *Pandosto*. The reunion with daughter and then wife is deeply touching as in *Pericles*, with the added magical touch that the audience does not know that Hermione is alive and in fact has been told that she is dead. Her wonderfully staged appearance as a statue coming to life is one of the great theatrical coups in Shakespeare, playing as it does with favorite Shakespearean themes in these late plays of the ministering daughter, the guilt-ridden husband, and the miraculously recovered wife. The story is all the more moving when one considers that Shakespeare may have had, or imagined, a similar experience of attempting to recover a relationship with his wife, Anne, whom he had left in Stratford during his many years in London.

In *Cymbeline* (c. 1608–1610) King Cymbeline drives his virtuous daughter, Imogen, into exile by his opposition to her marriage with Posthumus Leonatus. The wife in this case is Cymbeline's baleful queen, a stereotypical wicked stepmother, whose witless and lecherous son Cloten (Imogen's half brother) is the embodiment of everything that threatens and postpones the eventual happy ending of this tale. Posthumus, too, fails Imogen by being irrationally jealous of her, but he is eventually recovered to a belief in her goodness. The dark portraiture of the Queen illustrates how ambivalent is Shakespeare's view of the mother in his late plays. This Queen is the wicked step-mother, like Dionyza in *Pericles*; in her relentless desire for con-trol, she also brings to mind Lady Macbeth and the Weird Sisters in *Macbeth*, as well as Coriolanus's mother, Volumnia. The devouring mother is a forbidding presence in the late plays, though she is counterbalanced by redeeming maternal figures such as Hermione in *The Winter's Tale* and Thaisa in *Pericles*.

The Tempest (c. 1611) sums up much of what Shakespeare's mature art was all about. Once again we find a wifeless father with a daughter, in this case on a deserted island where the father, Prospero, is entirely responsible for his daughter's educa-tion. He behaves like a dramatist in charge of the whole play as well, arranging her life and that of the other characters. He employs a storm at sea to bring young Ferdinand into the com-pany of his daughter; Ferdinand is Prospero's choice, because such a marriage will resolve the bitter dispute between Milan and Naples—arising after the latter supported Prospero's usurping brother, Antonio, in his claim to the dukedom of Milan—that has led to Prospero's banishment. At the same time, Ferdinand is certainly Miranda's choice as well; the two fall instantly in love, anticipating the desired romantic happy ending. The ending will also mean an end to Prospero's career as artist and dramatist, for he is nearing retirement and senses that his gift will not stay with him forever. The imprisoned spirit Ariel, embodiment of that temporary and precious gift, must be freed in the play's closing moments. Caliban, too, must be freed, since Prospero has done what he could to educate and civilize this Natural Man. Art can only go so far.

The Tempest seems to have been intended as Shakespeare's farewell to the theater. It contains moving passages of reflection on what his powers as artist have been able to accomplish, and valedictory themes of closure. As a comedy, it demonstrates perfectly the way that Shakespeare was able to combine precise artistic construction (the play chooses on this farewell occasion to observe the classical unities of time, place, and action) with his special flair for stories that transcend the merely human and physical: *The Tempest* is peopled with spirits, monsters, and drolleries. This, it seems, is Shakespeare's summation of his art as comic dramatist.

But *The Tempest* proved not to be Shakespeare's last play after all. Perhaps he discovered, as many people do, that he was bored in retirement in 1613 or thereabouts. No doubt his acting company was eager to have him back. He wrote a history play titled *Henry VIII* (1613), which is extraordinary in a number of ways: it relates historical events substantially later chronologically than those of the 15th century that had been his subject in his earlier historical plays; it is separated from the last of those plays by perhaps 14 years; and, perhaps most significant, it is as much romance as history play. History in this instance is really about the birth of Elizabeth I, who was to become England's great queen. The circumstances of Henry VIII's troubled marital affairs, his meeting with Anne Boleyn, his confrontation with the papacy, and all the rest turn out to be the humanly unpredictable ways by which Providence engineers the miracle of Elizabeth's birth. The play ends with this great event and sees in it a justification of and necessity for all that has proceeded. Thus history yields its providential meaning in the shape of a play that is both history and romance.

Marston, John

One of the most vigorous satirists of the Shakespearean era, John Marston (1576–1634) is an English dramatist best known for *The Malcontent* (1604), in which he rails at the iniquities of a lascivious court. He wrote it, as well as other major works, for a variety of children's companies, organized groups of boy actors popular during Elizabethan and Jacobean times.

Marston was educated at the University of Oxford and resided from 1595 at the Middle Temple, London. He began his literary career in 1598 with *The Metamorphosis of Pigmalions Image and Certaine Satyres*, an erotic poem in the newly fashionable Ovidian style. In the same year, the rough-hewn, obscure verses of *The Scourge of Villanie*, in which Marston referred to himself as a "barking satirist," were widely acclaimed.

In 1599 Marston began writing for the theater, producing *Histrio-mastix* (published in 1610), probably for performance at the Middle Temple. In his character Chrisoganus, a "Master Pedant" and "translating scholler," the audience was able to recognize the learned Ben Jonson. A brief, bitter literary feud developed between Marston and Jonson—part of "the war of the theaters." In *Poetaster* (produced 1601) Jonson depicted Marston as Crispinus, a character with red hair and small legs who was given a pill that forced him to disgorge a pretentious vocabulary.

For the Children of Paul's, a theater company, Marston wrote *Antonio and Mellida* (1600), its sequel, *Antonio's Revenge* (1601), and *What You Will* (1601). The most memorable is *Antonio's Revenge*, a savage melodrama of a political power struggle with elements of parody and fantasy.

In 1604 Marston transferred his allegiance to the boy company at the Blackfriars Theatre (i.e., the Children of the Queen's Revels, later Children of the Blackfriars), for which he wrote his remaining plays. *The Dutch Courtezan* (produced 1603–1604), as well as *The Malcontent*, earned him his place as a dramatist. The former, with its coarse, farcical counterplot, was considered one of the cleverest comedies of its time. Although Marston used all the apparatus of contemporary revenge tragedy in *The Malcontent*, the wronged hero does not kill any of his tormentors and regains power by sophisticated Machiavellian strategems.

In 1605 Marston collaborated with Jonson and with George Chapman on *Eastward Ho*, a comedy of the contrasts within the life of the city. But the play's satiric references to opportunistic Scottish countrymen of the newly crowned James I gave offense, and all three authors were imprisoned.

After another imprisonment, presumably once again for libel, in 1608, Marston left unfinished *The Insatiate Countesse*, his most erotic play, and entered the Church of England. He took orders in 1609, married the daughter of James I's chaplain, and in 1616 accepted an ecclesiastical post in Christchurch, Hampshire. In 1633 he apparently insisted upon the removal of his name from the collected edition of six of his plays, *The Workes of John Marston*, which was reissued anonymously the same year as *Tragedies and Comedies*.

▌ Massinger, Philip

English playwright Philip Massinger (1583–c. 1640) is noted for his gifts of comedy, plot construction, social realism, and satirical power.

In addition to the documentation of his baptism at St. Thomas' Church, Salisbury, it is known that Massinger attended St. Alban Hall, Oxford, in 1602, but nothing certain is known about his life from then until 1613, when he was in prison for debt. Bailed out by the theatrical impresario Philip Henslowe, he spent a period working as the junior partner in coauthored plays, collaborating with established dramatists such as Thomas Dekker and John Fletcher, eventually graduating to his own independent productions. In 1625 he succeeded Fletcher, some of whose plays he revised, as the chief playwright of the King's Men (formerly the Lord Chamberlain's Men). Though apparently not as successful as Fletcher, he remained with the King's Men until his death, producing plays marked by a high moral tone and elevated philosophic character.

Among the plays Massinger collaborated on with Fletcher is *The False One* (c. 1620), a treatment of the story of Caesar and Cleopatra. Two other important plays written in collaboration are *The Fatal Dowry* (1616–1619, with Nathan Field), a domestic tragedy in a French setting, and *The Virgin Martyr* (1620?, with Thomas Dekker), a historical play about the persecution of Christians under the Roman emperor Diocletian. Fifteen plays written solely by Massinger have survived, but many of their dates can only be conjectured. The four tragedies are *The Duke of Milan* (1621–1622) and *The Unnatural Combat* (1624?)—both skillfully told mystery stories of a melodramatic type—and *The Roman Actor* (1626) and *Believe As You List* (1631)—each a historical tragedy in a classical setting. *The Roman Actor* is considered his best serious play.

The Bondman (1623), about a slave revolt in the Greek city of Syracuse, is one of Massinger's seven tragicomedies and shows his concern for state affairs. *The Renegado* (1624), a tragicomedy with a heroic Jesuit character, gave rise to the still disputed theory that he became a Roman Catholic. Another tragicomedy, *The Maid of Honour* (1621?), combines political realism with the courtly refinement of later Caroline drama. The tendency of his serious plays to conform to Caroline fashion, however, is contradicted by the mordant realism and satirical force of his two great comedies—*A New Way to Pay Old Debts*, his most popular and influential play, in which he expresses genuine indignation at economic oppression and social disorder, and *The City Madam* (1632?), dealing with similar evils but within a more starkly contrived plot that curiously combines naturalistic and symbolic modes. One of his last plays, *The King and the Subject* (1638), had politically objectionable lines cut from it by King Charles himself.

Measure for Measure

This "dark" comedy in five acts was written about 1603–1604 and published in the First Folio of 1623 from a transcript of an authorial draft. The play examines the complex interplay of mercy and justice. Shakespeare adapted the story from *Epitia*, a tragedy by Italian dramatist Giambattista Giraldi (also called Cinthio), and especially from a two-part play by George Whetstone titled *Promos and Cassandra* (1578).

The play opens with Vincentio, the benevolent duke of Vienna, commissioning his deputy Angelo to govern the city while he travels to Poland. In actuality, the duke remains in Vienna disguised as a friar in order to watch what unfolds. Following the letter of the law, Angelo passes the death sentence on Claudio, a nobleman convicted for impregnating his betrothed, Juliet. Claudio's sister Isabella, a novice in a nunnery, pleads his case to Angelo. This new deputy ruler, a man of stern and rigorous self-control, finds to his consternation and amazement that he lusts after Isabella; her virgin purity awakens in him a desire that more profligate sexual opportunities could not. Hating himself for doing so, he offers to spare Claudio's life if Isabella will have sex with him. She refuses and is further outraged when her brother begs her to reconsider. On the advice of the disguised Duke Vincentio, Isabella schedules the rendezvous but secretly arranges for her place to be taken by Mariana, the woman Angelo was once engaged to marry but whom he then disavowed because her dowry had been lost. Afterward, Angelo reneges on his promise to save Claudio, fearing that the young man knows too much and is therefore dangerous. Vincentio, reemerging at last from his supposed journey, presides over a finale in which Angelo is discredited and ordered to marry Mariana. Claudio, having been saved from execution by the secret substitution of one who has died in prison, is allowed to marry Juliet. Lucio, an engaging but irresponsible woman chaser and scandalmonger, is reproved by Vincentio and obliged to marry a whore with whom he has had a child. The rascally underworld figures (the bawd Mistress Overdone, her pimp Pompey, and her customer Froth) who have exploited the sexual freedom of Vienna despite the wonderfully inept policing attempts of Constable Elbow are finally brought to justice, partly through the careful supervision of the magistrate Escalus. Vincentio asks Isabella to give up her idea of being a nun in order to become his wife. (Whether she accepts is today a matter of theatrical choice.)

The Merchant of Venice

This comedy in five acts was written about 1596–1597 and printed in a quarto edition in 1600 from an authorial manuscript or a copy of one.

Bassanio, a noble but penniless Venetian, asks his wealthy merchant friend Antonio for a loan so that Bassanio can undertake a journey to woo the heiress Portia. Antonio, whose money is invested in foreign ventures, borrows the sum from Shylock, a Jewish moneylender, on the condition that if the loan cannot be repaid in time, Antonio will forfeit a pound of flesh. Antonio is reluctant to do business with Shylock, whom he despises for lending money at interest (unlike Antonio himself, who provides the money for Bassanio without any such financial obligation); Antonio considers that lending at interest violates the very spirit of Christianity. Nevertheless, he needs help in order to be able to assist Bassanio. Meanwhile, Bassanio has met the terms of Portia's father's will by selecting from three caskets the one that contains her portrait, and he and Portia marry. (Two previous wooers, the princes of Monaco and Aragon, have failed the casket test by choosing what many men desire or what the chooser thinks he deserves; Bassanio knows that he must paradoxically "give and hazard all he hath" to win the lady.) News arrives that Antonio's ships have been lost at sea. Unable to collect on his loan, Shylock attempts to use justice to enforce a terrible, murderous revenge on Antonio: he demands his pound of flesh. Part of Shylock's desire for vengeance is motivated by the way in which the Christians of the play have banded together to enable his daughter Jessica to elope from his house, taking with her a substantial portion of his wealth, in order to become the bride of the Christian Lorenzo. Shylock's revengeful plan is foiled by Portia, disguised as a lawyer, who turns the tables on Shylock by a legal quibble: he must take flesh only, and Shylock must die if any blood is spilled. Thus, the contract is canceled, and Shylock is ordered to give half of his estate to Antonio, who agrees not to take the money if Shylock converts to Christianity and restores his disinherited daughter to his will. Shylock has little choice but to agree. The play ends with the news that, in fact, some of Antonio's ships have arrived safely.

The character of Shylock has been the subject of modern scholarly debate over whether the playwright displays anti-Semitism or religious tolerance in his characterization, for despite his stereotypical usurious nature, Shylock is depicted as understandably full of hate, having been both verbally and physically abused by Christians, and he is given one of Shakespeare's most eloquent speeches ("Hath not a Jew eyes? . . .").

The Merry Wives of Windsor

This comedy in five acts was written sometime between 1597 and 1601 (probably near the earlier of these dates) and centers on the comic romantic misadventures of Falstaff. *The Merry Wives of Windsor* was published in a quarto edition in 1602 from a reported and abbreviated text. The First Folio version of 1623 is from a transcript by Ralph Crane (scrivener of the King's Men) of an authorial manuscript.

Although it contains elements of Plautus's comedies and Italian *novelle*, *The Merry Wives of Windsor* does not have a known source. The play differs from Shakespeare's other comedies of this period in that it is set not in an imaginary country but in Windsor and the small-town rural life of Shakespeare's own day.

Shakespeare's ploy in this engaging comedy is to introduce the character of Falstaff, already a household name in London in the late 1590s, into a nonhistorical plot where he occupies a very different role from that of the *Henry IV* plays. Along with him, Shakespeare also imports some other characters who appear in the *Henry IV* plays, such as Pistol, Bardolph, Nym, Mistress Quickly, and Justice Shallow. They are all in a delightfully new environment. Falstaff takes a fancy to two married women, Mistress Page and Mistress Ford, who are said to control their own financial affairs and thus to be moderately wealthy. He writes identical love letters to them, hoping to swindle some money from them while also enjoying them as sexual partners. He tries to engage the assistance of Pistol and Nym but is scorned by them. When he discharges them from his service, they go off and inform the husbands of Mistresses Page and Ford of Falstaff's plot. The wives compare their letters and resolve to trick the "greasy knight." Twice the wives fool Falstaff, and this results in his being dumped in a muddy ditch and, later, disguised as a witch and beaten. The trickery of the two women also serves to frustrate the jealous behavior of Master Ford. Mistress Ford lets her husband in on the joke at last, and the two couples, the Pages and the Fords, happily plan one more ruse at Falstaff's expense.

A secondary plot centers on the wooing of the Pages' charming daughter Anne. Doctor Caius, Slender, and Fenton are rivals for Anne's affection. To great comic effect, all three suitors use Caius's servant Mistress Quickly to argue their case to young Anne. Slender is favored by Master Page, who devises a plan for Slender and Anne to elope after the play's climactic scene. Mistress Page, who favors Caius as a son-in-law, devises a similar plan.

In the climactic scene, set in Windsor Forest, Falstaff dresses himself absurdly as Herne the Hunter, complete with stag's horns, expecting an assignation. The women and their husbands, however, have arranged for a group of friends, including Anne Page, in witch and fairy costumes, to frighten and tease him. The marriage plans conceived by Master and Mistress Page are foiled when Anne elopes with the suitor of her choice, Fenton. All identities are revealed at the end, and in an atmosphere of good humor, Fenton is welcomed into the Page family and Falstaff is forgiven.

Middleton, Thomas

A contemporary of Shakespeare, Thomas Middleton (1580–1627) was a late-Elizabethan dramatist who drew people as he saw them, with comic gusto or searching irony.

Thomas Middleton, detail of a woodcut from Two New Plays *by Middleton, 1657.*

By 1600 Middleton had spent two years at Oxford and had published three books of verse. He learned to write plays by collaborating with Thomas Dekker, John Webster, and others for the producer Philip Henslowe.

A popular playwright, he was often commissioned to write and produce lord mayor's pageants and other civic entertainments, and in 1620 he was appointed city chronologer. His chief stage success was *A Game at Chaess* (1625), in which the Black King and his men, representing Spain and the Jesuits, are checkmated by the White Knight, Prince Charles. This political satire drew crowds to the Globe until the Spanish ambassador protested and James I suppressed the play.

Middleton's masterpieces are two tragedies, *Women Beware Women* (1621?, published 1657) and *The Changeling* (1622, with William Rowley; published 1653). His comedies picture a society dazzled by money in which most people grasp for all they can get, by any means. *Michaelmas Terme* (1605?, published 1607) is one of the richest in irony. In *A Tricke to Catch the Old-one* (1606?, published 1608) two rival usurers are so eager to score over each other that both are taken in by a clever nephew. *A Tricke* was entered for licensing with an unattributed play entitled *The Revenger's Tragedie* (1607). Most recent scholarship now attributes the latter to Middleton, although Cyril Tourneur is still sometimes given as the author. In *A Mad World, My Masters* (1604?, published 1608) a delightful old country gentleman prides himself on his generosity to all except his grandson and heir.

A Chast Mayd In Cheape-side (1613?, published 1630) is an exuberant comedy that makes fun of naive or complacent London citizens.

The Roaring Girle (1604–1610?, with Dekker; published 1611) depicts events in the life of the notorious criminal Moll Frith (Moll Cutpurse), who dressed as a man and preferred her freedom to marriage.

Middleton's tragicomedies are farfetched in plot but strong in dramatic situations. *A Faire Quarrell* (1616?, with Rowley, published 1617) contains one of Middleton's few heroes, Captain Ager, with his conflicts of conscience.

Most of Middleton's other plays are comedies. He collaborated with Dekker in *The Honest Whore* (1604), and with Rowley and Massinger in *The Old Law* (1618?, published 1656).

▌ *A Midsummer Night's Dream*

This comedy in five acts was written about 1595–1596 and published in 1600 in a quarto edition from the author's manuscript, in which there are some minor inconsistencies. The version published in the First Folio of 1623 was taken from a second quarto edition, with some reference to a promptbook. One of the "great" or "middle" comedies, *A Midsummer Night's Dream*, with its multilayered examination of love and its vagaries, has long been one of the most popular of Shakespeare's plays.

Theseus, duke of Athens, has conquered Hippolyta, the Amazon queen, and is about to wed her. Meanwhile, two lovers, Hermia and Lysander, seek refuge in the forest near Athens when Hermia's father demands that she marry Demetrius. Hoping to win Demetrius's favor, Helena tells him their whereabouts and follows him to the forest, where he goes in search of Hermia. The forest is also full of fairies who have come for the duke's wedding. Oberon, the king of the fairies, quarrels with his queen, Titania, and bids his mischievous servant Puck to drop magic juice into her eyes as she sleeps; his intent is to punish her for her disobedience by causing her to fall hopelessly in love with whatever person or creature she happens to see when she awakes. Noting that the human lovers in the forest are also at odds, he orders Puck to drop the love juice into Demetrius's eyes so that Demetrius's onetime affection for Helena will be restored. Because the two young Athenian men look much alike, however, Puck mistakenly administers the love juice to Lysander, who then happens to see Helena when he awakes. He falls hopelessly in love with her. Now both young men are in love with Helena and neither with the poor, deserted Hermia. This situation does not make Helena any happier, though. She comes to the conclusion that they are all making fun of her. Hermia and Helena fall out over this contretemps, while the young men have become fierce and even would-be murderous rivals of one another for Helena. All is at sixes and sevens.

In the same woods a group of artisans are rehearsing an entertainment for Theseus's wedding. Ever playful, Puck gives one of the "mechanicals," Nick Bottom, an ass's head; when Titania awakens, she falls in love with Bottom. After much general confusion and comic misunderstanding, Oberon's magic restores Titania and the four lovers to their original states. Theseus invites the two couples to join him and Hippolyta in a triple wedding. The wedding celebration features Bottom's troupe in a comically inept performance of their play, *The Most Lamentable Comedy and Most Cruel Death of Pyramus and Thisbe*, which turns out to be a parody of the perilous encounters the various lovers have experienced in the forest and somehow managed to survive.

A CLOSER LOOK

Shakespeare and Opera

by Chantal Schütz

If William Shakespeare's ascendancy over Western theater has not extended to the opera stage—a fact explained by the want of Shakespeare-congenial librettists, the literary indifference of composers, and the difficulties involved in setting iambic pentameters to music—the Shakespeare canon has nonetheless established itself as one of the great inspirers of operas. This is clear from the 200-odd operas based on Shakespeare's plays, about half a dozen of which are among the rare monuments of operatic achievement. It is further demonstrated by an even more extended series of furtive references—moments of other operas that show signs of unmistakable Shakespearean family resemblance without any declared genealogical link to their source. Shakespeare's plays have thus given rise, side by side, to a "legitimate" operatic offspring and to an anonymous operatic dissemination, a recorded and an unrecorded history of Shakespeare on the opera stage.

Opera Derived from Shakespeare

The necessity of accommodating the formal unruliness and many-faceted characters of Shakespeare's theater to the succession of recitative and aria, elaborate scenery, and other conventions of opera makes adaptation of Shakespeare a hazardous business. Actor-manager David Garrick's opera version of *The Tempest* (1756) was accused of "castrating" Shakespeare's original play, while Lord Byron (in an 1818 letter to the poet Samuel Rogers) berated Gioacchino Rossini's librettist for "crucifying" *Othello* (1816).

Henry Purcell's *The Fairy Queen* (1692) is usually dubbed the first Shakespearean opera. Its music, however, is confined to interludes within a curtailed *A Midsummer Night's Dream*. Only in *Dido and Aeneas* (1689) did Purcell have the chance to write music for a tragic heroine of mythical status. Purcell's only real opera, written for a cast of young girls, displays distinctly Shakespearean influences that can be safely ascribed to his librettist, the poet and playwright Nahum Tate, who was familiar with the canon. Tate consistently "improved" Shakespeare to suit new audience tastes, the most famous instance being the happy ending he appended to *King Lear* (Tate's *King Lear* of 1681—in which Cordelia not only lives but marries Edgar—was in fact the only version to be presented on the English stage for the next 150 years). For *Dido and Aeneas*, Tate actually followed Virgil quite faithfully, with the exception of the addition of two *Macbeth*-inspired witch scenes that both complicate the action and introduce a considerable measure of doubt about the role of destiny in Aeneas's decisions; Mercury here becomes a mere decoy sent by the witches to trick Aeneas with the overall purpose of hurting Dido. Yet this addition established a Shakespearean dimension that made this short opera appropriate for use as a "play within a play" in performances of *Measure for Measure* on the London stage in 1700. Indeed, such insertions of musical pieces in or after Shakespeare's plays were customary in the 18th century: George Frideric Handel's pastoral *Acis and*

Galatea, for example, was performed at Drury Lane in 1724 as an afterpiece for *The Tempest*.

Opera Seria and Opera Buffa

It is tantalizing, with regard to Shakespearean dramaturgy, to note that opera was born in Florence in 1600—about the time that Hamlet first voiced Shakespeare's views on acting. Shakespeare and the theorists of opera expressed similar concerns about language and performance. Opera prospered, and Venice started opening public opera houses in 1637; in 1642 Puritan London closed its theaters. Italian opera reached London only at the beginning of the 18th century, when it immediately became a fashion and divided the public. Shakespeare was called upon in this contest: the "rude mechanicals'" play from *A Midsummer Night's Dream* was turned into a caricature of Italian opera in Richard Leveridge's *A Comick Masque of Pyramus and Thisbe* (1716). Some 30 years later (1745), J. F. Lampe revived the book as a "mock opera," complete with rage aria and contrived happy ending.

More antagonistic still were the reactions to Italian operas written on Shakespearean librettos. Francesco Gasparini's *Ambleto* (*Hamlet*), having been played throughout Europe, was taken to London in 1712 by the celebrated castrato Nicolini but quickly disappeared from the scene. Francesco Maria Veracini's *Rosalinda* (1744)—*As You Like It* staged as a polite Italian pastoral and written for a cast of female and castrato sopranos—suffered the same fate. *Gli equivoci*, an opera buffa by Wolfgang Amadeus Mozart's only English disciple, Stephen Storace, presents a different case. Written on a libretto by Lorenzo Da Ponte (much in the spirit of his—and Mozart's—*The Marriage of Figaro*) and auspiciously received in 1786 at the Vienna Burgtheater (now the Hofburgtheater) and throughout Germany, *Gli equivoci*, which is the only known setting of *The Comedy of Errors*, was considered too "Mozartian" and never made its way to London.

Others, such as J. C. Smith and the aforementioned David Garrick, both used and challenged the Italian opera fashion. While their opera on *The Tempest*, as well as *The Fairies* (1755), where the Prologue jokingly attributes authorship to a "Signor Shakespearelli," were poorly received, Garrick's *Tempest* book was successfully revived in 1777 with music by the remarkable Thomas Linley (1756–1778). Throughout the 18th century, *The Tempest*, like *A Midsummer Night's Dream*, was never actually performed except as a musical entertainment.

After the turn of the century, composers of opera buffa (such as Antonio Salieri) and German singspiel (such as Carl Ditters von Dittersdorf) turned their eyes to Shakespeare's more farcical vein. In 1849 Otto Nicolai, having declared that only Mozart could do justice to Shakespeare, wrote a successful opera on *Die lustigen Weiber von Windsor* (*The Merry Wives of Windsor*). Hermann Goetz's *Der Widerspenstigen Zähmung* (1874; *The Taming of the Shrew*) made Kate fall in love with Petruchio almost at first sight—mutating Shakespeare's self-confident anti-heroine into a *hochdramatisch* 19th-century hysteric.

Women from Theater to Opera

The twilight of opera seria and the advent of Romantic opera are epitomized by the emergence of the prima donna and the female conquest of the formerly castrato-dominated soprano region. Shakespeare's female roles, because they were played by boys, were usually less developed than his male roles; with the notable exceptions of Rosalind (in *As You Like It*) and Cleopatra (in *Antony and Cleopatra*), Shakespeare's female roles were far less significant. But the 19th-century primacy of the soprano extends to many other Shakespearean female roles, turning them into major parts.

Rossini's *Otello* (1816), the first opera seria with a tragic ending, poises three tenors—Iago (the villain), Rodrigo (the rejected lover), and Otello (the interloper)—against a besieged Desdemona who outweighs them all—and her basso father, Brabantio, to boot. Following the 18th-century French "translation" of

Othello by Jean-François Ducis, Rossini replaces the handkerchief, that shockingly intimate piece of female lingerie, with the more acceptable misdelivered, unaddressed letter of Italian comedy. The French poets Victor Hugo and Alfred de Vigny made endless fun of this "improvement," yet the painter Eugène Delacroix was so impressed by this reading that his paintings show Desdemona, not Othello, as the protagonist. Most of the action in the first acts is indeed forced into the mold of conventional opera seria. It contains bravura arias for all the soloists and dramatic grand finales that only distantly relate to the subtle progression of the Shakespearean narrative. Contrary to the stage version, which travels from Venice to Cyprus and involves lowlife characters such as prostitutes and gulls, the whole opera is set in magnificent palaces in Venice, staging mostly polite exchanges between members of a single noble class of individuals governed by acceptable passions. Yet in the final act of this seminal opera, Rossini introduced a quotation from Dante's *Inferno*, sung by a passing gondolier, which prompts Desdemona to sing an elaborate Willow Song that she accompanies on her harp, followed by a very moving prayer, leading on to the murder scene and a terse conclusion. *Otello* is the only Rossini opera to end in this manner, and the influence of this last act on 19th-century opera has proved enduring and far-reaching.

The passionate "Shakespearien" Hector Berlioz put the sopranos in the forefront in his last work, *Béatrice et Bénédict* (1862), based on the "merry war" subplot of *Much Ado about Nothing*. Shakespeare was a never-ending inspiration to Berlioz, notably in his *Roméo et Juliette* choral symphony (composed 1839). *Romeo and Juliet* has proved to be an all-time favorite for opera composers, prompting more than 20 versions. In adaptations by such composers as Nicola Antonio Zingarelli and Nicola Vaccai, the part of Romeo is sung by a mezzo-soprano, to the disapproval of Berlioz, who preferred, for this and other reasons, Daniel Steibelt's *Roméo et Juliette* (1793). *I Capuleti*, a vehicle for the famous Grisi sisters (Giuditta and Giulia), privileged female ensembles and conquered the public in the lovers' final duet by means of a timely awakening of Giulietta—an ending popularized by Garrick. Juliette is a sophisticated coloratura in Charles Gounod's 1867 opera (termed by Rossini "a duet in three parts: one before, one during, and one after"), overdeveloped, like the Ophelia of Ambroise Thomas's *Hamlet* (1868), at the expense of male partners. Other examples of that tendency include Saverio Mercadante's *Amleto* (1822), where the part of Hamlet is sung by a woman, and a verismo opera renamed *Giulietta e Romeo* (1922) by Riccardo Zandonai.

Both Gounod's and Thomas's librettos were written by the successful team of Jules Barbier and Michel Carré, who together and separately or with others authored the librettos of some of the most enduring French operas. The plot of Gounod's *Roméo et Juliette* is fairly faithful to the original, doing away with many secondary characters and expanding others (the page Stefano, for example, who is unnamed in Shakespeare's tragedy, has a memorable aria). The major departure from the original plot is once again the reawakening of Juliette just in time for a pathetic duet with Romeo before both die, begging God's forgiveness for their unchristian suicide.

The opera, which begins with the ball scene at the Capulets', overdramatizes several episodes, including the first appearance of Juliet, the revelation (by Tybalt rather than her nurse) of Romeo's identity to Juliet, and Juliet's fake death, which occurs just as her father has taken her arm to lead her to the chapel to marry Paris. In short, it possessed all the ingredients for success and was an immediate hit. It has remained in repertoire along with *Faust*, Gounod's other adaptation from a literary masterpiece.

In the early 1990s Thomas's *Hamlet*, after a long period of neglect, began once again to be performed by celebrated singers on prestigious stages and to be recorded. The opera poises Hamlet mostly against Gertrude, his mother, and his beloved Ophelia, but it also offers interesting insights into the political questions that troubled France at the time it was written, two years before the end of the Second Empire: Gertrude knows all about the murder of her former husband by Claudius (her current husband), and Hamlet rejects Ophelia only when he realizes that Polonius was an accomplice in the deed. In the "mousetrap" scene the seemingly mad Hamlet pulls the crown off Claudius's head, prompting a finale of epic proportion, as the Court comments on this act of lèse-majesté. In the final scene, at the graveyard, the ghost of Hamlet's father appears for a third time, visible to all this time, demanding action from Hamlet, who immediately kills King Claudius, thus restoring legitimacy to the throne and bringing stability to his tormented country. The opera ends to the sound of the people shouting "Vive Hamlet! Vive notre roi!"

In *Das Liebesverbot* (1836), Richard Wagner's only Shakespeare opera and the only extant setting of *Measure for Measure*, the Duke's role is entirely devolved to Isabella, who secretly loves the freethinker Lucio. The original performances were a complete failure, and the piece all but disappeared from the repertoire. Some performances in the mid and late 20th century, as well as recordings, however, have saved the work from utter oblivion and shed light on Wagner's formative years, when he was still attempting to write mainstream music.

As for the prominent role of the soprano in Giuseppe Verdi's *Macbeth* (1847), it is due to Shakespeare himself: Verdi simply recognized that Lady Macbeth's soliloquies read exactly like opera solos. His instruction that she "should not sing at all" is echoed in Ernest Bloch's *Macbeth* (1910), where the orchestra plays the leading part, providing counterpoint, depth, and tragic irony that voices alone cannot convey. Like Thomas's *Hamlet*, Verdi's *Macbeth* reflects the political situation in the composer's homeland in more ways than one: the tyrannical authority of the usurpers is opposed by Scottish exiles clamoring for liberty. The chorus of the Profughi Scozzesi is an echo of "Va, pensiero," the famous chorus from *Nabucco* that became an anthem in the struggle for Italian unity—prompting Verdi's name to become an acronym for the motto "Vittorio Emmanuele, Re d'Italia."

Rossini's *Otello* was saved by the memory of Shakespeare's, as Stendhal put it. Twentieth-century adaptations swung in the opposite direction: in Mario Zafred's *Amleto* (1961) or Frank Martin's *Der Sturm* (1956), the parlando music encumbers Shakespeare's words; literal readings by Reynaldo Hahn (1935) and Mario Castelnuovo-Tedesco (1961) have resulted in two disproportionately lengthy versions of *The Merchant of Venice*.

Opera Inspired by Shakespeare

The slower pace of operatic plots—the result of the singing of the dialogue and the interruption of the action by arias—imposes simplification. Composers therefore have been faced with the task of filling the gaps in most Shakespeare-based librettos. Their problem is that, as W. H. Auden pointed out, contrary to plays, operas cannot easily present characters who are "potentially good and bad." However, opera has other advantages: music speaks directly to the emotions, and its means are expanded by ensemble singing and the support of the orchestra. The simultaneous expression of different ideas and feelings thus made possible was first fully applied to Shakespearean opera in Verdi's *Otello* (1887) and *Falstaff* (1893), composed when the operatic form had reached its full maturity, just before the musical revolutions of Richard Strauss, Arnold Schoenberg, and Igor Stravinsky.

The first and definitive attempt to challenge Rossini's work, *Otello* is the only Shakespeare opera that generates the same critical response as the original, including G. B. Shaw's quip that "instead of *Otello* being an Italian opera written in the style of Shakespeare, *Othello* is a play written by Shakespeare in the style of Italian opera." Verdi's librettist, Arrigo Boito, a composer in his own right, took the opposite stance to Rossini's librettist and set the whole opera in Cyprus. He dropped altogether the confrontation between the lovers and Desdemona's father in the Doges' Palace, which had occupied so much of the earlier opera. Instead, he transposed Othello's tale of the wooing of Desdemona to an extended love duet, one of the most beautiful in the operatic canon. Jago (Iago), all trills and chromaticism, is epitomized by his *Credo*—a piece in line with the 19th century's fascination with Mephistophelian characters (Boito himself wrote an opera called *Mefistofele*)—which concludes with the nihilistic line "la morte è il nulla" ("death is nothingness"). It takes its cue from some of Iago's quizzical statements and "motiveless malignity" but definitely steps outside Elizabethan conceptions and presents a distinctly 19th-century air. The degradation of Otello's heroic stature, which was established in his terse entrance aria (*Esultate*), is depicted by his gradual appropriation of Jago's style and his distortion of Desdemona's lyrical phrases. In the tradition of Italian opera, *Otello* includes a "state scene" with a grand finale, in which stunned onlookers comment on the passions opposing the protagonists, but, like Rossini's final act, Verdi's reaches heights of simplicity and emotion unlike any opera that had gone before. Desdemona's "Willow Song," followed by a Prayer, becomes a poignant lull before the stormy denouement. Otello, who has often been compared to Wagner's Tristan, dies on the interrupted word *bacio* ("kiss"), in a rapturous recall of the theme developed in the earlier love duet.

The plot of Verdi's *Falstaff* tightens *The Merry Wives of Windsor* while integrating elements from the Henry IV plays— such as Falstaff's well-known speech on honor—which give more depth to the main character. Verdi was thus able to develop in parallel the comedy involving Falstaff and his acolytes on one side and Mistress Quickly and her friends on the other, as well as the darker undertones of the scenes involving the jealous Ford, and the lyrical development of the love interest of Fenton and Nannetta. The final fugue, "Tutto nel mondo è burla," is loosely based on the "Seven Ages of Man" speech from *As You Like It* ("all the world's a stage" becomes "all the world's a joke"). It celebrates against all evidence the victory of the "fat knight," who both invokes and provokes the liberating force of laughter. Like *Otello*, *Falstaff* moves imperceptibly from aria to duet or ensemble, unhampered by recitative, as if Shakespearean inspiration had helped the old master to free himself from the conventions on which he had thrived.

Credited with being the only successful setting of Shakespeare's words, Benjamin Britten's *A Midsummer Night's Dream* (1960) shares a nostalgia for Elizabethan England with two earlier, Falstaff-inspired works: Ralph Vaughan Williams's *Sir John in Love* (1929) and Gustav Holst's *At the Boar's Head* (1925). Both of these integrate "old English melodies," while Frederick Delius's *A Village Romeo and Juliet* (1900–1901) transposes the mythical "star-crossed lovers" into a supposedly more realistic context.

Britten's *A Midsummer Night's Dream* is the work of a mature opera composer who was able to devise the libretto himself, with the help of Peter Pears (who sang the part of Lysander), trimming the play without altering the text and making bold choices in the musical treatment of the characters. Opening in the woods with the fairies, in a musical atmosphere akin to that of Ravel's *L'Enfant et les sortilèges*, Britten takes his audience without mediation into the world of the supernatural, where misrule and desire are given free rein. Britten's fascination with the alternation and occasional interaction between three groups of very different characters provides the key to the opera: the fairies seem to embody nostalgia, sung as they are by boys accompanied by harps and percussion, while the role of Oberon is devolved to a countertenor, Titania to a coloratura— perhaps a subtle reference to Mozart's Queen of the Night in *Die Zauberflöte* (*The Magic Flute*). It is interesting to note that the part of Oberon was written for Alfred Deller, the performer who played an essential part in the rediscovery of the countertenor tessitura and the popularization of the Elizabethan repertoire. Puck, the mediator between the three worlds of court, country, and supernatural and between the stage world and the audience, is a spoken role usually given to a teenager.

The roles of the lovers, on the other hand, are characterized by an absence of arias or set pieces, making them hard to tell apart, following Shakespeare's deliberately confusing design but also in the spirit of the first acts of Mozart's *Così fan tutte*. Finally, the Mechanicals, whom Britten called the Rustics, provide the composer with a delightful opportunity for parody, underlined by the use of brass and bassoon. The opera ends with marriage and reconciliation at the court of Theseus and Hippolyta, but the musical climax is the love scene between Titania and Bottom, at the very heart of the piece. The gradual blending of two radically opposed musical styles into the most exquisitely lyrical language can be deciphered as a musical interpretation of Victor Hugo's Shakespeare-inspired theory that the sublime is often born of the grotesque.

Eminent recent European adaptations include Aribert Reimann's *Lear* (1978), based on an extraordinarily austere rendering of Shakespeare's hitherto unadapted play, and Luciano Berio's *Un re in ascolto* (1984; *A King Listens*), a reflection on creation and the complex workings of memory that is based on *The Tempest*. The French composer Pascal Dusapin's *Roméo et Juliette* (1988) is a metatheatrical opera built around a rehearsal of Shakespeare's play. *Wintermärchen* (1999) by the Belgian composer Philippe Boesmans (born 1936) is an adaptation in German of *The Winter's Tale*, a kaleidoscopic work that develops the game of contrasts provided by the Shakespearean plot. One great originality of the new version of *The Tempest* by Thomas Adès (born 1971), first performed at the Royal Opera House Covent Garden in 2004, resides in its libretto by Meredith Oakes, a completely rewritten text following the original plot but allowing an English-speaking composer to benefit from the same distance as Continental musicians working with translations. Adès adopts an eminently lyrical and introspective approach, with a gentle Caliban who seems to be Prospero's doppelgänger. The opera, which in 2005 won an Olivier Award for Outstanding Achievement in Opera, is notable for the instrumental treatment of the part of Ariel, whose coloratura vocalizing contributes to creating the supernatural atmosphere that underscores the whole piece.

More than 200 operas based on Shakespeare's plays have been written since 1945, but very few of them have remained in repertory. Coming a few years after Cole Porter's *Kiss Me, Kate* (1948; a lighthearted version of *The Taming of the Shrew*), Leonard Bernstein's *West Side Story* (1957) was a landmark at the frontier between musical and opera that transposed the story of Romeo and Juliet to a mid-20th-century New York torn apart by rival gangs, but it circumvented many key elements of the Shakespearean original, most notably Juliet's suicide.

A Tip of the Hat to Shakespeare

It is doubtful that Claudio Monteverdi knew the work of Shakespeare, yet his last opera, *L'Incoronazione di Poppea* (1643), is arguably closer to *Antony and Cleopatra* than are the settings of that work by Gian Francesco Malipiero (1938) or Samuel Barber (1966). The constant formal invention displayed by Monteverdi mirrors Shakespeare's fast succession of contrasting scenes: both pieces combine comic, tragic, ironic, and sentimental elements; both portray ambition and lust, shedding poetic light on the unbridled passions of a Roman leader, the repudiation of a virtuous empress (named Octavia in both pieces), and her replacement by a scheming courtesan; both include comic nurses—usually sung by male performers—belonging to the same tradition as the character in *Romeo and Juliet*.

It has long been recognized that Mozart's *Die Zauberflöte* and Shakespeare's *The Tempest* share many features: initiation, the supernatural, the power of music, the wise magician and his uncouth servant. Mozart, it seems, planned to write the music to a singspiel based on August Wilhelm von Schlegel's translation of *The Tempest*. The proposed book was actually set four times and, like most other German *Tempest* operas, resembles a sequel of *Die Zauberflöte*. It is also worth noting that Mozart's

Così fan tutte was reworked into a French version (1863) of *Love's Labour's Lost* by Léo Delibes, although one might contend that it is closer to other Shakespearean comedies involving cross-dressing or a love-quartet, such as *Twelfth Night* or *A Midsummer Night's Dream*. Berlioz conceived *Les Troyens* (1863), he said, according to the "Shakespearean system." The only words by Shakespeare in the opera are in Didon and Enée's love duet, which uses the "On such a night" dialogue of Lorenzo and Jessica in Act V, scene 1 of *The Merchant of Venice*, but other traceable borrowings are the ghosts that persuade the hero to leave Carthage and the comic scene that precedes Enée's tempestuous confrontation with Didon. The latter scene provides the only moment of comic relief in this highly dramatic work. All in all, the opera's epic force derives as much from Shakespeare's histories as from the *Aeneid*.

Modest Mussorgsky's *Boris Godunov* (first performed 1874) is a literal setting of a play by Aleksandr Pushkin, itself modeled on Shakespeare's histories, to which the composer added the *Macbeth*-inspired hallucination scene. The opera navigates in Shakespearean style between epic and drama, between the tragedy of the Russian people and the guilt-harrowed Tsar Boris, between popular comedy and the fate of the realm. The character of the Innocent can be seen as a direct echo of the Fool and Poor Tom in *King Lear*, while the murdered tsarevitch and his living counterpart point to characters and situations in *Richard III*.

One might think that Mussorgsky's masterpiece is an unlikely beneficiary of Shakespearean inspiration. The point, however, is that, unlike most adapters who have been wary of being defeated by their model, Pushkin was not afraid of Shakespeare. And Mussorgsky was not afraid of Pushkin, whose lines are set mostly as they were written. Librettists have tended for various reasons to avoid direct contact with Shakespeare's text and have turned not to *Hamlet* or *Romeo and Juliet* but back to Shakespeare's sources, using Saxo Grammaticus's *Gesta*

Danorum or Matteo Bandello's novella of the lovers of Verona. However, it seems to be of little doubt that, even in these two cases, not the venerable older authors but Shakespeare's master-pieces provided the original inspiration.

Chantal Schütz is a lecturer in English at the École Polytechnique, Paris. From 1995 to 1998 she was a Leverhulme Research Fellow at the University of Reading, Berkshire, England, then heavily involved in the reconstruction of the Globe Theatre.

Much Ado about Nothing

This comedy in five acts was written probably in 1598–1599 and printed in a quarto edition from the author's own manuscript in 1600. The play takes an ancient theme—that of a woman falsely accused of unfaithfulness—to brilliant comedic heights. Shakespeare used as his main source for the Claudio-Hero plot a story from Matteo Bandello's *Novelle* (1554–1573); he also may have consulted Ludovico Ariosto's *Orlando Furioso* and Edmund Spenser's *The Faerie Queene*. The Beatrice-Benedick plot is essentially Shakespeare's own, though he must have had in mind his own story of wife taming in *The Taming of the Shrew*.

Shakespeare sets up a contrast between the conventional Claudio and Hero, who have the usual expectations of each other, and Beatrice and Benedick, who are highly skeptical of romance and courtship and, seemingly, each other. Claudio is deceived by the jealous Don John into believing that Hero is prepared to abandon him for Claudio's friend and mentor, Don Pedro. This malicious fiction is soon dispelled, but Claudio seems not to have learned his lesson; he believes Don John a second time, and on a much more serious charge—that Hero is actually sleeping with other men, even on the night before her impending wedding to Claudio. Supported by Don Pedro, who also accepts the story (based on seeming visual evidence),

Claudio publicly rejects Hero at the wedding ceremony. She is so shamed that her family is obliged to report that she is dead. Don John's plot is eventually unveiled by the bumbling constable Dogberry and his comically inept fellow constable, but not before the story of Hero has taken a nearly tragic turn. Claudio's slanders of Hero have so outraged her cousin Beatrice that she turns to Benedick, pleading with him to kill Claudio. Former friends are near the point of mayhem until the revelations of the night watch prove the villainy of Don John and the innocence of Hero.

Meanwhile, Beatrice and Benedick carry on "a kind of merry war" that tests their wits in clever but crushing repartees. Both have a reputation for being scornful and wary of marriage. Though attracted to each other for many reasons, they find it virtually impossible to get beyond the game of one-upping each other. Eventually their friends have to intervene with a virtuous ruse designed to trick each of them into believing that the other is hopelessly but secretly suffering the pangs of love. The ruse works because it is essentially true. At the play's end, both couples are united.

▌ *Othello*

This tragedy in five acts was written in 1603–1604 and published in 1622 in a quarto edition from a transcript of an authorial manuscript. The text published in the First Folio of 1623 seems to have been based on a version revised by Shakespeare himself that sticks close to the original almost line by line but introduces numerous substitutions of words and phrases, as though Shakespeare copied it over himself and rewrote as he copied. The play derives its plot from Giambattista Giraldi's *De gli Hecatommithi* (1565), which Shakespeare appears to have known in the Italian original; it was available to him in French but had not been translated into English.

The play is set in motion when Othello, a heroic black general in the service of Venice, appoints Cassio and not Iago as his chief lieutenant. Jealous of Othello's success and envious of Cassio, Iago plots Othello's downfall by falsely implicating Othello's wife, Desdemona, and Cassio in a love affair. With the unwitting aid of Emilia, his wife, and the willing help of Roderigo, a fellow malcontent, Iago carries out his plan. Making use of a handkerchief belonging to Desdemona and found by Emilia when Othello has unwittingly dropped it, Iago persuades Othello that Desdemona has given the handkerchief to Cassio as a love token. Iago also induces Othello to eavesdrop on a conversation between himself and Cassio that is in fact about Cassio's mistress, Bianca, but which Othello is led to believe concerns Cassio's infatuation with Desdemona. These slender "proofs" confirm what Othello has been all too inclined to believe—that, as an older black man, he is no longer attractive to his young white Venetian wife. Overcome with jealousy, Othello kills Desdemona. When he learns from Emilia, too late, that his wife is blameless, he asks to be remembered as one who "loved not wisely but too well" and kills himself.

Oxford, Edward de Vere, 17th Earl of

An English lyric poet and patron of an acting company, Oxford's Men, Oxford (1550–1604) became, in the 20th century, the strongest candidate proposed (next to William Shakespeare himself) for the authorship of Shakespeare's plays.

Succeeding to the earldom as a minor in 1562, Oxford lived for eight years as a royal ward under the care of William Cecil (later Lord Burghley) and in December 1571 married Burghley's daughter, Anne Cecil. Along the way he studied at Queens' College and St. John's College, Cambridge. By the early 1580s his financial position had become very straitened, perhaps chiefly through his lack of financial sense. His younger children were provided for by Burghley, with whom he remained friendly even after Anne's death (June 1588) and his own remarriage in 1591 or 1592. In 1586 Queen Elizabeth granted him an annuity of £1,000.

He was never appointed to any important office or command, though he was named on the commissions of some noted trials of peers and was said to have been made a privy councilor by James I. It has therefore been suggested that the annuity may have been granted for his services in maintaining a company of actors (from 1580) and that the obscurity of his later life is to be explained by his immersion in literary pursuits. He was indeed a notable patron of writers. He employed John Lyly, the author of the novel *Euphues*, as his secretary for many years.

That Oxford might be the author of Shakespeare's plays was first advanced in a major way in *"Shakespeare" Identified in Edward de Vere, the Seventeenth Earl of Oxford* (1920), a study by J. Thomas Looney. Looney argued that there was a biographical similarity between Oxford and both Bertram (in *All's Well That Ends Well*) and Hamlet and that Oxford's poems resembled Shakespeare's early work. Oxford's interest in the drama extended beyond noble patronage, for he himself wrote some plays, though there are no known examples extant. His 23 acknowledged poems were written in his youth, and because he was born in 1550, Looney proposed that they were the prelude to his mature work and that this began in 1593 with *Venus and Adonis*. This theory is supported by the coincidence that Oxford's poems apparently ceased just before Shakespeare's work began to appear. A further claim is that Oxford assumed a pseudonym in order to protect his family from the social stigma attached to the stage and also because extravagance had brought him into disrepute at court. A major difficulty in the Oxfordian theory, however, is his death date (1604), because, according to standard chronology, 14 of Shakespeare's plays, including many of the most important ones, were apparently written after that time. The debate, however, remained lively in the late 20th century.

▌*Pericles, Prince of Tyre*

This play in five acts was written about 1606–1608 and published in a quarto edition in 1609, a defective and at times nearly unintelligible text that shows signs of having been reconstructed from memory. The editors of the First Folio of 1623 did not include *Pericles* in that edition, which suggests that they did not think it to be all or substantially by Shakespeare. The play was based on the classical tale of Apollonius of Tyre as told in Book VIII of *Confessio amantis* by John Gower and in *The Pattern of Painful Adventures* by Laurence Twine.

The spirit of Gower opens the play and sets the stage with the title character in Antioch seeking to marry the princess. Pericles, however, discovers the truth about King Antiochus's incestuous love for his own daughter and flees, leaving the loyal Helicanus to rule Tyre in his absence. After aiding the starving people of Tarsus, Pericles is shipwrecked near Pentapolis, where he wins the hand of the beautiful Thaisa, daughter of King Simonides. As the couple sail back to Tyre, Thaisa gives birth to Marina during a violent storm. Pericles, believing his wife has died in childbirth, buries her at sea, but she is rescued and joins the temple of the goddess Diana at Ephesus. Pericles leaves his newborn daughter with Cleon, the governor of Tarsus, and his wife, Dionyza.

Marina, grown to young womanhood, is hated by Dionyza, who orders her murder. Instead, she is kidnapped by pirates and sold to a brothel, where she earns her keep by singing and doing needlework. Marina is reunited with her father when he is brought to her, mute and sick from years of grief. Pericles then has a vision of Diana, who sends them to Ephesus to be reunited with Thaisa.

The play is episodic, highly symbolic, and filled with imagery of the stormy seas. The most significant recurring theme is the proper relationship between parent and child, especially between father and daughter. Shakespeare returned to this theme often in his other late plays.

Poetry

Shakespeare seems to have wanted to be a poet as much as he sought to succeed in the theater. His plays are wonderfully and poetically written, often in blank verse. And when he experienced a pause in his theatrical career about 1592–1594, the plague having closed down much theatrical activity, he wrote poems. *Venus and Adonis* (1593) and *The Rape of Lucrece* (1594) are the only works that Shakespeare seems to have shepherded through the publishing process. Both owe a good deal to Ovid, the Classical poet whose writings Shakespeare encountered repeatedly in school. These two poems are the only works for which he wrote dedicatory prefaces. Both are to Henry Wriothesley, earl of Southampton. This young man, a favorite at court, seems to have encouraged Shakespeare and to have served, for a brief time at least, as his sponsor. The dedication to the second poem is measurably warmer than the first. An unreliable tradition supposes that Southampton gave Shakespeare the stake he needed to buy into the newly formed Lord Chamberlain's acting company in 1594. Shakespeare became an actor-sharer, one of the owners in a capitalist enterprise that shared the risks and the gains among them. This company succeeded brilliantly; Shakespeare and his colleagues, including Richard Burbage, John Heminge, Henry Condell, and Will Sly, became wealthy through their dramatic presentations.

Shakespeare may also have written at least some of his sonnets to Southampton, beginning in these same years of 1593–1594 and continuing on through the decade and later. The question of autobiographical basis in the sonnets is much debated, but Southampton at least fits the portrait of a young gentleman who is being urged to marry and produce a family. (Southampton's family was eager that he do just this.) Whether the account of a strong, loving relationship between the poet and his gentleman friend is autobiographical is more difficult still to determine. As a narrative, the sonnet sequence tells of strong attachment, of jealousy, of grief at separation, of joy at being together and sharing beautiful experiences. The emphasis on the importance of poetry as a way of eternizing human achievement and of creating a lasting memory for the poet himself is appropriate to a friendship between a poet of modest social station and a friend who is better-born. When the sonnet sequence introduces the so-called Dark Lady, the narrative becomes one of painful and destructive jealousy. Scholars do not know the order in which the sonnets were composed—Shakespeare seems to have had no part in publishing them—but no order other than the order of publication has been proposed, and as the sonnets stand, they tell a coherent and disturbing tale. The poet experiences sex as something that fills him with revulsion and remorse, at least in the lustful circumstances in which he encounters it. His attachment to the young man is a love relationship that sustains him at times more than the love of the Dark Lady can do, and yet this loving friendship also dooms the poet to disappointment and self-hatred. Whether the sequence reflects any circumstances in Shakespeare's personal life, it certainly is told with an immediacy and dramatic power that bespeak an extraordinary gift for seeing into the human heart and its sorrows.

Raleigh, Sir Walter

English adventurer and writer, and a contemporary of Shakespeare, Sir Walter Raleigh (c. 1554–1618) was a favorite of Queen Elizabeth I, who knighted him in 1585. Accused of treason by Elizabeth's successor, James I, he was imprisoned in the Tower of London and eventually put to death.

Raleigh was a younger son of Walter Raleigh (d. 1581) of Fardell in Devon, by his third wife, Katherine Gilbert (née Champernowne). In 1569 he fought on the Huguenot (French Protestant) side in the Wars of Religion in France, and he is known later to have been at Oriel College, Oxford (1572), and at the Middle Temple law college (1575). In 1580 he fought against the Irish rebels in Munster, and his outspoken criticism of the way English policy was being implemented in Ireland brought him to the attention of Queen Elizabeth. By 1582 he had become the monarch's favorite, and he began to acquire lucrative monopolies, properties, and influential positions. His Irish service was rewarded by vast estates in Munster. In 1583 the queen secured him a lease of part of Durham House in the Strand, London, where he had a monopoly of wine

Sir Walter Raleigh, engraving by Simon Pass for the title page of the first edition of Raleigh's The History of the World *(1614).*

licenses (1583) and of the export of broadcloth (1585); and he became warden of the stannaries (the Cornish tin mines), lieutenant of Cornwall, and vice admiral of Devon and Cornwall and frequently sat as a member of Parliament. In 1587, two years after he had been knighted, Raleigh became captain of the queen's guard. His last appointment under the crown was as governor of Jersey (one of the Channel Islands) in 1600.

In 1592 Raleigh acquired the manor of Sherborne in Dorset. He wanted to settle down and start a family. His marriage to Elizabeth, daughter of Sir Nicholas Throckmorton, possibly as early as 1588, had been kept a secret from the jealous queen. In 1592 the birth of a son betrayed him, and he and his wife were both imprisoned in the Tower of London. Raleigh bought his release with profits from a privateering voyage in which he had invested, but he never regained his ascendancy at court. The child did not survive; a second son, Walter, was born in 1593 and a third son, Carew, in 1604 or 1605.

Although Raleigh was the queen's favorite, he was not popular. His pride and extravagant spending were notorious, and he was attacked for unorthodox thought. A Jesuit pamphlet in 1592 accused him of keeping a "School of Atheism," but he was not an atheist in the modern sense. He was a bold talker, interested in skeptical philosophy, and a serious student of mathematics as an aid to navigation. He also studied chemistry and compounded medical formulas. The old idea that Shakespeare satirized Raleigh's circle under the name of the "School of Night" is now entirely discredited.

Raleigh's breach with the queen widened his personal sphere of action. Between 1584 and 1589 he had tried to establish a colony near Roanoke Island (in present North Carolina), which he named Virginia, but he never set foot there himself. In 1595 he led an expedition to what is now Venezuela, in South America, sailing up the Orinoco River in the heart of Spain's colonial empire. He described the expedition in his book *The Discoverie of Guiana* (1596). Spanish documents and stories told by Indians had convinced him of the existence of Eldorado (El Dorado), the ruler of Manoa, a supposedly fabulous city of gold in the interior of South America. He did locate some gold mines, but no one supported his project for colonizing the area. In 1596 he went with Robert Devereux, 2nd earl of Essex, on an unsuccessful expedition to the Spanish city of Cádiz, and he was Essex's rear admiral on the Islands voyage in 1597, an expedition to the Azores.

Raleigh's aggressive policies toward Spain did not recommend him to the peace-loving King James I (reigned 1603–1625). His enemies worked to bring about his ruin, and in 1603 he and others were accused of plotting to dethrone the king. Raleigh was convicted on the written evidence of Henry Brooke, Lord Cobham, and, after a last-minute reprieve from the death sentence, was consigned to the Tower. He fought to save Sherborne, which he had conveyed in trust for his son, but a clerical error invalidated the deed. In 1616 he was released but not pardoned. He still hoped to exploit the wealth of Venezuela, arguing that the country had been ceded to England by its native chiefs in 1595. With the king's permission, he financed and led a second expedition there, promising to open a gold mine without offending Spain. A severe fever prevented his leading his men upriver. His lieutenant, Lawrence Kemys, burned a Spanish settlement but found no gold. Raleigh's son Walter died in the action. King James invoked the suspended sentence of 1603, and in 1618, after writing a spirited defense of his acts, Raleigh was executed.

Popular sentiment had been on Raleigh's side ever since 1603. After 1618 his occasional writings were collected and published, often with little discrimination. The authenticity of some minor works attributed to him is still unsure. Some 560 lines of verse in his hand are preserved. They address the queen as "Cynthia" and complain of her unkindness, probably with reference to his imprisonment of 1592. His best-known prose works in addition to *The Discoverie of Guiana* are *A Report of the Truth of the Fight About the Iles of Açores This Last Sommer* (1591; generally known as *The Last Fight of the Revenge*) and *The History of the World* (1614). The last work, undertaken in the Tower, proceeds from the Creation to the second century BC. History is shown as a record of God's Providence, a doctrine that pleased contemporaries and counteracted the charge of atheism. King James was meant to note the many warnings that the injustice of kings is always punished.

Raleigh survives as an interesting and enigmatic personality rather than as a force in history. He can be presented either as a hero or as a scoundrel. His vaulting imagination, which could envisage both North and South America as English territory, was supported by considerable practical ability and a persuasive pen, but some discrepancy between the vision and the deed made him less effective than his gifts had promised.

▌*Richard II*

This chronicle play in five acts was written in 1595–1596 and published in a quarto edition in 1597 and in the First Folio of 1623. The quarto edition omits the deposition scene in Act IV, almost certainly as a result of censorship. The play is the first in a sequence of four history plays (the other three being *Henry IV, Part 1*, *Henry IV, Part 2*, and *Henry V*) known collectively as the "second tetralogy," treating major events in English history of the late 14th and early 15th centuries. The story of Richard II was taken mainly from Raphael Holinshed's *Chronicles*. While much of the play is true to the facts of Richard's life, Shakespeare's account of his murder rests on no reliable authority.

Richard begins the play as an extravagant, self-indulgent king. He exiles two feuding noblemen, Thomas Mowbray and Henry Bolingbroke, seemingly because Mowbray has been implicated along with Richard himself in the murder of Richard's uncle Thomas of Woodstock, duke of Gloucester, while Bolingbroke, Richard's first cousin, is a threat to the king because he is intent on avenging the death of Gloucester. When John of Gaunt, Bolingbroke's father, dies, Richard seizes his properties to finance a war against the Irish. The seizure gives Bolingbroke an excuse to invade England with his own armies; he insists that his return in arms is solely to regain his illegally seized dukedom. Powerful earls, especially the Earl of Northumberland and his family, support Bolingbroke because of their intense disapproval of Richard's invasion of baronial rights. Richard's last surviving uncle, Edmund of Langley, duke of York, serves as regent while the king is fighting in Ireland. York, however, recognizes that change is inevitable and swears allegiance to Bolingbroke. York's son, the Duke of Aumerle, remains loyal to Richard despite his father's change of allegiance.

Unable to defeat Bolingbroke militarily, Richard reluctantly agrees to surrender and abdicate the throne. In prison, lonely, miserable, and forgotten, he soliloquizes on the meaning of his suffering. From this moment of truth, he rediscovers pride, trust, and courage, so that, when he is murdered, he dies with access to strength and an ascending spirit. Bolingbroke, now King Henry IV, performs his first royal act (and displays his pragmatic approach to governing) by acquiescing to the Duchess of York's pleas for Aumerle's life while the zealous

York demands his "disloyal" son's execution. The play ends with Henry inquiring about his own wastrel son, Prince Hal, and swearing to make a pilgrimage to the Holy Land to atone for his part in Richard's murder.

▋*Richard III*

This chronicle play in five acts was written about 1592–1594 and published in 1597 in a quarto edition seemingly reconstructed from memory by the acting company when a copy of the play was missing. The text in the First Folio of 1623 is substantially better, having been heavily corrected with reference to an independent manuscript. *Richard III* is the last in a sequence of four history plays (the others being *Henry VI, Part 1; Henry VI, Part 2;* and *Henry VI, Part 3*) known collectively as the "first tetralogy," treating major events of English history during the late 14th and early 15th centuries. For the events of the play, Shakespeare relied mainly on the chronicles of Raphael Holinshed and, to a lesser extent, Edward Hall.

The dissembling and physically deformed Richard, duke of Gloucester, reveals his true purpose in the opening soliloquy of *Richard III*:

> And therefore, since I cannot prove a lover
> To entertain these fair well-spoken days,
> I am determined to prove a villain.

Having killed King Henry VI and Henry's son, the prince of Wales, in *Henry VI, Part 3*, Richard sets out to kill all who stand between him and the throne of England. He woos and marries Lady Anne, whose husband (Edward, prince of Wales) and father-in-law he has murdered, and then arranges for Anne's death as well once she is no longer useful to him. He displays his animosity toward King Edward's wife and then widow, Queen Elizabeth, by arranging for the deaths of her sons, the Marquess of Dorset and Lord Grey, and her brother, Anthony Woodville, Earl Rivers. He orders the execution of Lord Hastings when that courtier proves loyal to King Edward's children.

At first Richard is ably assisted by the Duke of Buckingham, who readily persuades Cardinal Bourchier to remove the young Duke of York from the protection of sanctuary and place him and his brother under their uncle's "protection" in the Tower. Buckingham further arranges for and later explains away the hurried execution of Hastings, spreads ugly rumors about the bastardy of the young princes and of Edward himself, and stage-manages Richard's apparently reluctant acceptance of the crown. The nefarious partnership between Richard and Buckingham ends when Buckingham balks at killing the young princes and then flees to escape the same fate. An army led by Henry Tudor, earl of Richmond, challenges Richard's claim to the throne. On the night before the Battle of Bosworth Field, Richard is haunted by the ghosts of all whom he has murdered. After a desperate fight, Richard is killed, and Richmond becomes King Henry VII.

▌ *Romeo and Juliet*

This play was written about 1594–1596 and first published in an unauthorized quarto in 1597. An authorized quarto appeared in 1599, substantially longer and more reliable. A third quarto, based on the second, was used by the editors of the First Folio of 1623. The characters of Romeo and Juliet have been depicted in literature, music, dance, and theater. The appeal of the young hero and heroine—whose families, the Montagues and the Capulets, respectively, are implacable enemies—is such that they have become, in the popular imagination, the exemplar of star-crossed lovers.

Shakespeare's principal source for the plot was *The Tragicall Historye of Romeus and Juliet* (1562), a long narrative poem by the English poet Arthur Brooke, who had based his poem on a French translation of a tale by the Italian Matteo Bandello.

Shakespeare sets the scene in Verona, Italy. Juliet and Romeo meet and fall instantly in love at a masked ball of the Capulets, and they profess their love when Romeo, unwilling to leave, climbs the wall into the orchard garden of her family's house and finds her alone at her window. Because their well-to-do families are enemies, the two are married secretly by Friar Laurence. When Tybalt, a Capulet, seeks out Romeo in revenge for the insult of Romeo's having dared to shower his attentions on Juliet, an ensuing scuffle ends in the death of Romeo's dearest friend, Mercutio. Impelled by a code of honor among men, Romeo kills Tybalt and is banished to Mantua by the Prince of Verona, who has been insistent that the family feuding cease. When Juliet's father, unaware that Juliet is already secretly married, arranges a marriage with the eminently eligible Count Paris, the young bride seeks out Friar Laurence for assistance in her desperate situation. He gives her a potion that will make her appear to be dead and proposes that she take it and that Romeo rescue her. She complies. Romeo, however, unaware of the friar's scheme because a letter has failed to reach him, returns to Verona on hearing of Juliet's apparent death. He encounters a grieving Paris at Juliet's tomb, reluctantly kills him when Paris attempts to prevent Romeo from entering the tomb, and finds Juliet in the burial vault. There he gives her a last kiss and kills himself with poison. Juliet awakens, sees the dead Romeo, and kills herself. The families learn what has happened and end their feud.

A CLOSER LOOK

Viewing Shakespeare on Film

by Kenneth S. Rothwell

At the end of the 19th and the start of the 20th centuries, when William Shakespeare was becoming an academic institution, so to speak—a subject for serious scholarly study—a revolutionary search began in the world outside the universities for the means to present his great dramas in the new medium of film. Pioneer French filmmakers had begun to produce primitive *actualités* (i.e., brief film clips of parading soldiers and umbrella dancers), which were screened between the live acts in vaudeville houses in London and New York City. Among these early films was a remarkable production of 1899 (still available) by the London studio of the British Mutoscope and Biograph Company: a scene from Shakespeare's *King John*—then on the boards at Her Majesty's Theatre and featuring Sir Herbert Beerbohm Tree— recorded on 68-mm film. Of four excerpts shot and later exhibited at London's Palace Theatre to promote the stage production, only the death scene (Act V, scene 2), long thought lost, resurfaced in 1990 in an Amsterdam film archive. Like all silent films, the scene from *King John* might well have been accompanied by some variation of live music, sound effects, phonograph records, intertitles, recitations, or supplementary lectures, as filmmakers sought to compensate for a silenced Shakespeare.

Cineasts in France, the United States, Italy, and Germany soon began making other Shakespeare movies. In 1900 Sarah Bernhardt appeared on-screen at the Paris Exposition in the duel scene from *Hamlet*, and in 1907 Georges Méliès attempted to make a coherent one-reel *Hamlet* that distilled the essence of the story. Emulating the high culture of the Comédie-Française, French filmmakers organized a Film d'Art movement that cast high-profile actors in adaptations of famous plays, a movement that was limited by its deference to the theater.

By 1913, however, in one of the last Film d'Art releases, *Shylock* (a version of *The Merchant of Venice*), the actors had successfully adapted their stage talents to film. In Italy Giovanni Pastrone, whose monumental *Cabiria* (1914) later inspired D. W. Griffith's *Intolerance* (1916), brought the sense of grand opera spectacle to his *Giulio Cesare* (1909; *Julius Caesar*). Italian audiences in 1910 saw *Il mercante di Venezia* (*The Merchant of*

Venice), directed by Gerolamo Lo Savio, and in 1913 they saw *Una tragedia alla corte di Sicilia* ("A Tragedy of the Court of Sicily"; a version of *The Winter's Tale*), directed by Baldassare Negroni.

Meanwhile, in Brooklyn, New York, the Vitagraph production company had moved the camera off the stage and into the city parks. Brooklyn's Prospect Park served as one location for *A Midsummer Night's Dream* (1909), and Central Park's Bethesda Fountain doubled as a Veronese street in *Romeo and Juliet* (1908).

The Americans, like their European counterparts, began making longer movies for the grander "palace" movie houses that were putting the old nickelodeons and penny gaffs out of business. One of the earliest feature-length movies surviving in North America is a Shakespeare movie, James Keane (Kcene) and M. B. Dudley's *Richard III* (1912), also rediscovered in the late 20th century. A veteran Shakespearean actor and lecturer

Francis X. Bushman (Romeo) and Beverly Bayne (Juliet) in a silent version of Romeo and Juliet *(1916), directed by Francis X. Bushman and John W. Noble.*

on the Chautauqua circuit, Frederick Warde, played the film's Richard. He toured with the movie, providing appropriate recitations and commentary.

Many film directors had difficulty moving beyond filmed stage performances. Sir Frank Benson's *Richard III* (1911), filmed at the Stratford Theatre, even revealed the front line of the floorboards. Other directors, however, were more creative; E. Hay Plumb, for example, took the cast of the London Drury Lane Company to the Dorset coast to film the castle scenes in a *Hamlet* (1913) that featured the 60-year-old Johnston Forbes-Robertson as the gloomy prince. Directors Svend Gade and Heinz Schall came up with a gender-bending *Hamlet* (1920), which starred the famous actress Asta Nielsen as a cross-dressing prince. The internationally known actor Emil Jannings played the title role in *Othello* (1922) to Werner Krauss's Iago. Krauss also portrayed Shylock in a free adaptation of *The Merchant of Venice* (1923; *Der Kaufmann von Venedig*).

In the United States Mary Pickford played a saucy Kate in *The Taming of the Shrew* (1929), the first feature-length sound movie of Shakespeare. With her sly wink to Bianca during the "submission" speech to Petruchio, she showed how film could subvert the Shakespearean text. Warner Brothers' *A Midsummer Night's Dream* (1935), directed by émigrés Max Reinhardt and William Dieterle, revealed the influence of Weimar Expressionism, but it combined the incidental music of Felix Mendelssohn with the presence of contract actors James Cagney and Mickey Rooney, who played Bottom and Puck, respectively. Almost immediately thereafter, producer Irving Thalberg and director George Cukor offered a reverential *Romeo and Juliet* (1936), with Norma Shearer and Leslie Howard and a supporting cast of actors from the Hollywood expatriate British colony. Joseph L. Mankiewicz and John Houseman produced a spectacular "newsreel"-style *Julius Caesar* (1953) that may have been a covert attack on McCarthyism. Marlon Brando was formidable as the film's Mark Antony.

*Leslie Howard (Romeo) and Norma Shearer (Juliet) in
George Cukor's* Romeo and Juliet *(1936).*

In Laurence Olivier's landmark *Henry V* (1944), the camera participated in the action rather than merely recording it. Olivier began with the gritty "actualities" of an opening scene at the boisterous Globe playhouse, moved from there to a realistic 19th-century stage set for the Boar's Head Inn, and then soared off into a mythical France as portrayed in the 1490 manuscript *Les Très Riches Heures du Duc de Berry*. In *Hamlet* (1948) Olivier used a probing, interrogating camera and deep-focus photography to ferret out every nook and cranny of Elsinore. His brilliant performance as the title character in a filmed and subsequently televised *Richard III* (1955) identified him to millions of viewers as "that bottled spider . . . this poisonous bunch-back'd toad" (Act I, scene 3, line 245).

The American Orson Welles rivaled Olivier in the production of Shakespeare films. Despite its crudities, Welles's *Macbeth* (1948) captures the essence of the play's wild imaginings. In *Chimes at Midnight* (1966), based on the Henriad, Falstaff becomes self-referentially Welles himself, a misunderstood genius. Welles's cinematic masterpiece is *Othello* (1952; restored 1992). Its skewed camera angles and film noir texture mirror Othello's agony.

*Orson Welles (Othello) and Suzanne Cloutier (Desdemona)
in Welles's* Othello *(1952).*

In France two loose adaptations, André Cayatte's *Les Amants de Vérone* (1949; "The Lovers of Verona") and Claude Chabrol's *Ophélia* (1962), captured essences of *Romeo and Juliet* and *Hamlet*.

In the late 1960s a golden age for Shakespeare movies emerged, beginning with Franco Zeffirelli's exuberant *The Taming of the Shrew* (1966), featuring Richard Burton and Elizabeth Taylor. Soon thereafter Zeffirelli offered a hugely popular *Romeo and Juliet* (1968) that reinvented the young lovers (played for once by actors of an age appropriate to their roles) as alienated youth in rebellion against intransigent parents; they behave much like the feuding street gangs in *West Side Story* (1961), the Robert Wise–Jerome Robbins musical adaptation of *Romeo and Juliet*.

During the same period, the Russian director Grigory Kozintsev directed a production of *Hamlet* titled *Gamlet* (1964) and one of *King Lear* titled *Karol Lear* (1970), which employed

Olivia Hussey (Juliet) and Leonard Whiting (Romeo) in Franco Zeffirelli's Romeo and Juliet *(1968).*

grim charcoal textures. Another bleak *King Lear* of 1970, which featured Paul Scofield as the aged king, was filmed by British director Peter Brook in frozen Jutland. Roman Polanski's *Macbeth* (1971) displayed raw filmic energy and bravura. The voracious eye of Polanski's camera roams over the barnyard details of a 10th-century Scottish castle that in its squalor mirrors the inner psyches of the Macbeths. The Japanese director Akira Kurosawa presented his own version of *Macbeth* in *Kumonosu-jo* (1957; *Throne of Blood*), a translation of the play into stylized Noh drama. As Washizu Taketori (Macbeth) rides in circles, the swirling forest mist becomes a metaphor for the intricate web of fate that drives his destiny, while the demureness of Asaji (Lady Macbeth) masks a terrifying savagery. *Ran* (1985; also known as *Chaos*), Kurosawa's adaptation of *King Lear*, sets the action in pre-Tokugawa Japan, where the aging warlord Ichimonji Hidetora divides his wealth between two of his ambitious sons; the third son is banished for pointing out his father's foolishness. The film's formality and epic sweep serve beautifully to underline the Shakespearean tragedy.

In the 1970s and 1980s young British artists angered by "the Establishment" made transgressive Shakespeare movies. Derek Jarman's *The Tempest* (1979) filtered the play through the lens of a camp-gay sensibility that, in depicting Prospero's impossible struggle to govern benevolently in a malevolent world, shared the attitudes of Polish critic Jan Kott's influential book *Shakespeare, Our Contemporary* (1966). Jarman's *Tempest* was outdone by the avant-garde antics of Celestino Coronado's *A Midsummer Night's Dream* (1984). At the same time, in other circles, orthodoxy prevailed in Stuart Burge's waxworks *Julius Caesar* (1970), with Charlton Heston as Mark Antony. Two years later Heston's own ambitious *Antony and Cleopatra* proved a better "toga epic."

An unprecedented number of expensively produced Shakespeare movies were released in the 1990s. After decades Franco Zeffirelli returned to filming Shakespeare but for *Hamlet* (1990) abandoned his Italianate settings in favor of medieval English castles. In it Mel Gibson proved an action-oriented prince. The following year Peter Greenaway's beautiful but obscure *Prospero's Books*, starring an octogenarian John Gielgud, pioneered not only in bringing computer-based imagery into the Shakespeare movie but also in establishing ideological and artistic independence from the classic Hollywood film.

With his *Henry V* (1989) and *Much Ado about Nothing* (1993), Kenneth Branagh rapidly assumed the mantle left by Olivier. In contrast to Olivier's phlegmatic warrior figure, Branagh created a Prince Hal who was Hamlet-like in his introspection. His *Much Ado*, featuring such popular American actors as Denzel Washington and Michael Keaton, privileged the play's sentimental side over its ironic side. Branagh's four-hour "uncut" *Hamlet* (1996) combined the 1623 First Folio version with passages from the 1605 quarto. The film was spectacularly photographed, with exterior scenes shot at Blenheim Palace in Oxfordshire. Branagh used flashbacks and fades, as he did in *Henry V*, to "explain" what is left unexplained in Shakespeare's play, showing a torrid affair between Ophelia and Hamlet. The hall of mirrors in the grand palace (filmed in the studio) underscores the tension between the worlds of illusion and reality at the heart of the play: "Seems, madam? Nay, it is. I know not 'seems,'" says Hamlet to his mother (Act I, scene 2, line 76). A later offering is Branagh's amusing musical comedy version of *Love's Labour's Lost* (2000), in which he played Berowne and comic actor Nathan Lane played Costard.

Oliver Parker's *Othello* (1995) paired a black actor, Laurence Fishburne, as a dynamic Othello, with Irène Jacob as a plucky Desdemona, but the film as a whole—despite Branagh's menacing Iago—was disappointingly stagy. Richard Loncraine's *Richard III* (1995) presented Ian McKellen as the evil Richard in a 1930s London teetering on the edge of fascism. Shakespeare's language works well with the suave cultural codes of high society before World War II, while the whiff of decadence in the palace ballroom makes a perfect setting for the hoggish schemes of the master manipulator.

*Andrey Popov (Iago, left) and Yevgeny Vesnik (Roderigo)
in Sergey Yutkevich's* Othello *(1955).*

The line between "high" and "low" culture became increasingly blurred with director Baz Luhrmann's postmodern
William Shakespeare's Romeo + Juliet (1996), starring Leonardo
DiCaprio and Claire Danes. The young lovers inhabit a world of
drugs, cars, MTV, and violence. The high mimetic language of
the play belies the ironic mise-en-scène. This melding of "high"
and "low" continued not so much in the full-scale adaptations
of Shakespeare as in the many derivative movies that displaced
plots or snippets or echoes from Shakespeare into surprising
contexts. Gus Van Sant's *My Own Private Idaho* (1991) updated
the Henriad's court/tavern dualities by locating the film in Port-
land, Oregon, where the mayor's prodigal son falls in with dis-
solute street people. Al Pacino's *Looking for Richard* (1996) is a
witty film essay about the history of Shakespeare's *Richard III*.
An earlier Branagh film, *In the Bleak Midwinter* (1995; U.S.
title, *A Midwinter's Tale*), explores *Hamlet* as it is rehearsed in
an abandoned church by a band of struggling actors. Other

derivative movies include the cerebral *Last Action Hero* (1993), which is Pirandello-like in its interplay between *Hamlet* and the film's hero (played by Arnold Schwarzenegger); *10 Things I Hate About You* (1999), based on *The Taming of the Shrew*; and *The King Is Alive* (2000), in which tourists stranded in a desert perform *King Lear*.

The early 1990s witnessed a spate of interest in Shakespeare's comedies, not generally favored by filmmakers. Christine Edzard's *As You Like It* (1992) displayed a gritty realism. Whereas Paul Czinner's 1936 version, starring Olivier and Elisabeth Bergner, gloried in the "poetic realism" of designer Lazare Meerson, Edzard used a daring ploy in transforming Shakespeare's forest of Arden into a hobo jungle in East London.

Trevor Nunn followed his notable television achievements— with Janet Suzman in *Antony and Cleopatra* (first broadcast in 1974) and Judi Dench and McKellen in *Macbeth* (first broadcast in 1979)—with a splendid *Twelfth Night* (1996). Shot in Cornwall, it enfolds the fragile world of Illyria within the nostalgic atmosphere of a Chekhovian comedy.

Two major versions of *A Midsummer Night's Dream*, the first directed by Adrian Noble and the second by Michael Hoffman, were released in 1996 and 1999. In Noble's flawed film, the audience experiences the action through the eyes of a small boy who dreams about the play. This trope dates at least to Jane Howell's BBC televised production of *Titus Andronicus* (1985), and it persists in Julie Taymor's *Titus* (1999). Despite some sublime visual moments, Noble's movie is unsatisfying—neither transgressive enough in its homoerotic innuendos nor regressive enough to suit those who prefer a more innocent approach.

Hoffman's version removed the play from Shakespeare's Athens to a fin-de-siècle setting in northern Italy. The film's musical score begins conventionally enough with the incidental music by Mendelssohn but yields to an anachronistic yet delightful medley of airs from Italian grand opera. Like a true New Woman of the 1890s, feisty Helena rides a bicycle, as do other characters. The effervescent music for the ballroom scene in

Giuseppe Verdi's *La Traviata* enlivens the townspeople's after-noon promenade in the village square. Hoffman's lovely movie is also a lesson in art history; the film's designer, Luciana Arrighi, drew inspiration from the Pre-Raphaelites, Gian Lorenzo Bernini's sculptures, Etruscan relics, and Greek mythology.

At the turn of the 21st century, two costume movies, *Eliza-beth* (1998) and *Shakespeare in Love* (1998), presented heavily fictionalized versions of Shakespeare's life and times. *Elizabeth*, by Pakistani director Shekhar Kapur, starred Cate Blanchett as the beleaguered queen hemmed in by a chilling array of schemers and plotters. John Madden's *Shakespeare in Love* proved the more popular movie. Its witty screenplay by Marc Norman and Tom Stoppard portrays Will Shakespeare (played by Joseph Fiennes) as a starving young hack with a terrible case of writer's block, struggling to write an absurd play called *Romeo and Ethel, the Pirate's Daughter.* The farcical plot, how-ever, conceals a substrata of learned in-jokes playing on such matters as Shakespeare's literary debt to Christopher Marlowe and, through the young playwright's doodling, the various sig-natures that are attributed to him. A vicious adolescent who enjoys feeding mice to cats turns out to be the macabre Jacobean playwright John Webster. When Shakespeare's love, Viola De Lesseps (played by Gwyneth Paltrow), cross-dressed as a male actor, auditions before the playwright at the Rose The-atre, she uses verses from *Two Gentlemen of Verona* ("What light is light, if Sylvia be not seen?" [Act III, scene 1, line 174]) and for a few numinous moments reasserts the supremacy of word over image.

Two versions of Shakespeare's most violent play, *Titus Andronicus*, appeared in 1999, as if to affirm that apocalypse would attend the turn of the century. The first of these, directed by Christopher Dunne, was described by its marketers as "a sav-age epic of brutal revenge." The film is a Götterdämmerung marked by beheading, amputation, and stabbing, but Shake-speare's language has been kept meticulously intact.

The second version, *Titus*, was offered by the theatrical director Taymor, who had staged the play Off Broadway in 1994. She collaborated with cinematographer Luciano Tovoli and others to make brilliant Fellini-like images out of Shakespeare's lurid melodrama. In the film Taymor's haikulike montages blur the line between illusion and reality, making the savagery aesthetically bearable. Anthony Hopkins played Titus, Jessica Lange a passionate Tamora, and Alan Cumming the decadent and utterly villainous Saturninus.

Michael Almereyda's *Hamlet* (2000), starring Ethan Hawke, replaced the Danish court with the Denmark Corporation in Manhattan. Elsinore is a nearby luxury hotel. Hawke played a surly Prince Hamlet disgusted by his stepfather's greed and his mother's veneer of innocence. An amateur filmmaker, Hamlet lives in a world of television and cinema, delivering the "To be or not to be" soliloquy in the Action aisle of a video store. In one of several whimsical touches, while jetting to England Hamlet discovers Claudius's orders for his execution on the hard drive of a laptop stored in the luggage bin over the sleeping Rosencrantz and Guildenstern.

When all is said and done, this flourishing body of work is a singular testament to Shakespeare's universality and humanity. More than 400 years have passed since he put quill to paper, yet, centuries after he first brought them to life on the small outdoor stage near the River Thames, Shakespeare's scenes, characters, and poetry continue to fuel a rich industry for film, literary, and music scholars and critics. Ultimately, of course, Shakespeare's commercial value rests on his immeasurable ability, then and now, to captivate readers, music and theater lovers, filmmakers, and moviegoers alike in his own "strong toil of grace."

Kenneth S. Rothwell is emeritus professor of English at the University of Vermont, Burlington. He is the author of A History of Shakespeare on Screen.

▌Royal Shakespeare Company (RSC)

This English theatrical company has a long history of Shakespearean performance. The company is based in Stratford-upon-Avon, where it maintains three venues—the Royal Shakespeare Theatre, the Swan Theatre (fashioned after the Elizabethan-era theater of the same name), and the Other Place (a studio theater). Its repertoire continues to center on works by William Shakespeare and other Elizabethan and Jacobean playwrights. Modern works are also produced.

The company was founded in 1875 and was originally attached to Stratford's Shakespeare Memorial Theatre (opened

Royal Shakespeare Theatre, Stratford-upon-Avon, Warwickshire, England.

1879; destroyed by fire 1926), which had been built through the efforts of Charles Edward Flower. This theater was the site of an annual festival of Shakespeare's plays, and its resident, seasonal company was called the Shakespeare Memorial Company. In 1925 the company, which had by then become one of the most prestigious in Great Britain, was granted a royal charter. The new Shakespeare Memorial Theatre (opened 1932) was renamed the Royal Shakespeare Theatre in 1961, and the company too was renamed. Under the direction of Peter Hall, the RSC expanded its repertoire.

At the same time it established a second unit in London, which it maintained for several decades at the Barbican and which enabled its players to develop into a professional ensemble working year-round. Although it no longer has residence at a particular theater, the RSC maintains a base in London as well as (since 1977) in Newcastle, and the company also tours internationally.

Sexuality

Like so many circumstances of Shakespeare's personal life, the question of his sexual nature is shrouded in uncertainty. At age 18, in 1582, he married Anne Hathaway, a woman who was eight years older than he. Their first child, Susanna, was born on May 26, 1583, about six months after the marriage ceremony. A license had been issued for the marriage on November 27, 1582, with only one reading (instead of the usual three) of the banns, or announcement of the intent to marry in order to give any party the opportunity to raise any potential legal objections. This procedure and the swift arrival of the couple's first child suggest that the pregnancy was unplanned, as it was certainly premarital. The marriage thus appears to have been a "shotgun" wedding. Anne gave birth some 21 months after the arrival of Susanna to twins, named Hamnet and Judith, who were christened on February 2, 1585. Thereafter William and Anne had no more children. They remained married until his death in 1616.

Were they compatible, or did William prefer to live apart from Anne for most of this time? When he moved to London at some point between 1585 and 1592, he did not take his family with him. Divorce was nearly impossible in this era. Were there medical or other reasons for the absence of any more children? Was he was present in Stratford when his only son, Hamnet, died in 1596 at age 11? He bought a fine house for his family in Stratford and acquired real estate in the vicinity. He was eventually buried in Holy Trinity Church in Stratford, where Anne joined him in 1623.

Shakespeare seems to have retired to Stratford from London in about 1612. He had lived apart from his wife and children, except presumably for occasional visits in the course of a very busy professional life, for at least two decades. His bequeathing in his last will and testament of his "second best bed" to Anne, with no further mention of her name in that document, has suggested to many scholars that the marriage was a disappointment necessitated by an unplanned pregnancy. Other interpretations have been offered, to be sure: that the "second-best bed" may have been the couple's own bed and thus evidence of their conjugality, and that Shakespeare need not have made more bequests in his will specifically to Anne since she was legally entitled to one third of his goods and real estate and the use of their home for life. Still, in the estimation of at least one scholar (Ernst Honigmann), the will, when compared with the wills of other theatrical persons of that period, is notably laconic and perhaps even churlish with regard to the wife.

What was Shakespeare's love life like during those decades in London, apart from his family? Knowledge on this subject is uncertain at best. According to an entry in the commonplace book of a law student named John Manningham, dated March 13, 1602, Shakespeare had a brief affair when he happened to overhear a female citizen at a performance of *Richard III* making an assignation with Richard Burbage, the leading actor of the acting company to which Shakespeare also belonged. Taking advantage of having overheard their conversation, Shakespeare allegedly hastened to the place where the assignation had been arranged, was "entertained" by the woman, and was "at his game" when Burbage showed up. When a message was brought that "Richard the Third" had arrived, Shakespeare is supposed to have "caused return to be made that William the Conqueror was before Richard the Third. Shakespeare's name William." This diary entry of Manningham's must be regarded with much skepticism, since it is verified by no other evidence and since it may simply speak to the timeless truth that actors are regarded as free spirits and bohemians. Indeed, the story was so amusing that it was retold, embellished, and printed in Thomas Wilkes's *A General View of the Stage* (1759) well before Manningham's diary was discovered. It does at least suggest, at any rate, that Manningham imagined it to be true that Shakespeare was heterosexual and not averse to an occasional infidelity to his marriage vows. The film *Shakespeare in Love* (1998) plays amusedly with this idea in its purely fictional presentation of Shakespeare's torchy affair with a young woman named Viola De Lesseps who was eager to become a player in a professional acting company and who inspired Shakespeare in his writing of *Romeo and Juliet*—indeed, giving him some of his best lines.

Apart from these intriguing circumstances, little evidence survives other than the poems and plays that Shakespeare wrote. Can anything be learned from them? The sonnets, written perhaps over an extended period from the early 1590s into the 1600s, chronicle a deeply loving relationship between the speaker of the sonnets and a well-born young man. At times the poet-speaker is greatly sustained and comforted by a love that seems reciprocal. More often, the relationship is one that is troubled by painful absences, by jealousies, by the poet's perception that other writers are winning the young man's affection, and finally by the deep unhappiness of an outright desertion in which the young man takes away from the poet-speaker the dark-haired beauty whose sexual favors the poet-speaker has enjoyed (though not without some revulsion at his own unbridled lust; see Sonnet 129). This narrative would seem to posit heterosexual desire in the poet-speaker, even if of a troubled and guilty sort; but do the earlier sonnets suggest also a desire for the young man? The relationship is portrayed as indeed deeply emotional and dependent; the poet-speaker cannot live without his friend and that friend's returning the love that the poet-speaker so ardently feels. Yet readers today cannot easily tell whether that love is aimed at physical completion; indeed, Sonnet 20 seems to deny that possibility by insisting that Nature's having equipped the friend with "one thing to my purpose nothing," that is, a penis, means that physical sex must be regarded as solely in the province of the friend's relationship with women: "But since she [Nature] pricked thee out for women's pleasure, / Mine be thy love and thy love's use their treasure." The bawdy pun on "pricked" underscores the sexual meaning of the sonnet's concluding couplet. Critic Joseph Pequigney has argued at length that the sonnets nonetheless do commemorate a consummated physical relationship between the poet-speaker and the friend, but most commentators have backed away from such a bold assertion.

A significant difficulty is that one cannot be sure that the sonnets are autobiographical. Shakespeare is such a masterful dramatist that one can easily imagine him creating such an intriguing story line as the basis for his sonnet sequence. Then, too, are the sonnets printed in the order that Shakespeare would have intended? He seems not to have been involved in their publication in 1609, long after most of them had been written. Even so, one can perhaps ask why such a story would have appealed to Shakespeare. Is there a level at which fantasy and dreamwork may be involved?

The plays and other poems lend themselves uncertainly to such speculation. Loving relationships between two men are sometimes portrayed as extraordinarily deep. Antonio, in *Twelfth Night*, protests to Sebastian that he needs to accompany

Sebastian on his adventures even at great personal risk: "If you will not murder me for my love, let me be your servant" (Act II, scene 1, lines 33–34). That is to say, I will die if you leave me behind. Another Antonio, in *The Merchant of Venice*, risks his life for his loving friend Bassanio. Actors in today's theater regularly portray these relationships as homosexual, and indeed actors are often incredulous toward anyone who doubts that to be the case. In *Troilus and Cressida*, Patroclus is rumored to be Achilles's "masculine whore" (Act V, scene 1, line 17), as is suggested in Homer, and certainly the two are very close in friendship, though Patroclus does admonish Achilles to engage in battle by saying, "A woman impudent and mannish grown / Is not more loathed than an effeminate man / In time of action" (Act III, scene 3, lines 218–220). Again, on the modern stage this relationship is often portrayed as obviously, even flagrantly, sexual; but whether Shakespeare sees it as such, or valorizes homosexuality or bisexuality, is another matter.

Certainly his plays contain many warmly positive depictions of heterosexuality, in the loves of Romeo and Juliet, Orlando and Rosalind, and Henry V and Katharine of France, among many others. At the same time, Shakespeare is astute in his representations of sexual ambiguity. Viola, in disguise as a young man, Cesario, in *Twelfth Night*, wins the love of Duke Orsino in such a delicate way that what appears to be the love between two men morphs into the heterosexual mating of Orsino and Viola. The ambiguity is reinforced by the audience's knowledge that in Shakespeare's theater Viola/Cesario was portrayed by a boy actor of perhaps 16. All the cross-dressing situations in the comedies, including Portia in *The Merchant of Venice*, Rosalind/Ganymede in *As You Like It*, Imogen in *Cymbeline*, and many others, playfully explore the uncertain boundaries between the genders. Rosalind's male disguise name in *As You Like It*, Ganymede, is that of the cupbearer to Zeus of whom the god was enamored; the ancient legends assume that Ganymede was Zeus's catamite. Shakespeare is characteristically delicate on that score, but he does seem to delight in the frisson of sexual suggestion.

Sidney, Sir Philip

Elizabethan courtier, statesman, soldier, poet, and patron of scholars and poets, Sir Philip Sidney (1554–1586) is considered the ideal gentleman of his day. After Shakespeare's sonnets, Sidney's *Astrophel and Stella* is considered the finest Elizabethan sonnet cycle. His *Defence of Poesie* introduced the critical ideas of Renaissance theorists to England.

Sidney was the eldest son of Sir Henry Sidney and his wife, Lady Mary Dudley, daughter of the duke of Northumberland, and godson of King Philip II of Spain. After Elizabeth I succeeded to the throne, his father was appointed lord president of Wales (and later served three times as lord deputy of Ireland), while his uncle, Robert Dudley, was created earl of Leicester and became the queen's most trusted adviser. In keeping with his family background, the young Sidney was intended for a career as a statesman and soldier. At age 10 he entered Shrewsbury School, where his classmate was Fulke Greville (later a court official under Elizabeth), who became his lifelong friend and was his early biographer. In February 1568 he began a three-year period of studies at Christ Church, Oxford, afterward traveling in Europe between May 1572 and June 1575, perfecting his knowledge of Latin, French, and Italian. He also gained firsthand knowledge of European politics and became acquainted with many of Europe's leading statesmen.

His first court appointment came in the spring of 1576, when he succeeded his father as cupbearer to the queen, a ceremonial position. Then in February 1577, when he was only 22, he was sent as ambassador to the German emperor Rudolf II and the elector palatine Louis VI, carrying Queen Elizabeth's condolences on the deaths of their fathers. But along with this formal task, he also had secret instructions to sound out the German princes on their attitude toward the formation of a Protestant league—the chief political aim being to protect England by associating it with other Protestant states in Europe, which would counterbalance the threatening power of Roman Catholic

Spain. Sidney apparently brought back enthusiastic reports on the possibilities of forming such a league, but the cautious queen sent other emissaries to check on his reports, and they returned with less optimistic accounts of the German princes' reliability as allies. He did not receive another major official appointment until eight years later.

He nevertheless continued to busy himself in the politics and diplomacy of his country. In 1579 he wrote privately to the queen, advising her against a proposal that she enter into a marriage with the duke of Anjou, the Roman Catholic heir to the French throne. Sidney, moreover, was a member of Parliament for Kent in 1581 and 1584–1585. He corresponded with foreign statesmen and entertained important visitors—including the French Protestant envoy Philippe de Mornay in 1577, the German Calvinist prince Casimir in 1578, the Portuguese pretender Dom Antônio in 1581, and, later, a number of Scottish lords. Sidney was among the few Englishmen of his time with any interest in the newly discovered Americas, and he supported maritime explorations by the navigator Sir Martin Frobisher. In 1582 Richard Hakluyt, who published accounts of English explorers' enterprises, dedicated his *Divers Voyages Touching the Discoverie of America* to him. Sidney later became interested in the project to establish the American colony of Virginia, sent out by Sir Walter Raleigh, and he intended to set out himself in an expedition with Sir Francis Drake against the Spaniards. He had wide-ranging intellectual and artistic interests, discussed art with the painter Nicholas Hilliard and chemistry with the scientist John Dee, and was a great patron of scholars and men of letters. More than 40 works by English and European authors were dedicated to him—works of divinity, ancient and modern history, geography, military affairs, law, logic, medicine, and poetry—indicating the breadth of his interests. Among the many poets and prose writers who sought his patronage were Edmund Spenser, Abraham Fraunce, and Thomas Lodge.

Sidney was an excellent horseman and became renowned for his participation in tournaments—elaborate entertainments, half athletic contest and half symbolic spectacle, that were a chief amusement of the court. He hankered after a life of heroic action, but his official activities were largely ceremonial—attending on the queen at court and accompanying her on her progresses about the country. In January 1583 he was knighted, not because of any outstanding accomplishment but in order to give him the qualifications needed to stand in for his friend Prince Casimir, who was to receive the honor of admittance to the Order of the Garter but was unable to attend the ceremony. In September he married Frances, daughter of Queen Elizabeth's secretary of state, Sir Francis Walsingham. They had one daughter, Elizabeth.

Because the queen would not give him an important post, he turned to literature as an outlet for his energies. In 1578 he composed a pastoral playlet, *The Lady of May*, for the queen. By 1580 he had completed a version of his heroic prose romance, the *Arcadia*. It is typical of his gentlemanly air of assumed nonchalance that he should call it "a trifle, and that triflingly handled," whereas it is in fact an intricately plotted narrative of 180,000 words.

Early in 1581 his aunt, the countess of Huntington, had brought to court her ward, Penelope Devereux, who later that year married the young Lord Rich. Whether or not Sidney really did fall in love with her, during the summer of 1582 he composed a sonnet sequence, *Astrophel and Stella*, which recounts a courtier's passion in delicately fictionalized terms: its first stirrings, his struggles against it, and his final abandonment of his suit to give himself instead to the "great cause" of public service. These sonnets, witty and impassioned, brought Elizabethan poetry at once of age. About the same time, he wrote *The Defence of Poesie*, an urbane and eloquent plea for the social value of imaginative fiction, which remains the finest work of Elizabethan literary criticism. In 1584 he began a radical revision of his *Arcadia*, transforming its linear dramatic plot into a many-stranded, interlaced narrative. He left it half finished, but it remains the most important work of prose fiction in English of the 16th century. He also composed other poems and later began a paraphrase of the Psalms. He wrote for his own amusement and for that of his close friends; true to the gentlemanly code of avoiding commercialism, he did not allow his writings to be published in his lifetime.

The incomplete revised version of his *Arcadia* was not printed until 1590; in 1593 another edition completed the story by adding the last three books of his original version (the complete text of the original version remained in manuscript until 1926). His *Astrophel and Stella* was printed in 1591 in a corrupt text, his *Defence of Poesie* in 1595, and a collected edition of his works in 1598, reprinted in 1599 and nine times during the 17th century.

Although in July 1585 he finally received his eagerly awaited public appointment, his writings were to be his most lasting accomplishment. He was appointed, with his uncle, the earl of Warwick, as joint master of the ordnance, an office that administered the military supplies of the kingdom. In November the queen was finally persuaded to assist the struggle of the Dutch against their Spanish masters, sending them a force led by the earl of Leicester. Sidney was made governor of the town of Flushing (Dutch: Vlissingen) and was given command of a company of cavalry. But the following 11 months were spent in ineffective campaigns against the Spaniards, while Sidney was hard put to maintain the morale of his poorly paid troops. He wrote to his father-in-law that if the queen did not pay her soldiers, she would lose her garrisons but that, for himself, the love of the cause would never make him weary of his resolution, because he thought "a wise and constant man ought never to grieve while he doth play his own part truly, though others be out."

On September 22, 1586, he volunteered to serve in an action to prevent the Spaniards from sending supplies into the town of Zutphen. The supply train was heavily guarded, and the English were outnumbered; but Sidney charged three times through the enemy lines, and even though his thigh was shattered by a bullet, he rode his horse from the field. He was carried to Arnhem, where his wound became infected, and he prepared himself religiously for death. In his last hours he confessed:

> There came to my remembrance a vanity wherein I had taken delight, whereof I had not rid myself. It was the Lady Rich. But I rid myself of it, and presently my joy and comfort returned.

He was buried at St. Paul's Cathedral in London on February 16, 1587, with an elaborate funeral of a type usually reserved for great noblemen. The Universities of Oxford and Cambridge and scholars throughout Europe issued memorial volumes in his honor, while almost every English poet composed verses in his praise. He won this adulation even though he had accomplished no action of consequence; it would be possible to write a history of Elizabethan political and military affairs without so much as mentioning his name. It is not what he did but what he was that made him so widely admired: the embodiment of the Elizabethan ideal of gentlemanly virtue.

▐ Social and Intellectual Context

Shakespeare lived at a time when ideas and social structures established in the Middle Ages still informed human thought and behavior. Queen Elizabeth I was God's deputy on earth, and lords and commoners had their due places in society under her, with responsibilities up through her to God and down to those of more humble rank. The order of things, however, did not go unquestioned. Atheism was still considered a challenge to the beliefs and way of life of a majority of Elizabethans, but the Christian faith was no longer a monolithic entity. Rome's authority had been challenged by Martin Luther, John Calvin, a multitude of small religious sects, and, indeed, the English church itself. Royal prerogative was challenged in Parliament; the economic and social orders were disturbed by the rise of capitalism, by the redistribution of monastic lands under Henry VIII, by the expansion of education, and by the influx of new wealth from discovery of new lands.

An interplay of new and old ideas was typical of the time: official homilies exhorted the people to obedience; the Italian political theorist Niccolò Machiavelli was expounding a new, practical code of politics that caused Englishmen to fear the Italian "Machiavillain" and yet prompted them to ask what men do, rather than what they should do. In *Hamlet*, disquisitions—on man, belief, a "rotten" state, and times "out of joint"—clearly reflect a growing disquiet and skepticism. The translation of Montaigne's *Essays* in 1603 gave further currency, range, and finesse to such thought, and Shakespeare was one of many who read them, making direct and significant quotations in *The Tempest*. In philosophical inquiry the question "How?" became the impulse for advance, rather than the traditional "Why?" of Aristotle. Shakespeare's plays written between 1603 and 1606 unmistakably reflect a new, Jacobean distrust. James I, who, like Elizabeth, claimed divine authority, was far less able than she to maintain the authority of the throne. The so-called Gunpowder Plot (1605) showed a determined challenge by a small minority in the state; James's struggles with the House of Commons in successive Parliaments, in addition to indicating the strength of the "new men," also revealed the inadequacies of the administration.

The Latin comedies of Plautus and Terence were familiar in Elizabethan schools and universities, and English translations or adaptations of them were occasionally performed by students. Seneca's rhetorical and sensational tragedies, too, had been translated and often imitated. But there was also a strong native dramatic tradition deriving from the medieval miracle plays, which had continued to be performed in various towns until forbidden during Elizabeth's reign. This native drama had been able to assimilate French popular farce, clerically inspired morality plays on abstract themes, and interludes or short entertainments that made use of the "turns" of individual clowns and actors. Although Shakespeare's immediate predecessors were known as the "university wits," their plays were seldom structured in the manner of those they had studied at Oxford or Cambridge; instead, they used and developed the more popular narrative forms.

The English language at this time was changing and extending its range. The poet Edmund Spenser led with the restoration of old words, and schoolmasters, poets, sophisticated courtiers, and travelers all brought further contributions from France, Italy, and the Roman classics, as well as from farther afield. Helped by the growing availability of cheaper, printed books, the language began to become standardized in grammar and vocabulary and, more slowly, in spelling. Ambitious for a European and permanent reputation, the essayist and philosopher Francis Bacon wrote in Latin as well as in English; but if he had lived only a few decades later, even he might have had total confidence in his own tongue.

Shakespeare's most obvious debt was to Raphael Holinshed, whose *Chronicles* (the second edition, published in 1587) furnished story material for several plays, including *Macbeth* and *King Lear*. In Shakespeare's earlier works other debts stand out clearly: to Plautus for the structure of *The Comedy of Errors*; to the poet Ovid and to Seneca for rhetoric and incident in *Titus Andronicus*; to morality drama for a scene in which a father mourns his dead son and a son his father, in *Henry VI*; to Christopher Marlowe for sentiments and characterization in *Richard III* and *The Merchant of Venice*; to the Italian popular tradition of commedia dell'arte for characterization and dramatic style in *The Taming of the Shrew*; and so on. Soon, however, there was no line between their effects and his. In *The Tempest* (perhaps the most original of all his plays in form, theme, language, and setting) folk influences may also be traced, together with a newer and more obvious debt to a courtly diversion known as the masque, as developed by Ben Jonson and others at the court of King James.

Theatrical Conditions

The Globe and its predecessor, the Theatre, were public play-houses run by the Lord Chamberlain's Men, a leading theater company of which Shakespeare was a member. Almost all classes of citizens, excepting many Puritans and like-minded Reformers, came to them for afternoon entertainment. The players were also summoned to court, to perform before the monarch and assembled nobility. In times of plague, usually in the summer, they might tour the provinces, and on occasion they performed at London's Inns of Court (associations of law students), at universities, and in great houses. Popularity led to an insatiable demand for plays: early in 1613 the King's Men— as the Lord Chamberlain's Men were then known—could present "fourteen several plays." The theater soon became fashionable, too, and in 1608–1609 the King's Men started to perform on a regular basis at the Blackfriars, a "private" indoor theater where high admission charges assured the company a more select and sophisticated audience for their performances.

Shakespeare's first associations with the Lord Chamberlain's Men seem to have been as an actor. He is not known to have acted after 1603, and tradition gives him only secondary roles, such as the ghost in *Hamlet* and Adam in *As You Like It*, but his continuous association must have given him direct working knowledge of all aspects of theater. Numerous passages in his plays show conscious concern for theater arts and audience reactions. Hamlet gives expert advice to visiting actors in the art of playing. Prospero in *The Tempest* speaks of the whole of life as a kind of "revels," or theatrical show, that, like a dream, will soon be over. The Duke of York in *Richard II* is conscious of how

> . . . in a theatre, the eyes of men,
> After a well-graced actor leaves the stage
> Are idly bent on him that enters next,
> Thinking his prattle to be tedious.

In Shakespeare's day there was little time for group rehearsals, and actors were given the words of only their own parts. The crucial scenes in Shakespeare's plays, therefore, are between two or three characters only or else are played with one character dominating a crowded stage. Most female parts were written for young male actors or boys, so Shakespeare did not often write big roles for them or keep them actively engaged on stage for lengthy periods. Writing for the clowns of the company—who were important popular attractions in any play—presented the problem of allowing them to use their comic personalities and tricks and yet have them serve the immediate interests of theme and action.

Also, since the days of Shakespeare, the English language has changed, and so have audiences, theaters, actors, and customary patterns of thought and feeling. Time has placed an ever-increasing cloud before the mirror he held up to life, and it is here that scholarship can help.

Problems are most obvious in single words. In the 21st century, *presently*, for instance, does not mean "immediately," as it usually did for Shakespeare, or *will* mean "lust," or *rage* mean "folly," or *silly* denote "innocence" and "purity." In Shakespeare's day, words sounded different, too, so that *ably* could rhyme with *eye* or *tomb* with *dumb*. Syntax was often different, and, far more difficult to define, so was response to meter and phrase. What sounds formal and stiff to a modern hearer might have sounded fresh and merry to an Elizabethan.

Ideas have changed, too, most obviously political ones. Shakespeare's contemporaries almost unanimously believed in authoritarian monarchy and recognized divine intervention in history. Most of them would have agreed that a man should be burned for ultimate religious heresies. It is the office of linguistic and historical scholarship to aid the understanding of the multitude of factors that have significantly affected the impressions made by Shakespeare's plays.

None of Shakespeare's plays has survived in his handwritten manuscript, and in the printed texts of some plays, notably *King*

Lear and *Richard III*, there are passages that are manifestly corrupt, with only an uncertain relationship to the words Shakespeare once wrote. Even if the printer received a good manuscript, small errors could still be introduced. Compositors were less than perfect; they often "regularized" the readings of their copy, altered punctuation in accordance with their own preferences or "house" style or because they lacked the necessary pieces of type, or made mistakes because they had to work too hurriedly. Even the correction of proof sheets in the printing house could further corrupt the text, since such correction was usually effected without reference to the author or to the manuscript copy; when both corrected and uncorrected states are still available, it is sometimes the uncorrected version that is preferable. Correctors were responsible for some errors now impossible to right.

Sources

With a few exceptions, Shakespeare did not invent the plots of his plays. Sometimes he used old stories (*Hamlet*, *Pericles*). Sometimes he worked from the stories of comparatively recent Italian writers, such as Giovanni Boccaccio—using both well-known stories (*Romeo and Juliet*, *Much Ado about Nothing*) and little-known ones (*Othello*). He used the popular prose fictions of his contemporaries in *As You Like It* and *The Winter's Tale*. In writing his historical plays, he drew largely from Sir Thomas North's translation of Plutarch's *Lives of the Noble Grecians and Romans* for the Roman plays and the chronicles of Edward Hall and Raphael Holinshed for the plays based upon English history. Some plays deal with rather remote and legendary history (*King Lear*, *Cymbeline*, *Macbeth*). Earlier dramatists had occasionally used the same material (there were, for example, the earlier plays called *The Famous Victories of Henry the Fifth* and *King Leir*). But because many plays of Shakespeare's time have been lost, it is impossible to be sure of the relation between an earlier, lost play and Shakespeare's surviving one: in the case of *Hamlet* it has been plausibly argued that an "old play," known to have existed, was merely an early version of Shakespeare's own.

Shakespeare was probably too busy for prolonged study. He had to read what books he could, when he needed them. His enormous vocabulary could only be derived from a mind of great celerity, responding to the literary as well as the spoken language. It is not known what libraries were available to him. The Huguenot family of Mountjoys, with whom he lodged in London, presumably possessed French books. Moreover, he seems to have enjoyed an interesting connection with the London book trade. The Richard Field who published Shakespeare's two poems *Venus and Adonis* and *The Rape of Lucrece*, in 1593–1594, seems to have been (as an apprenticeship record describes him) the "son of Henry Field of Stratford-upon-Avon in the County of Warwick, tanner." When Henry Field the tanner died in 1592, John Shakespeare the glover was one of the three appointed to value his goods and chattels. Field's son, bound apprentice in 1579, was probably about the same age as Shakespeare. From 1587 he steadily established himself as a printer of serious literature—notably of North's translation of Plutarch (1595, reprinted in 1603 and 1610). There is no direct evidence of any close friendship between Field and Shakespeare. Still, it cannot escape notice that one of the important printer-publishers in London at the time was an exact contemporary of Shakespeare at Stratford, that he can hardly have been other than a schoolmate, that he was the son of a close associate of John Shakespeare, and that he published Shakespeare's first poems. Clearly, a considerable number of literary contacts were available to Shakespeare, and many books were accessible.

That Shakespeare's plays had "sources" was already apparent in his own time. An interesting contemporary description of a performance is to be found in the diary of a young lawyer of the Middle Temple, John Manningham, who kept a record of his experiences in 1602 and 1603. On February 2, 1602, he wrote:

At our feast we had a play called *Twelfth Night*; or,
What You Will, much like *The Comedy of Errors*, or
Menaechmi in Plautus, but most like and near to
that in Italian called *Inganni*.

The first collection of information about sources of Elizabethan plays was published in the 17th century—Gerard Lang-
baine's *Account of the English Dramatick Poets* (1691) briefly
indicated where Shakespeare found materials for some plays.
But during the course of the 17th century, it came to be felt that
Shakespeare was an outstandingly "natural" writer, whose intellectual background was of comparatively little significance: "he
was naturally learn'd; he needed not the spectacles of books to
read nature," wrote John Dryden in 1668. It was nevertheless
obvious that the intellectual quality of Shakespeare's writings
was high and revealed a remarkably perceptive mind. The
Roman plays, in particular, gave evidence of careful reconstruction of the ancient world.

The first collection of source materials, arranged so that
they could be read and closely compared with Shakespeare's
plays, was made by Charlotte Lennox in the 18th century. More
complete collections appeared later, notably those of John
Payne Collier (*Shakespeare's Library*, 1843; revised by W. Carew
Hazlitt, 1875). These earlier collections have been superseded
by a seven-volume version edited by Geoffrey Bullough as *Narrative and Dramatic Sources of Shakespeare* (1957–1972).

It has become steadily more possible to see what was original in Shakespeare's dramatic art. He achieved compression and
economy by the exclusion of undramatic material. He developed characters from brief suggestions in his source (Mercutio,
Touchstone, Falstaff, Pandarus), and he developed entirely new
characters (the Dromio brothers, Beatrice and Benedick, Sir
Toby Belch, Malvolio, Paulina, Roderigo, Lear's Fool). He
rearranged the plot with a view to more effective contrasts of
character, climaxes, and conclusions (*Macbeth*, *Othello*, *The
Winter's Tale*, *As You Like It*). A wider philosophical outlook

was introduced (*Hamlet, Coriolanus, All's Well That Ends Well, Troilus and Cressida*). And everywhere an intensification of the dialogue and an altogether higher level of imaginative writing transformed the older work.

But quite apart from evidence of the sources of his plays, it is not difficult to get a fair impression of Shakespeare as a reader, feeding his own imagination by a moderate acquaintance with the literary achievements of other men and of other ages. He quotes his contemporary Christopher Marlowe in *As You Like It*. He casually refers to the *Aethiopica* ("Ethiopian History") of Heliodorus (which had been translated by Thomas Underdown in 1569) in *Twelfth Night*. He read the translation of Ovid's *Metamorphoses* by Arthur Golding, which went through seven editions between 1567 and 1612. George Chapman's vigorous translation of Homer's *Iliad* impressed him, though he used some of the material rather sardonically in *Troilus and Cressida*. He derived the ironical account of an ideal republic in *The Tempest* from one of Montaigne's essays. He read (in part, at least) Samuel Harsnett's *Declaration of Egregious Popish Impostors* and remembered lively passages from it when he was writing *King Lear*. The beginning lines of one sonnet (106) indicate that he had read Edmund Spenser's poem *The Faerie Queene* or comparable romantic literature.

He was acutely aware of the varieties of poetic style that characterized the work of other authors. A brilliant little poem he composed for Prince Hamlet (Act V, scene 2, line 115) shows how ironically he perceived the qualities of poetry in the last years of the 16th century, when poets such as John Donne were writing love poems uniting astronomical and cosmogonic imagery with skepticism and moral paradoxes. The eight-syllable lines in an archaic mode written for the 14th-century poet John Gower in *Pericles* show his reading of that poet's *Confessio amantis*. The influence of the great figure of Sir Philip Sidney, whose *Arcadia* was first printed in 1590 and was widely read for generations, is frequently felt in Shakespeare's writings. Finally, the importance of the Bible for Shakespeare's style and range of allusion is not to be underestimated. His works show a pervasive familiarity with the passages appointed to be read in church on each Sunday throughout the year, and a large number of allusions to passages in Ecclesiasticus (Wisdom of Jesus the Son of Sirach) indicates a personal interest in one of the deuterocanonical books.

Southampton, Henry Wriothesley, 3rd Earl of

Southampton (1573–1624) was an English nobleman best remembered for being Shakespeare's patron.

Henry Wriothesley succeeded to his father's earldom in 1581 and became a royal ward under the care of Lord Burghley. Educated at the University of Cambridge and at Gray's Inn, London, he was 17 years old when he was presented at court, where he was favored by Queen Elizabeth I and befriended by Robert Devereux, 2nd earl of Essex. Southampton became a munificent patron of writers, including Barnabe Barnes, Thomas Nashe, and Gervase Markham. He is best known, however, as the patron of Shakespeare, who dedicated the poems *Venus and Adonis* (1593) and *The Rape of Lucrece* (1594) to him. It has also been argued, albeit inconclusively, that the sonnets were addressed to him. If so, the earlier sonnets, urging marriage, must have been written before the beginning (in 1595) of Southampton's intrigue with Elizabeth Vernon, one of the queen's waiting women, which culminated with their hasty marriage in 1598, incurring the queen's wrath and leading to their brief imprisonment.

In 1596 and 1597 Southampton accompanied Essex on his expeditions to Cádiz and to the Azores. In 1599 he went to Ireland with Essex, but the queen insisted that Southampton return to London. He was deeply involved in the Essex rebellion (February 1601), on the eve of which he induced players at the

Globe Theatre to revive *Richard II* (a play dealing with the deposition of a king) in order to stir up the populace. He was tried for treason on February 19, 1601; his titles were forfeited and he was condemned to death, but his sentence was commuted to life imprisonment through the intervention of Sir Robert Cecil.

On the accession of James I, Southampton resumed his place at court. He was made a Knight of the Garter and captain of the Isle of Wight in 1603 and was restored to the peerage by act of Parliament. In 1603 he entertained Queen Anne with a performance of Shakespeare's *Love's Labour's Lost* by the Lord Chamberlain's Men, soon to be known as the King's Men.

Southampton was an active member of the Virginia Company and the East India Company. He was a volunteer in support of German Protestants in 1614, and in 1617 he proposed fitting out an expedition against the Barbary pirates. He became a privy councilor in 1619 but fell into disgrace through his determined opposition to the royal favorite, the duke of Buckingham. In 1624 he and his elder son volunteered to fight for the United Provinces against Spain, but on landing in the Netherlands they were attacked with fever, and Southampton died a few days after the death of his son.

▌ Spenser, Edmund

A contemporary of Shakespeare, Edmund Spenser (1552/53–1599) was an English poet whose long allegorical poem *The Faerie Queene* is one of the greatest in the English language. It was written in what came to be called the Spenserian stanza.

Little is certainly known about Spenser. He was related to the noble Midlands family of Spencer, whose fortune had been made through sheep raising. His own immediate family was not wealthy. He was entered as a "poor boy" in the Merchant Taylors' grammar school, where he would have studied mainly Latin, with some Hebrew, Greek, and music.

In 1569, when Spenser was about 16 years old, his English versions of poems by the 16th-century French poet Joachim du Bellay and his translation of a French version of a poem by the Italian poet Petrarch appeared at the beginning of an anti-Catholic prose tract, *A Theatre for Voluptuous Worldlings*; they were no doubt commissioned by its chief author, the wealthy Flemish expatriate Jan Baptista van der Noot. (Some of these poems Spenser later revised for his *Complaints* volume.)

Edmund Spenser, oil painting by an unknown artist.

From May 1569 Spenser was a student in Pembroke Hall (now Pembroke College) of the University of Cambridge, where, along with perhaps a quarter of the students, he was classed as a sizar—a student who, out of financial necessity, performed various menial or semi-menial duties. He received a Bachelor of Arts degree in 1573. Because of an epidemic, Spenser left Cambridge in 1574, but he received a Master of Arts degree in 1576.

His best-known friend at Cambridge was the slightly older Gabriel Harvey, a fellow of Pembroke, who was learned, witty, and enthusiastic about ancient and modern literature but also pedantic, devious, and ambitious. There is no reason to believe that Spenser shared the most distasteful of these qualities, but in the atmosphere of social mobility and among the new aristocracy of Tudor England, it is not surprising that he hoped for preferment to higher position.

Spenser's period at the University of Cambridge was undoubtedly important for the acquisition of his wide knowledge not only of the Latin and some of the Greek classics but also of the Italian, French, and English literature of his own and earlier times. His knowledge of the traditional forms and themes of lyrical and narrative poetry provided foundations for him to build his own highly original compositions. Without the Roman epic poet Virgil's *Aeneid*, the 15th-century Italian Ludovico Ariosto's *Orlando furioso*, and, later, Torquato Tasso's *Gerusalemme liberata* (1581), Spenser could not have written his heroic, or epic, poem *The Faerie Queene*. Without Virgil's *Bucolics* and the later tradition of pastoral poetry in Italy and France, Spenser could not have written *The Shepheardes Calender*. And without the Latin, Italian, and French examples of the highly traditional marriage ode and the sonnet and canzone forms of Petrarch and succeeding sonneteers, Spenser could not have written his greatest lyric, *Epithalamion*, and its accompanying sonnets, *Amoretti*. The patterns of meaning in Spenser's poetry are frequently woven out of the traditional interpretations—developed through classical times and his own—of pagan myth, divinities, and philosophies and out of an equally strong experience of the faith and doctrines of Christianity; these patterns he further enriched by the use of medieval and contemporary story, legend, and folklore.

Spenser's religious training was a most important part of his education. He could not have avoided some involvement in the bitter struggles that took place in his university over the path the new Church of England was to tread between Roman Catholicism and extreme Puritanism, and his own poetry repeatedly engages with the opposition between Protestantism and Catholicism and the need to protect the national and moral purity of the Elizabethan church. Contrary to a former view, there is little reason to believe that he inclined toward the Puritanical side. His first known appointment (after a blank of several years, when he may have been in the north of England) was in 1578 as secretary to Bishop John Young of Rochester, former master of Spenser's college at Cambridge. Spenser's first important publication, *The Shepheardes Calender* (1579 or 1580), is more concerned with the bishops and affairs of the English church than is any of his later work.

The Shepheardes Calender can be called the first work of the English literary Renaissance. Following the example of Virgil and of many later poets, Spenser was beginning his career with a series of eclogues (literally "selections," usually short poems in the form of pastoral dialogues), in which various characters, in the guise of innocent and simple shepherds, converse about life and love in a variety of elegantly managed verse forms, formulating weighty—often satirical—opinions on questions of the day. The paradoxical combination in pastoral poetry of the simple, isolated life of shepherds with the sophisticated social ambitions of the figures symbolized or discussed by these shepherds (and of their probable readership) has been of some interest in literary criticism.

The *Calender* consists of 12 eclogues, one named after each month of the year. One of the shepherds, Colin Clout, who excels in poetry but is ruined by his hopeless love for one Rosalind, is Spenser himself. The eclogue "Aprill" is in praise of the shepherdess Elisa, really the queen (Elizabeth I) herself. "October" examines the various kinds of verse composition and suggests how discouraging it is for a modern poet to try for success in any of them. Most of the eclogues, however, concern good or bad shepherds—that is to say, pastors—of Christian congregations. The *Calender* was well received in its day, and it is still a revelation of what could be done poetically in English after a long period of much mediocrity and provinciality. The archaic quality of its language, sometimes deplored, was partly motivated by a desire to continue older English poetic traditions, such as that of Geoffrey Chaucer. Archaic vocabulary is not so marked a feature of Spenser's later work.

The years 1578–1580 probably produced more changes in Spenser's life than did any other corresponding period. He appears by 1580 to have been serving the fascinating, highly placed, and unscrupulous Robert Dudley, earl of Leicester, and to have become a member of the literary circle led by Sir Philip Sidney, Leicester's nephew, to whom the *Calender* was dedicated and who praised it in his important critical work *The Defence of Poesie* (1595). Spenser remained permanently devoted to this brilliant writer and good nobleman, embodied him variously in his own poetry, and mourned his early death in an elegy. By 1580 Spenser had also started work on *The Faerie Queene*, and in the previous year he had apparently married one Machabyas Chylde. Interesting sidelights on his personal character, of which next to nothing is known, are given in a small collection of letters between Spenser and Gabriel Harvey that was printed in 1580. The ironies in that exchange of letters are so intricate, however, as to make it difficult to draw many conclusions from them about Spenser, except that he was young, ambitious, accomplished, and sincerely interested in the theory and practice of poetry. In 1580 Spenser was made secretary to the new lord deputy of Ireland, Arthur Lord Grey, who was a friend of the Sidney family.

Sixteenth-century Ireland and the Irish were looked on by the English as a colony, although the supposed threat of an invasion by Spain and the conflict between an imposed English church and the Roman Catholicism of the Irish were further complicating factors. Irish chieftains and the Anglo-Irish nobility encouraged native resistance to newly arrived English officials and landowners. As Grey's secretary, Spenser accompanied the lord deputy on risky military campaigns as well as on more routine journeys. He may have witnessed the Smerwick massacre (1580), and his poetry is haunted by nightmare characters who embody a wild lawlessness. The conflict between Grey's direct, drastic governmental measures and the queen's characteristic procrastinating and temporizing style soon led to Grey's frustration and recall. But Spenser, like many others, admired and defended Grey's methods. His later tract, *A View of the Present State of Ireland* (written 1595–1596, published 1633), argues lucidly for a typically 16th-century theory of rule: firm measures, ruthlessly applied, with gentleness only for completely submissive subject populations.

For four or five years from roughly 1584, Spenser carried out the duties of a second important official position in Ireland, deputizing for his friend Lodowick Bryskett as clerk of the lords president (governors) of Munster, the southernmost Irish province. The fruits of his service in Ireland are plain. He was given a sinecure post and other favors, including the right to dispose of certain forfeited parcels of land (he no doubt indulged in profitable land speculation). For a time he leased the small property of New Abbey, County Kildare, and on this basis was first designated "gentleman." Finally, he obtained a much larger estate in Munster. One of the chief preoccupations of the presidents of this province, scarred as it was by war and starvation, was to repopulate it. To this end, large "plantations" were awarded to English "undertakers," who undertook to make them self-sustaining by occupying them with Englishmen of various trades. In 1588 or 1589 Spenser took over the 3,000-acre (1,200-hectare) plantation of Kilcolman, about 25 miles (40 km) to the north and a little to the west of Cork. No doubt he took there his son and daughter and his wife, if she was still alive (she is known to have died by 1594, when Spenser married Elizabeth Boyle, a "kinswoman" of the earl of Cork and one of Ireland's wealthiest men). By acquiring this estate, Spenser made his choice for the future: to rise into the privileged class of what was, to all intents, a colonial land of opportunity rather than to seek power and position on the more crowded ground of the homeland, where he had made his poetic reputation. In his new situation he, like other undertakers, had much conflict with the local Anglo-Irish aristocracy and had limited success in filling the plantations with English families. Nevertheless, it was under these conditions that Spenser brought his greatest poetry to completion.

In its present form, *The Faerie Queene* consists of six books and a fragment (known as the "Mutabilitie Cantos"). According to Spenser's introductory letter in the first edition (1590) of his great poem, it was to contain 12 books, each telling the adventure of one of Gloriana's knights. Like other poets, Spenser must have modified his general plan many times, yet this letter, inconsistent though it is with various plot details in the books that are extant, is probably a faithful mirror of his thinking at one stage. The stories actually published were those of Holiness (the Red Cross Knight), Temperance (Sir Guyon), Chastity

(Britomart, a female knight), Friendship (ostensibly concerning Triamond and Cambello, although these play a small part), Justice (Artegall), and Courtesy (Calidore). As a setting Spenser invented the land of Faerie and its queen, Gloriana. To express himself he invented a nine-line stanza, the first eight of five stresses and the last of six, whose rhyme pattern is ababbcbcc.

What is most characteristic of Spenser in *The Faerie Queene* is his serious view of the capacity of the romance form to act as a paradigm of human experience: the moral life as quest, pilgrimage, aspiration; as eternal war with an enemy, still to be known; and as encounter, crisis, the moment of illumination—in short, as ethics, with the added dimensions of mystery, terror, love, and victory and with all the generous virtues exalted. Modern readers' impatience with the obscure allusions in the poem, with its political and ecclesiastical topicalities, is a failure to share the great conflict of Spenser's time between Protestant England and Roman Catholic Spain; to Spenser, the war between good and evil was here and now. In *The Faerie Queene* Spenser proves himself a master: picture, music, meter, story—all elements are at one with the deeper significance of his poem, providing a moral heraldry of colors, emblems, legends, folklore, and mythical allusion, all prompting deep, instinctive responses.

The poem was published with the help of Sir Walter Raleigh, who owned large lands to the east of Spenser's estate. He and the poet came together at Kilcolman in 1589 and became well acquainted with each other's poetry. Spenser implies that Raleigh persuaded Spenser to accompany him back to England to present the completed portion of *The Faerie Queene* to Queen Elizabeth herself. The history of this episode is charmingly evoked in *Colin Clouts Come Home Againe* (completed 1595), which is also one of Spenser's most effective pastoral embodiments of a provincial innocent up against the sophistications of a center of power, with subsequent reflections on false, superficial love and the true love that finally animates a concordant universe.

Arriving thus in London with the support of the queen's

favorite, Spenser was well received—not least by Elizabeth herself. The first three books of *The Faerie Queene* were duly published in 1590, together with a dedication to her and commendatory sonnets to notables of the court. Spenser saw the book through the press, made a hurried visit to Ireland, and returned speedily to London—presumably in the hope of preferment. At this time he supervised the printing of certain other of his poems in a collection called *Complaints* (1591), many of which had probably been written earlier in his career and were now being published so as to profit from the great success of his new heroic poem. It is difficult to believe that the many titles of poems that have not survived but were mentioned earlier in his career were not published in revised form and under other titles in his known work, for *Complaints* suggests by its miscellaneous and uneven character that Spenser was hastily bringing to the light of day nearly every last shred that he had to offer; early translations, an elegy, and the delightful mock-heroic poem *Muiopotmos* are contained in it. Another item, the beast fable "Prosopopoia; or, Mother Hubberd's Tale," apparently caused the authorities to withdraw unsold copies of the volume (perhaps in 1592) because it contained a covert attack on Lord Burghley, who was one of the most powerful figures of the court. Nevertheless, in 1591 Queen Elizabeth gave Spenser a small pension for life.

Back in Ireland, Spenser pressed on with his writing, in spite of the burdens of his estate. In early 1595 he published *Amoretti* and *Epithalamion*, a sonnet sequence and a marriage ode celebrating his marriage to Elizabeth Boyle after what appears to have been an impassioned courtship in 1594. This group of poems is unique among Renaissance sonnet sequences in that it celebrates a successful love affair culminating in marriage. The *Epithalamion* further idealizes the marriage by building into its structure the symbolic numbers 24 (the number of stanzas) and 365 (the total number of long lines), allowing the poem to allude to the structure of the day and of the year. The marriage is thus connected with the encompassing harmonies of the universe, and the cyclical processes of change and renewal expressed in the procreation of the two mortal lovers. However, matters were less harmonious in books IV, V, and VI of *The Faerie Queene*, which appeared in 1596 and are strikingly more ambiguous and ironic than the first three books. Book V includes much direct allegory of some of the most problematical political events of Elizabeth's reign, and book VI's Sir Calidore is a far less confident and effective fairy knight than his predecessors are. In the only surviving fragment of a projected seventh book (published posthumously in 1609), Spenser represents Elizabeth herself as subject to Mutability, the inexorable processes of aging and change.

This burst of publication was the last of his lifetime. His early death may have been precipitated by the penetration into Munster of the Irish uprising of 1598. The undertakers and other loyalists failed to make headway against this. Kilcolman was burned, and Spenser, probably in despair despite the Privy Council's having just recommended his appointment to the important post of sheriff of Cork, carried official letters about the desperate state of affairs from the president to London, where he died. He was buried with ceremony in Westminster Abbey close by the grave of Geoffrey Chaucer.

Spenser was considered in his day to be the greatest of English poets, who had glorified England and its language by his long allegorical poem *The Faerie Queene*, just as Virgil had glorified Rome and the Latin tongue by his epic poem the *Aeneid*. Spenser had a strong influence upon his immediate successors, and the sensuous features of his poetic style, as well as his nine-line stanza form, were later admired and imitated by such poets as Lord Byron and Percy Bysshe Shelley in the Romantic period of the late 18th and early 19th centuries. He is widely studied today as one of the chief begetters of the English literary Renaissance and as a master who embodied in poetic myth a view of the virtuous life in a Christian universe.

▌Stratford-upon-Avon

Stratford-upon-Avon stands where a Roman road forded the River Avon, and a 19th-century bridge still spans the river alongside a 15th-century arched stone bridge. The first royal charter was granted in 1553. Shakespeare was born in 1564 in a half-timbered house on Henley Street. He attended the local grammar school adjoining the medieval Chapel of the Guild of the Holy Cross. In 1597 Shakespeare returned from London to the house known as New Place, where he died in 1616. His grave is in the parish church of Holy Trinity. It was not until 1769—more than a century and a half after the playwright's death, when the actor-producer David Garrick inaugurated the first of the annual birthday celebrations—that an attempt was made to preserve buildings and other memorials of Shakespeare's life in the town.

By the river the group of modern buildings known as the Shakespeare Centre includes a library and art gallery (opened in 1881) and a theater (opened in 1932). April 23—the date of Shakespeare's death and, approximately, also of his birth—is celebrated annually in Stratford-upon-Avon, and every year from March until October there is a festival during which his plays are acted in the Royal Shakespeare Theatre.

▌*The Taming of the Shrew*

This comedy in five acts was written sometime in 1590–1594 and first published in the First Folio of 1623. The play describes the volatile courtship between the shrewish Katharina (Kate) and the canny Petruchio, who is determined to subdue Katharina's legendary temper and win her dowry. The main story is offered as a play within a play; the frame plot consists of an initial two-scene "induction" in which a whimsical lord decides to play a practical joke on a drunken tinker, Christopher Sly, by inducing him to believe that he is in fact a nobleman who has suffered from amnesia and is only now awaking from it. The main body of the play is presented to Sly as an entertainment for his delectation.

The source of the Petruchio-Katharina plot is unknown, although a number of analogues exist in ballads about the "taming" of shrewish women. The play's other plot involving Bianca and her many suitors was derived from George Gascoigne's comedy *Supposes* (1566), itself a translation of *I suppositi* (1509) by Ludovico Ariosto.

Following the induction, the play opens in Padua, where several eligible bachelors have gathered to claim the hand of Bianca, the youngest daughter of the wealthy Baptista. But Baptista has stated that Bianca will not be wed before her older sister, Katharina. The plot of "the taming of the shrew" then begins when Petruchio arrives in Padua in search of a rich wife. His friend Hortensio sets Petruchio's sights on Katharina (the shrew). Although Katharina responds hostilely to Petruchio, he woos, wins, and tames her by the sheer force of his manly insistence and by his wit; Katharina is attracted to Petruchio in spite of herself, since clearly he is her match in a way that other men could not be. After their bizarre marriage ceremony, in which Petruchio dresses in a wild fashion and abuses the priest, Katharina's taming continues. In order to show her a picture of her own willfulness, Petruchio obliges her to forgo food, sleep, and fancy clothing. He abuses his own servants, notably Grumio, as a way of demonstrating how unattractive a sharp temper can be. Katharina learns, however reluctantly, that the only way she can find peace is to agree with anything that Petruchio says and do whatever he insists. At the play's end, Petruchio wins a bet from the other gentlemen that Katharina will be more obedient than their new wives. To show that she is indeed now more obedient, on Petruchio's orders Katharina delivers a short sermon on the virtues of wifely obedience.

The play's other plot follows the competition between Hortensio, Gremio, and Lucentio for Bianca's hand in marriage. The only serious candidate is Lucentio, the son of a wealthy Florentine gentleman. He is so smitten with Bianca's charms that he exchanges places with his clever servant, Tranio, in order to gain access to the woman he loves. He does so disguised as a tutor. So does the less successful Hortensio. Gremio has nothing to recommend his suit except his wealth; he is an old man, unattractive to Bianca. In order to fend off this claim of wealth (since Baptista has vowed to bestow Bianca on the suitor with the greatest wealth), Tranio poses as the son of a wealthy gentleman and steps into the competition for Bianca's hand. Needing a father to prove his claim, Tranio persuades a pedant (or merchant) from Mantua to play the role. This ruse fools Baptista, and so the formal arrangements for the marriage proceed. Tranio's tricks are eventually exposed, but not before Lucentio and Bianca have taken the occasion to marry in secret. Hortensio, in the meantime, has forsaken his pursuit of Bianca and married a wealthy widow. In the play's final scene, both Bianca and Hortensio's new wife ironically prove to be shrewish.

The Tempest

This drama in five acts was first written and performed about 1611 and published in the First Folio of 1623 from an edited transcript, by Ralph Crane (scrivener of the King's Men), of the author's papers after they had been annotated for production.

The play opens with a storm raised by Prospero, who years earlier, as the rightful duke of Milan, had been set adrift in a boat with his three-year-old daughter, Miranda, by his usurping brother, Antonio. Prospero, more interested in his books and his magic than in the pragmatics of ruling Milan, had left himself vulnerable to this overthrow. Arriving at an island, Prospero proceeded to make good use of his magic by freeing the sprite Ariel from the torment of imprisonment to which Ariel had been subjected for refusing to carry out the wicked behests of the sorceress Sycorax. Prospero and Miranda found no living person on the island other than Sycorax's son Caliban. They took Caliban into their little family and lived in harmony until Caliban attempted to rape Miranda. Prospero then confined Caliban to a rock and to the status of slave, requiring him to attend to their needs by performing such tasks as gathering firewood. As the play begins, Prospero raises the tempest in order to cast onto the shores of his island a party of Neapolitans returning to Naples from a wedding in Tunis: King Alonso of Naples, his son Ferdinand, his brother Sebastian, and Prospero's brother, Antonio.

With the arrival of the outsiders, the process of testing and eventual reconciliation begins. The party is brought to shore by Ariel, but Ferdinand is separated from the others and is believed drowned. Ariel helps foil plots against Prospero by Caliban and against Alonso by Antonio. Ariel then appears to Alonso and Antonio as a harpy and reproaches them for their treatment of Prospero. Alonso, believing Ferdinand dead, is certain that his death was punishment for Alonso's crime and has a change of heart. Prospero, convinced that Antonio and company are repentant (or at least chastened), reconciles all and prepares to return to Milan to reclaim his throne.

Young Ferdinand meantime has encountered Miranda, and the two have fallen instantly in love. Their courtship is watched carefully by Prospero, who, though insistent that they proceed carefully and preserve their virginity until they are actually married, welcomes this love relationship as a way of making Miranda happy and at the same time of reconciling Milan and Naples; their marriage will unite the two contending kingdoms.

▌ The Theatre

The first public playhouse of London, it was located in the parish of St. Leonard's, Shoreditch. Designed and built by James Burbage (the father of actor Richard Burbage), the Theatre was a roofless, circular building with three galleries surrounding a yard. It opened in 1576, and several companies performed there, including Leicester's Men (1576–1578), the Admiral's Men (1590–1591), and the Lord Chamberlain's Men (1594–1596), who were associated with William Shakespeare. The Theatre also was the site of fencing and athletic competitions. After the death of James Burbage in February 1597, the theater's lease ended. In 1598 the building was dismantled, and Burbage's sons, Cuthbert and Richard, used its timbers to construct the first Globe Theatre.

▌*Timon of Athens*

This tragedy in five acts was probably written sometime in 1605–1608 and was published in the First Folio of 1623 from an authorial manuscript, probably unfinished. Some parts of the play may be by Thomas Middleton. It belongs to Shakespeare's late experimental period, when he explored a new kind of tragic form.

Unlike the plots of his great tragedies, the story of *Timon of Athens* is simple and lacks development. It demonstrates events in the life of Timon, a man known for his great and universal generosity, who spends his fortune and then is spurned when he needs help. He puts on a feast, invites his fair-weather friends, serves them warm water, and throws it in their faces. Leaving Athens filled with hatred, he goes to live in a cave. There he is visited by his loyal servant Flavius, by the churlish philosopher Apemantus, and by two mistresses of the general Alcibiades, all of whom sympathize to some degree with Timon's plight, but to no avail; Timon has turned his back on ungrateful humankind. While digging for roots to eat, Timon uncovers gold, most of which he gives to Alcibiades' mistresses and to Alcibiades himself for his war against Athens. Word of his fortune reaches Athens, and, as a variety of Athenians importune Timon again, he curses them and dies.

▌ *Titus Andronicus*

This early, experimental tragedy was written sometime in 1589–1592 and published in a quarto edition from an incomplete draft in 1594. The First Folio version was prepared from a copy of the quarto, with additions from a manuscript that had been used as a promptbook. The play's crude, melodramatic style and its numerous savage incidents led many critics to believe it was not written by Shakespeare. Modern criticism, however, tends to regard the play as authentic. Although not ranked with Shakespeare's other great Roman plays, *Titus Andronicus* relates its story of revenge and political strife with a uniformity of tone and consistency of dramatic structure. Sources for the story include Euripides' *Hecuba*, Seneca's *Thyestes* and *Troades*, and parts of Ovid and Plutarch. More important, an 18th-century chapbook titled *The History of Titus Andronicus*, though clearly too late to have served as Shakespeare's source, may well have been derived from a very similar prose version that Shakespeare could have known.

Titus Andronicus returns to Rome after having defeated the Goths, bringing with him Queen Tamora, whose eldest son he sacrifices to the gods. The late emperor's son Saturninus is supposed to marry Titus's daughter, Lavinia; however, when his brother, Bassianus, runs away with her instead, Saturninus marries Tamora. Saturninus and Tamora then plot revenge against Titus. Lavinia is raped and mutilated by Tamora's sadistic sons, Demetrius and Chiron, who cut off her hands and cut out her tongue so that she will be unable to testify against them. She nonetheless manages, by holding a stick in her mouth and guiding it with the stumps of her hands, to reveal the names of her ravishers. Titus now emerges as the revenger who must bring Tamora's brutal family to account. Tamora takes as her lover a black man named Aaron the Moor; between them they produce a mulatto child of whom Aaron is intensely proud. Titus's garish revenge begins as he puts on the guise of madness. He pretends to accept Demetrius and Chiron as the personifications of Rape and Murder, invites them into his house, and murders them, with Lavinia holding a basin to catch their blood. Titus then prepares a feast in which, acting as cook, he serves up to Tamora her own sons baked in a dish. Titus kills Lavinia to end her shame, stabs Tamora, and is cut down by Saturninus, at which Titus's son Lucius responds by delivering Saturninus a fatal blow. Aaron the Moor is to be executed as well for his villainies. The blood-filled stage is presided over finally by Lucius and Titus's brother, Marcus, as the sole survivors of Titus's much-wronged family.

Troilus and Cressida

This drama in five acts was written about 1601–1602 and printed in a quarto edition in two different "states" in 1609, probably from the author's working draft. The editors of the First Folio of 1623 may have had copyright difficulties in obtaining permission to include this play in their collection; it is anomalously placed between the histories and the tragedies, almost entirely without pagination. Its genre is indeed anomalous; many scholars prefer to classify it with the "problem plays" or the "dark" comedies. Based on George Chapman's translation of the *Iliad* and on 15th-century accounts of the Trojan War by John Lydgate and William Caxton, *Troilus and Cressida* is an often cynical exploration of the causes of strife between and within the Greek and Trojan armies—the betrayal of love, the absence of heroism, and the emptiness of honor. The play was also influenced by Geoffrey Chaucer's love poem *Troilus and Criseyde*, although Shakespeare's treatment of the lovers and his attitude toward their dilemma is in sharp contrast to Chaucer's.

Cressida, a Trojan woman whose father has defected to the Greeks, pledges her love to Troilus, one of King Priam's sons. However, when her father demands her presence in the Greek camp, she reluctantly accepts the attentions of Diomedes, the Greek officer who has been sent to escort her to the Greek side. Given her situation in an enemy camp and being an attractive woman among sex-starved warriors, she has few choices. The love between Troilus and Cressida, begun on such a hopeful note, is at last overwhelmed by the circumstances of war that they cannot control. Meanwhile, the war itself is presented in all its seamy aspects, since it is at bottom a senseless war fought over the possession of Helen, wife of Menelaus of Sparta but now the mistress of the Trojan prince Paris. Their one scene together presents Helen and Paris as vapid and self-centered. Other figures fare no less well. The legendary Greek hero Achilles is depicted as petulant and greedy for honor, so much so that he brutally massacres the great Hector when that warrior is unarmed. Hector, for his part, is at once the wisest of the Trojans and a captive of his own sense of honor, which obliges him to go into battle when his wife and family all warn him of ominous prognostications. The Greek general Agamemnon is given to long-winded speeches; so is old Nestor. Ulysses, the most astute of the Greek generals, is right-minded about many things but also cynical and calculating. Ajax, another Greek officer, is an oaf, easily put upon by his colleagues. Thersites, a deformed Greek, comments wryly on the actions of the other characters, while Pandarus, the bawdy go-between of the lovers, enjoys watching their degradation. The drama ends on a note of complete moral and political disintegration.

Twelfth Night

This comedy in five acts was written about 1600–1602 and published in the First Folio of 1623 from a transcript of an authorial draft or possibly a playbook. One of Shakespeare's finest comedies, *Twelfth Night* precedes the great tragedies and problem plays in order of composition. The original source appears to have been the story "Apollonius and Silla" in Barnabe Riche's

Riche His Farewell to Military Profession (1581), based in turn on a number of Continental versions that included an Italian comedy called *Gl'ingannati* (1531; "The Deceived"), published anonymously, and a story in Matteo Bandello's *Novelle* (1554–1573).

Twins Sebastian and Viola are separated during a shipwreck off the coast of Illyria; each believes the other dead. Viola disguises herself as a boy named Cesario and enters the service of Duke Orsino, who thinks he is in love with the lady Olivia. Orsino sends Viola/Cesario to plead his cause to Olivia, who promptly falls in love with the messenger. Viola, meanwhile, is in love with Orsino, and, when her twin, Sebastian, is rediscovered, many comic situations of mistaken identity ensue. There is a satiric subplot involving the members of Lady Olivia's household—Feste the jester, Maria, Olivia's uncle Sir Toby Belch, and Sir Toby's friend Sir Andrew Aguecheek—who scheme to undermine the high-minded, pompous Malvolio by planting a love letter purportedly written by Olivia to Malvolio urging him to show his affection for her by smiling constantly and dressing himself in cross-garters and yellow. Malvolio is thoroughly discomfited and even locked up for a time as a supposed madman—a fate ironically suited to one who has set himself up as the apostle of sobriety and decorum. Malvolio's animosity toward merriment is a challenge not only to the merrymakers but to the play's more serious characters as well; all must learn to embrace life's joys before those joys are overtaken by aging and death. At the play's end, Malvolio is the only solitary figure among the pairs of happy lovers.

The Two Gentlemen of Verona

This early play in five acts was written perhaps in 1590–1594 and was published in the First Folio of 1623 from an authorial manuscript. It is a pastoral story about two young friends who travel to Milan, where they are educated in courtly behavior.

The main source of the play's plot was a translation of a long Spanish prose romance titled *Los siete libros de la Diana* (1559?; "The Seven Books of the Diana") by Jorge de Montemayor. Shakespeare is thought to have adapted the relationship of the two gentlemen of the title and the ending of the play from various possible sources, including Richard Edwards's play *Damon and Pythias* (1565), Geoffrey Chaucer's *The Knight's Tale* in *The Canterbury Tales*, and especially the story of Titus and Gisippus in Sir Thomas Elyot's *The Boke Named the Governour* (1531).

Valentine (one of the two gentlemen of the title) opens the play by chiding his closest friend, Proteus (the other gentleman), for remaining idly at home with his beloved Julia rather than venturing to Milan with him. Shortly thereafter Proteus's plans change, because of his father's insistence, and he too heads for Milan after proclaiming his undying love and fidelity to Julia.

Mayhem erupts in the third act after the fickle Proteus arrives in Milan and abruptly becomes enamoured of Silvia, the Duke's fair daughter, with whom Valentine plans secretly to elope. Proteus treacherously betrays Valentine's plan to the Duke, who promptly banishes Valentine. The Duke is assisted in all this by Thurio, a wealthy and most unwelcome suitor to Silvia. Concurrently, Julia disguises herself as a boy and travels to Milan to be reunited with Proteus, only to discover him wooing Silvia for himself.

As the love entanglements ensue, the setting shifts from the civilized city to the forest. Silvia sets out to find Valentine, who has been captured by bandits and has agreed to become their leader. Silvia is accosted by the outlaws but is rescued by Proteus, who has been relentlessly following her with his page, the still-disguised Julia. Proteus then attempts to rape Silvia but is prevented by Valentine. The latter shames Proteus into penitence for his ruthless actions and inconstancy. In an extreme show of forgiveness, Valentine offers to give up Silvia for Proteus, causing Julia to faint and her identity to be revealed. In the end, the men resolve to marry their original loves and live in "mutual happiness."

▌ *The Two Noble Kinsmen*

This tragicomedy in five acts is the result of a collaboration by William Shakespeare and John Fletcher. The play was probably written and first performed about 1612–1614. It was published in quarto in 1634 with a title page identifying Fletcher and Shakespeare as joint authors. It was included in the second folio of works by Fletcher and Francis Beaumont in 1679, and schol ars have long debated the extent of Shakespeare's contribution. One commonly held theory is that he wrote all or most of Act I and Act V, with Fletcher responsible for most of the three intervening acts. The primary source for the story was *The Knight's Tale* from Geoffrey Chaucer's *Canterbury Tales*, but earlier plays concerning the friendship of Palamon and Arcite are known to have been performed. The playwrights may also have been familiar with Chaucer's source, Giovanni Boccaccio's *Tescida delle nozze di Emilia*.

Theseus, duke of Athens, is preparing to marry Hippolyta, queen of the Amazons, accompanied by her sister, Emilia, and his friend, Pirithous, when he is called upon to wage war on the corrupt Theban king, Creon. Palamon and Arcite, two noble nephews of Creon, are captured. As they languish in prison, their protestations of eternal friendship stop the instant they glimpse Emilia through a window, and they quarrel over her. Arcite is unexpectedly released and banished, but he returns in disguise; Palamon escapes with the help of the lovelorn Jailer's Daughter. The youths continue quarreling over Emilia, and when Emilia is unable to choose between them, Theseus announces a tournament for her hand—the loser to be executed. Arcite wins but is killed in a fall from his horse. Before he dies, the two young noblemen are reconciled, and Arcite bequeaths his bride to his friend. Meanwhile, the abandoned Jailer's Daughter, distraught from love for Palamon and fear for her father's safety, goes mad. She is saved by a devoted but unnamed Wooer, who courts her disguised as Palamon.

The theme of love versus friendship is evident throughout

the play, as is the recurring chivalric ideal, demonstrated by the cousins' generosity of spirit even as they prepare to fight to the death.

University Wits

This notable group of pioneer English dramatists wrote during the last 15 years of the 16th century and transformed the native interlude and chronicle play with their plays of quality and diversity.

The university wits included Christopher Marlowe, Robert Greene, Thomas Nashe (all graduates of Cambridge), and Thomas Lodge and George Peele (both of Oxford). Another of the wits, though not university-trained, was Thomas Kyd. Preceded by John Lyly (an Oxford man), they prepared the way for William Shakespeare. The greatest poetic dramatist among them was Marlowe, whose handling of blank verse gave the theater its characteristic voice for the next 50 years.

Wars of the Roses

This series of dynastic civil wars from English history served as the basis for a number of Shakespeare's history plays.

Fought between the Houses of Lancaster and York for the English throne, the wars were named many years afterward for the supposed badges of the contending parties: the white rose of York and the red of Lancaster.

Both houses claimed the throne through descent from the sons of Edward III. Since the Lancastrians had occupied the throne from 1399, the Yorkists might never have pressed a claim but for the near anarchy prevailing in the mid-15th century. After the death of Henry V in 1422 the country was subject to the long and factious minority of Henry VI. Great magnates with private armies dominated the countryside. Lawlessness was rife and taxation burdensome. Henry later proved to be feckless and simpleminded, subject to spells of madness, and dominated by his ambitious queen, Margaret of Anjou, whose party had allowed the English position in France to deteriorate.

Henry lapsed into insanity in 1453, causing a powerful baronial clique, backed by Richard Neville, the earl of Warwick (the "kingmaker"), to install Richard, duke of York, as protector of the realm. When Henry recovered in 1455, he reestablished the authority of Margaret's party, forcing York to take up arms for self-protection. The first battle of the wars, at St. Albans (May 22, 1455), resulted in a Yorkist victory and four years of uneasy truce. Civil war was resumed in 1459. The Yorkists were successful at Blore Heath (September 23) but were scattered after a skirmish at Ludford Bridge (October 12). In France Warwick regrouped the Yorkist forces and returned to England in June 1460, decisively defeating the Lancastrian forces at Northampton (July 10). York tried to claim the throne but settled for the right to succeed upon the death of Henry. This effectively disinherited Henry's son, Prince Edward, and caused Queen Margaret to continue her opposition.

Gathering forces in northern England, the Lancastrians surprised and killed York at Wakefield in December and then marched south toward London, defeating Warwick on the way at the Second Battle of St. Albans (February 17, 1461). Meanwhile, York's eldest son and heir, Edward, had defeated a Lancastrian force at Mortimer's Cross (February 2) and marched to relieve London, arriving before Margaret on February 26. The young duke of York was proclaimed King Edward IV at Westminster on March 4. Then Edward, with the remainder of Warwick's forces, pursued Margaret north to Towton. There, in the bloodiest battle of the war, the Yorkists won a complete victory. Henry, Margaret, and their son fled to Scotland. The first phase of the fighting was over, except for the reduction of a few pockets of Lancastrian resistance.

The next round of the wars arose out of disputes within the
Yorkist ranks. Warwick and his circle were increasingly passed
over at Edward's court; more seriously, Warwick differed with
the king on foreign policy. In 1469 civil war was renewed.
Warwick and Edward's rebellious brother George, duke of
Clarence, fomented risings in the north; and in July, at Edgecote
(near Banbury), defeated Edward's supporters, afterward holding the king prisoner. By March 1470, however, Edward
regained his control, forcing Warwick and Clarence to flee to
France, where they allied themselves with the French king Louis
XI and their former enemy, Margaret of Anjou. Returning to
England (September 1470), they deposed Edward and restored
the crown to Henry VI. Edward fled to the Netherlands with his
followers and, securing Burgundian aid, returned to England in
March 1471. Edward outmaneuvered Warwick, regained the
loyalty of Clarence, and decisively defeated Warwick at Barnet
on April 14. That very day, Margaret had landed at Weymouth.
Hearing the news of Barnet, she marched west, trying to reach
the safety of Wales; but Edward won the race to the Severn.
At Tewkesbury (May 4) Margaret was captured, her forces
destroyed, and her son killed. Shortly afterward, Henry VI was
murdered in the Tower of London. Edward's throne was secure
for the rest of his life (he died in 1483).

In 1483 Edward's brother Richard III, overriding the
claims of his nephew, the young Edward V, alienated many
Yorkists, who then turned to the last hope of the Lancastrians,
Henry Tudor (later Henry VII). With the help of the French
and of Yorkist defectors, Henry defeated and killed Richard at
Bosworth Field on August 22, 1485, bringing the wars to a
close. By his marriage to Edward IV's daughter Elizabeth of
York in 1486, Henry united the Yorkist and Lancastrian
claims. Henry defeated a Yorkist uprising supporting the pretender Lambert Simnel on June 16, 1487, a date that some historians prefer over the traditional 1485 for the termination of
the wars.

Webster, John

The White Devil (c. 1609– c. 1612) and *The Duchess of Malfi* (c. 1613, published 1623) by John Webster (1580–1632) are generally regarded as the paramount 17th-century English tragedies apart from those of Shakespeare.

Little is known of Webster's life. His preface to *Monuments of Honor*, his Lord Mayor's Show for 1624, says he was born a freeman of the Merchant Taylors' Company. He was probably a coachmaker, and possibly he was an actor. Apart from his two major plays and *The Devils Law-Case* (c. 1620; published 1623), his dramatic work consists of collaborations (not all extant) with leading writers. With Thomas Dekker, his main collaborator, he wrote *Westward Ho* (1604) and *Northward Ho* (1605), both of which were published in 1607. He is also believed to have worked to varying degrees with William Rowley, Thomas Middleton, John Fletcher, John Ford, and perhaps Philip Massinger. Eight extant plays and some nondramatic verse and prose are wholly or partly his; the most standard edition is *The Complete Works of John Webster,* ed. by F. L. Lucas, 4 vols. (1927).

The White Devil, like *Macbeth*, is a tragedy of action; and *The Duchess of Malfi*, like *King Lear*, is a tragedy of suffering.

W. H., Mr.

Mr. W. H., known only by his initials, is the person to whom William Shakespeare dedicated the first edition of his sonnets (1609):

TO THE ONLIE BEGETTER OF

THESE INSUING SONNETS

Mr. W.H. ALL HAPPINESSE

AND THAT ETERNITIE

PROMISED

BY

OUR EVER-LIVING POET

WISHETH

THE WELL-WISHING

ADVENTURER IN

SETTING

FORTH

The mystery of his identity has tantalized generations of biographers and critics, who have generally argued either that W. H. was the "fair youth" to whom many of the sonnets are addressed or that he was a friend or patron who earned the gratitude of one or both parties by procuring Shakespeare's manuscript for the printer, Thomas Thorpe. Among the names offered for consideration are those of Henry Wriothesley, 3rd earl of Southampton, who was a noted patron of several writers, and William Herbert, 3rd earl of Pembroke, with whom Shakespeare is believed to have had some connection, albeit slight. Also suggested are William Hatcliffe, who was Lord of Misrule during the celebrations at Gray's Inn (1587–1588), and William Hall (a printer) and Sir William Harvey (Southampton's stepfather), both of whom could well have conveyed the manuscript to Thorpe. The ambiguity with which the dedication is expressed presents additional problems, for apparently the person in question was both "wished" eternity by Thorpe and "promised" it by Shakespeare.

The Winter's Tale

This play in five acts was written about 1609–1611 and produced at the Globe Theatre in London. It was published in the First Folio of 1623 from a transcript, by Ralph Crane (scrivener of the King's Men), of an authorial manuscript or possibly the playbook. One of Shakespeare's final plays, *The Winter's Tale* is a romantic comedy with elements of tragedy.

The plot was based on a work of prose fiction called *Pandosto* (1588) by Robert Greene. The play opens with Leontes, the king of Sicilia, entertaining his old friend Polixenes, the king of Bohemia. Leontes jealously mistakes the courtesy between his wife, Hermione, and Polixenes as a sign of Hermione's adultery with him. In a fit of jealousy, he attempts to have Polixenes killed, but Polixenes escapes with Camillo, Leontes' faithful counselor, whom Leontes has sent to kill him. The pregnant Hermione is then publicly humiliated and thrown in jail, despite her protests of innocence. When the child, a girl, is born, Leontes rejects the child out of hand and gives her over to Antigonus, the husband of Hermione's attendant Paulina. Antigonus is instructed to abandon the baby in some wild place. Having learned of his mother's mistreatment, Leontes' beloved son, Mamillius, dies, and Hermione too is carried out and reported dead. Having lost everyone important to him and having realized the error of his ways, Leontes is left to his solitary despair. Meanwhile, the baby girl, named Perdita, is brought up by a shepherd and his wife in Polixenes' kingdom of Bohemia. She appears in Act IV as a young and beautiful shepherdess who has been discovered by Polixenes' son, Florizel. Needless to say, her true status is eventually discovered once she and Florizel have arrived at Leontes' court in Sicilia. In a climactic ending, Hermione is discovered to be alive after all. She had been sequestered by Paulina for some 16 years until the time for reunion and reconciliation arrived. Leontes is shown a seeming statue of Hermione, so lifelike that one might imagine it breathes. The "statue" comes to life, and Hermione is seen to have aged during her years of separation and waiting. Leontes, to his intense joy, realizes that he loves his wife more than ever. The recovery of the daughter he attempted to kill is no less precious to him. All is forgiven.

Chronology of the Plays

Despite much scholarly argument, it is often impossible to date a given play precisely. But there is a general consensus, especially for plays written in 1588–1601, in 1605–1607, and from 1609 onward. The following list of dates of composition is based on external and internal evidence, on general stylistic and thematic considerations, and on the observation that an output of no more than two plays a year seems to have been established in those periods when dating is rather clearer than others.

1. 1588–1597 *Love's Labour's Lost*
2. 1589–1592 *1 Henry VI, Titus Andronicus*
3. 1589–1594 *The Comedy of Errors*
4. 1590–1592 *2 Henry VI*
5. 1590–1593 *3 Henry VI*
6. 1590–1594 *The Taming of the Shrew, The Two Gentlemen of Verona*
7. 1590–1595 *Edward III*
8. 1592–1594 *Richard III*
9. 1594–1596 *King John, Romeo and Juliet*
10. 1595–1596 *A Midsummer Night's Dream, Richard II*
11. 1596–1597 *The Merchant of Venice, 1 Henry IV*
12. 1597–1598 *2 Henry IV*
13. 1597–1601 *The Merry Wives of Windsor*
14. 1598–1599 *Much Ado about Nothing*
15. 1598–1600 *As You Like It*
16. 1599 *Henry V*
17. 1599–1600 *Julius Caesar*
18. 1599–1601 *Hamlet*
19. 1600–1602 *Twelfth Night*
20. 1601–1602 *Troilus and Cressida*

21.   1601–1605 *All's Well That Ends Well*
22.   1603–1604 *Measure for Measure, Othello*
23.   1605–1606 *King Lear*
24.   1605–1608 *Timon of Athens*
25.   1606–1607 *Macbeth, Antony and Cleopatra*
26.   1606–1608 *Pericles*
27.   1608 *Coriolanus*
28.   1608–1610 *Cymbeline*
29.   1609–1611 *The Winter's Tale*
30.   1611 *The Tempest*
31.   1612–1614 *The Two Noble Kinsmen*
32.   1613 *Henry VIII*

Shakespeare's two narrative poems, *Venus and Adonis* and *The Rape of Lucrece*, can be dated with certainty to the years when the plague stopped dramatic performances in London, in 1592–1593 and 1593–1594, respectively, just before their publication. But the sonnets offer many and various problems; they cannot have been written all at one time, and most scholars set them within the period 1593–1600. *The Phoenix and the Turtle* can be dated 1600–1601.

Selected Filmography

Antony and Cleopatra

Antony and Cleopatra Spain, Switzerland, U.K.; 1972; 160 min. Director: Charlton Heston. Selected notable actors: Charlton Heston (Antony), Hildegard Neil (Cleopatra), Fernando Rey (Lepidus).

As You Like It

As You Like It U.K.; 1936; 97 min. Director: Paul Czinner. Selected notable actors: Henry Ainley (Duke Senior), Felix Aylmer (Duke Frederick), Laurence Olivier (Orlando), Elisabeth Bergner (Rosalind).

As You Like It U.K.; 1992; 117 min. Director: Christine Edzard. Selected notable actors: Andrew Tiernan (Orlando/Oliver), Emma Croft (Rosalind), Cyril Cusack (Adam), James Fox (Jaques).

Hamlet

Hamlet France; 1900; 3 min. Director: Clément Maurice. Selected notable actors: Sarah Bernhardt (Hamlet), Pierre Magnier (Laertes).

Hamlet France; 1907; 10 min. Director: Georges Méliès. Selected notable actor: Georges Méliès (Hamlet).

Hamlet U.K.; 1913, 54 min. Director: E. Hay Plumb. Selected notable actor: Johnston Forbes-Robertson (Hamlet).

Hamlet Germany; 1920; 117 min. Directors: Svend Gade, Heinz Schall. Selected notable actor: Asta Nielsen (Hamlet).

Hamlet U.K.; 1948; 152 min. Director: Laurence Olivier. Selected notable actors: Laurence Olivier (Hamlet), Jean Simmons (Ophelia), Eileen Herlie (Gertrude).

Ophélia France; 1962; 105 min. Director: Claude Chabrol. Selected notable actors: André Jocelyn (Yvan/Hamlet), Juliette Mayniel (Lucie/Ophelia), Alida Valli (Claudia Lesurf/Gertrude), Claude Cerval (Adrien Lesurf/Claudius).

Gamlet U.S.S.R.; 1964; 148 min. Director: Grigory Kozintsev. Selected notable actor: Innokenti Smoktunovsky (Hamlet).

Hamlet U.K.; 1969; 117 min. Director: Tony Richardson. Selected

notable actors: Nicol Williamson (Hamlet), Marianne Faithfull
(Ophelia), Judy Parfitt (Gertrude), Anthony Hopkins (Claudius).

Hamlet U.S.; 1990; 135 min. Director: Franco Zeffirelli. Selected
notable actors: Mel Gibson (Hamlet), Helena Bonham Carter
(Ophelia), Glenn Close (Gertrude), Alan Bates (Claudius).

Rosencrantz and Guildenstern Are Dead U.S., U.K.; 1990; 117 min.
Director: Tom Stoppard. Selected notable actors: Richard Dreyfuss
(Player), Gary Oldman (Rosencrantz), Tim Roth (Guildenstern).

Last Action Hero U.S.; 1993; 130 min. Director: John McTiernan.
Selected notable actors: Arnold Schwarzenegger (Jack Slater/
Himself), Ian McKellen (Death), Joan Plowright (Teacher).

In the Bleak Midwinter (*A Midwinter's Tale*) U.K.; 1995; 98 min.
Director: Kenneth Branagh. Selected notable actors: Richard Briers
(Henry Wakefield), Joan Collins (Margaretta D'Arcy).

Hamlet U.K., U.S.; 1996; 242 min. Director: Kenneth Branagh.
Selected notable actors: Kenneth Branagh (Hamlet), Kate Winslet
(Ophelia), Julie Christie (Gertrude), Charlton Heston (Player King),
Richard Briers (Polonius), Derek Jacobi (Claudius).

Hamlet U.S.; 2000; 123 min. Director: Michael Almereyda. Selected
notable actors: Ethan Hawke (Hamlet), Diane Venora (Gertrude),
Julia Stiles (Ophelia), Sam Shepard (Ghost), Bill Murray (Polonius).

Henry IV, Parts 1 and 2, and Henry V

Henry V U.K.; 1944; 137 min. Director: Laurence Olivier. Selected
notable actors: Laurence Olivier (Henry V), Robert Newton
(Pistol), Leslie Banks (Chorus), Renée Asherson (Katherine).

Chimes at Midnight Spain, Switzerland; 1966; 119 min. Director:
Orson Welles. Selected notable actors: Orson Welles (Falstaff),
Keith Baxter (Prince Hal), John Gielgud (Henry IV), Margaret
Rutherford (Mistress Quickly).

Henry V U.K.; 1989; 138 min. Director: Kenneth Branagh. Selected
notable actors: Kenneth Branagh (Henry V), Derek Jacobi (Chorus),
Ian Holm (Fluellen), Judi Dench (Mistress Quickly).

My Own Private Idaho U.S.; 1991; 102 min. Director: Gus Van Sant.
Selected notable actors: River Phoenix (Mike Waters), Keanu
Reeves (Scott Favor), William Richert (Bob Pigeon).

Julius Caesar

Julius Caesar U.S.; 1950; 90 min. Director: David Bradley. Selected
notable actor: Charlton Heston (Mark Antony).

Julius Caesar U.S.; 1953; 121 min. Director: Joseph L. Mankiewicz.

Selected notable actors: Marlon Brando (Mark Antony), James Mason (Brutus), John Gielgud (Cassius), Louis Calhern (Julius Caesar).

Julius Caesar U.K.; 1970; 117 min. Director: Stuart Burge. Selected notable actors: Charlton Heston (Mark Antony), Jason Robards (Brutus), John Gielgud (Julius Caesar), Diana Rigg (Portia).

King John

King John U.K.; 1899; 2 min. Director: W. K. Laurie Dickson. Selected notable actor: Sir Herbert Beerbohm Tree (King John).

King Lear

Karol Lear U.S.S.R.; 1970; 140 min. Director: Grigory Kozintsev. Selected notable actor: Yuri Yarvet (King Lear).

King Lear U.K., Denmark; 1971; 137 min. Director: Peter Brook. Selected notable actors: Paul Scofield (King Lear), Irene Worth (Goneril), Jack MacGowran (Fool), Anne-Lise Gabold (Cordelia).

Ran, or *Chaos* Japan, France; 1985; 160 min. Director: Akira Kurosawa. Selected notable actors: Tatsuya Nakadai (Lord Hidetora Ichimonji), Jinpachi Nezu (Jiro), Jun Tazaki (Suiji Ayabe), Hisashi Igawa (Shuri Kurogane).

The King Is Alive Denmark, Sweden, U.S.; 2000; 110 min. Director: Kristian Levring. Selected notable actors: Miles Anderson (Jack), David Bradley (Henry).

Love's Labour's Lost

Love's Labour's Lost U.K., France, U.S.; 2000; 93 min. Director: Kenneth Branagh. Selected notable actors: Kenneth Branagh (Berowne), Nathan Lane (Costard), Richard Briers (Nathaniel), Alicia Silverstone (The Princess).

Macbeth

Macbeth U.S.; 1948; 89 min. Director: Orson Welles. Selected notable actors: Orson Welles (Macbeth), Jeanette Nolan (Lady Macbeth), Dan O'Herlihy (Macduff).

Throne of Blood Japan; 1957; 105 min. Director: Akira Kurosawa. Selected notable actors: Toshiro Mifune (Taketori Washizu/Macbeth), Isuzu Yamada (Asaji Washizu/Lady Macbeth).

Macbeth U.K.; 1971; 140 min. Director: Roman Polanski. Selected notable actors: Jon Finch (Macbeth), Francesca Annis (Lady Macbeth).

Scotland, PA U.S.; 2001; 104 min. Director: Billy Morrissette. Selected notable actors: James LeGros (Joe "Mac" McBeth), Maura Tierney (Pat McBeth), Christopher Walken (Lt. Ernie McDuff).

Maqbool India; 2003; 132 min. Director: Vishal Bharadwaj. Selected notable actors: Irfan Khan (Maqbool/Macbeth), Tabu (Nimmi/Lady Macbeth), Pankaj Kapoor (Abbaji/Duncan).

The Merchant of Venice

Il mercante di Venezia Italy; 1910; 8 min. Director: Gerolamo Lo Savio. Selected notable actors: Ermete Novelli (Shylock), Francesca Bertini (Portia).

Shylock France; 1913; 22 min. Director: Henri Desfontaines. Selected notable actors: Harry Baur (Shylock), Pépa Bonafé (Portia).

Der Kaufmann von Venedig Germany; 1923; 64 min. Director: Peter Paul Felner. Selected notable actors: Werner Krauss (Shylock), Henny Porten (Portia), Max Schreck (Doge of Venice), Carl Ebert (Antonio).

The Maori Merchant of Venice New Zealand; 2002; 158 min. Director: Don Selwyn. Selected notable actors: Waihoroi Shortland (Shylock), Ngarimu Daniels (Portia).

The Merchant of Venice U.S., Italy, Luxembourg, U.K.; 2004; 138 min. Director: Michael Radford. Selected notable actors: Al Pacino (Shylock), Jeremy Irons (Antonio), Joseph Fiennes (Bassanio).

A Midsummer Night's Dream

A Midsummer Night's Dream U.S.; 1909; 8 min. Directors: Charles Kent, J. Stuart Blackton. Selected notable actors: Maurice Costello (Lysander), Dolores Costello (Fairy), William Ranous (Nick Bottom).

A Midsummer Night's Dream U.S.; 1935; 132 min. Directors: Max Reinhardt, William Dieterle. Selected notable actors: Dick Powell (Lysander), Olivia de Havilland (Hermia), Mickey Rooney (Puck), James Cagney (Nick Bottom).

A Midsummer Night's Dream Spain, U.K.; 1984; 80 min. Director: Celestino Coronado. Selected notable actors: Lindsay Kemp (Puck), Francois Testory (Changeling).

A Midsummer Night's Dream U.K.; 1996; 105 min. Director: Adrian Noble. Selected notable actors: Lindsay Duncan (Hippolyta/Titania), Alex Jennings (Theseus/Oberon), Desmond Barrit (Nick Bottom), Osheen Jones (The Boy).

A Midsummer Night's Dream Italy, U.K.; 1999; 115 min. Director:

Michael Hoffman. Selected notable actors: Kevin Kline (Nick Bottom), Michelle Pfeiffer (Titania), Rupert Everett (Oberon).

Much Ado about Nothing

Much Ado about Nothing U.K., U.S.; 1993; 110 min. Director: Kenneth Branagh. Selected notable actors: Kenneth Branagh (Benedick), Emma Thompson (Beatrice), Michael Keaton (Dogberry), Denzel Washington (Don Pedro).

Othello

Othello Germany; 1922; 80 min. Director: Dimitri Buchowetzki. Selected notable actors: Emil Jannings (Othello), Werner Krauss (Iago), Ica von Lenkeffy (Desdemona).

Othello Morocco; 1952; 91 min. Director: Orson Welles. Selected notable actors: Orson Welles (Othello), Micheál MacLiammóir (Iago), Suzanne Cloutier (Desdemona), Robert Coote (Roderigo).

Othello U.S.S.R.; 1955; 108 min. Director: Sergey Yutkevich. Selected notable actors: Sergey Bondarchuk (Othello), Andrey Popov (Iago), Irina Skobtseva (Desdemona).

Othello U.K.; 1965; 165 min. Directors: John Dexter, Stuart Burge. Selected notable actors: Laurence Olivier (Othello), Frank Finlay (Iago), Maggie Smith (Desdemona).

Othello U.K.; 1995; 124 min. Director: Oliver Parker. Selected notable actors: Laurence Fishburne (Othello), Kenneth Branagh (Iago), Irène Jacob (Desdemona).

O U.S.; 2001; 91 min. Director: Tim Blake Nelson. Selected notable actors: Mekhi Phifer (Odin James), Josh Hartnett (Hugo Goulding), Julia Stiles (Desi Brable).

Richard III

Richard III U.K.; 1911; 16 min. Director: Frank R. Benson. Selected notable actor: Frank R. Benson (Richard III).

Richard III U.S.; 1912; 55 min. Directors: M. B. Dudley, James Keane [Keene]. Selected notable actors: Frederick Warde (Richard III), James Keane [Keene] (Richmond).

Richard III U.K.; 1955; 157 min. Director: Laurence Olivier. Selected notable actors: Laurence Olivier (Richard III), John Gielgud (Clarence), Ralph Richardson (Buckingham), Claire Bloom (Lady Anne).

Richard III U.S.; 1995; 105 min. Director: Richard Loncraine. Selected notable actors: Ian McKellen (Richard III), Jim Broadbent

(Buckingham), Kristin Scott Thomas (Lady Anne), Annette Bening
(Queen Elizabeth).

Looking for Richard U.S.; 1996; 109 min. Director: Al Pacino. Selected
notable actors: Al Pacino (Richard III), Aidan Quinn (Richmond),
Alec Baldwin (Clarence), Winona Ryder (Lady Anne).

Romeo and Juliet

Romeo and Juliet U.S.; 1936; 126 min. Director: George Cukor.
Selected notable actors: Leslie Howard (Romeo), Norma Shearer
(Juliet), John Barrymore (Mercutio), Basil Rathbone (Tybalt).

Les Amants de Vérone France; 1949; 110 min. Director: André Cayatte. Selected notable actors: Serge Reggiani (Romeo), Anouk Aimée
(Juliet).

Giulietta e Romeo U.K., Italy; 1954; 138 min. Director: Renato Castel-
lani. Selected notable actors: Laurence Harvey (Romeo), Susan
Shentall (Juliet), Flora Robson (Nurse).

West Side Story U.S.; 1961; 151 min. Directors: Robert Wise, Jerome
Robbins. Selected notable actors: Natalie Wood (Maria), Richard
Beymer (Tony).

Giulietta e Romeo Italy, Spain; 1964; 90 min. Director: Riccardo
Freda. Selected notable actors: Gerald Meynier (Romeo), Rosemarie
Dexter (Juliet).

Romeo and Juliet Italy, U.K.; 1968; 152 min. Director: Franco Zeffirelli. Selected notable actors: Leonard Whiting (Romeo), Olivia
Hussey (Juliet), Michael York (Tybalt).

William Shakespeare's Romeo + Juliet U.S.; 1996; 120 min. Director:
Baz Luhrmann. Selected notable actors: Leonardo DiCaprio
(Romeo), Claire Danes (Juliet), Brian Dennehy (Montague), Paul
Sorvino (Capulet).

Tromeo and Juliet U.S.; 1996; 107 min. Director: Lloyd Kaufman.
Selected notable actors: Jane Jensen (Juliet), Will Keenan (Tromeo
Que).

The Taming of the Shrew

The Taming of the Shrew U.S.; 1929; 68 min. Director: Sam Taylor.
Selected notable actors: Mary Pickford (Katharina), Douglas Fair-
banks (Petruchio).

The Taming of the Shrew U.S., Italy; 1966; 122 min. Director: Franco
Zeffirelli. Selected notable actors: Elizabeth Taylor (Katharina),
Richard Burton (Petruchio).

10 Things I Hate About You U.S.; 1999; 97 min. Director: Gil Junger. Selected notable actors: Heath Ledger (Patrick Verona), Julia Stiles (Katarina Stratford), Larisa Oleynik (Bianca Stratford).

The Tempest

The Tempest U.K.; 1979; 96 min. Director: Derek Jarman. Selected notable actors: Heathcote Williams (Prospero), Karl Johnson (Ariel), Toyah Willcox (Miranda).

Prospero's Books U.K., Netherlands, France, Italy; 1991; 124 min. Director: Peter Greenaway. Selected notable actors: John Gielgud (Prospero), Isabelle Pasco (Miranda), Michael Clark (Caliban).

Titus Andronicus

William Shakespeare's Titus Andronicus U.S.; 1999; 147 min. Director: Christopher Dunne. Selected notable actors: Candy K. Sweet (Tamora), Lexton Raleigh (Aaron), Robert Reese (Titus Andronicus).

Titus U.S.; 1999; 162 min. Director: Julie Taymor. Selected notable actors: Jessica Lange (Tamora), Anthony Hopkins (Titus Andronicus).

Twelfth Night

Dvenadtsataya noch U.S.S.R.; 1955; 90 min. Director: Yakow Fried. Selected notable actors: Katya Luchko (Sebastian/Viola), Anna Larionova (Olivia).

Twelfth Night U.K., U.S.; 1996; 134 min. Director: Trevor Nunn. Selected notable actors: Imogen Stubbs (Viola), Helena Bonham Carter (Olivia), Richard E. Grant (Sir Andrew Aguecheek), Steven Mackintosh (Sebastian).

The Winter's Tale

Una tragedia alla corte di Sicilia Italy; 1913; 32 min. Director: Baldassare Negroni. Selected notable actors: Pina Fabbri (Paulina), V. Cocchi (Leontes).

The Winter's Tale U.K.; 1966; 151 min. Director: Frank Dunlop. Selected notable actors: Laurence Harvey (Leontes), Jane Asher (Perdita).

Bibliography

Bibliography

Many authors contributed to the material compiled in this book. They include especially David Bevington (University of Chicago), editor of *The Complete Works of Shakespeare* and other Shakespeare titles and author of *Action Is Eloquence: Shakespeare's Language of Gesture*; Anthony M. Quinton, Baron Quinton (Chairman, British Library Board), author of *The Nature of Things*; Stephen Greenblatt, author of *Renaissance Self-Fashioning: From More to Shakespeare* and *Will in the World: How Shakespeare Became Shakespeare*; Patricia Garland Pinka (Agnes Scott College), author of *This Dialogue of One: The Songs and Sonnets of John Donne*; M. H. Butler (University of Leeds), author of *Theatre and Crisis, 1632–1642*; Andrew J. Gurr (University of Reading), author of *Playgoing in Shakespeare's London*; A. Kent Hieatt (University of Western Ontario), author of *Short Time's Endless Monument: The Symbolism of the Numbers in Spenser's Epithalamion*; and Kenneth Rothwell (University of Vermont), author of *A History of Shakespeare on Screen*.

Modern Editions of Shakespeare

Late-20th-century collections of Shakespeare's works include Irving Ribner and George Lyman Kittredge, eds., *The Complete Works of Shakespeare* (1971); Sylvan Barnet, ed., *The Complete Signet Classic Shakespeare* (1972); Stanley Wells and Gary Taylor, eds., *William Shakespeare, The Complete Works* (1986, reissued as *The Complete Works*, 1998); G. Blakemore Evans and J. J. Tobin, eds., *The Riverside Shakespeare*, 2nd ed. (1997); David Bevington, ed., *The Complete Works of Shakespeare*, 4th ed., updated (1997); and Stephen Greenblatt, ed., *The Norton Shakespeare* (1997). Three series were in progress at the turn of the 21st century, with plays and poems in individual volumes: Stanley Wells, ed., *The Oxford Shakespeare* (1982–); Philip Brockbank, ed., *The New Cambridge Shakespeare* (1984–); and Richard Proudfoot, Ann Thompson, and David Scott Kastan, eds., *The Arden Shakespeare*, 3rd series (1995–).

288

Shakespeare Biography

The following are especially informative and up-to-date: S. Schoenbaum, William *Shakespeare. A Documentary Life* (1975) and *William Shakespeare: Records and Images* (1981); Richard Dutton, *William Shakespeare: A Literary Life* (1989); Dennis Kay, *Shakespeare: His Life, Work, and Era* (1992); Stanley Wells, *Shakespeare: A Life in Drama* (1995, reissued 1997); and Park Honan, *Shakespeare: A Life* (1998).

Shakespearean Staging and Acting Companies

W. W. Greg, ed., *Dramatic Documents from the Elizabethan Playhouses: Stage Plots, Actors' Parts, Prompt Books*, 2 vols. (1931, reissued 1969); M. Channing Linthicum, *Costume in the Drama of Shakespeare and His Contemporaries* (1936, reprinted 1972); Alfred Harbage, *Shakespeare's Audience* (1941, reissued 1969) and *As They Liked It* (1947, reissued 1972); G. E. Bentley, *The Jacobean and Caroline Stage*, 7 vols. (1941–1968) and *The Professions of Dramatist and Player in Shakespeare's Time, 1590–1642* (1986); Philip Henslowe, *Henslowe's Diary*, ed. by R. A. Foakes and R. T. Rickert (1961, reprinted 1968); M. C. Bradbrook, *The Rise of the Common Player: A Study of Actor and Society in Shakespeare's England* (1962, reissued 1979); Alan C. Dessen, *Elizabethan Drama and the Viewer's Eye* (1977) and *Recovering Shakespeare's Theatrical Vocabulary* (1995); Ann Jennalie Cook, *The Privileged Playgoers of Shakespeare's London, 1576–1642* (1981); R. A. Foakes, *Illustrations of the English Stage, 1580–1642* (1985); Richard Dutton, *Mastering the Revels: The Regulation and Censorship of English Renaissance Drama* (1991); David Mann, *The Elizabethan Player: Contemporary Stage Representation* (1991); David Bradley, *From Text to Performance in the Elizabethan Theatre: Preparing the Play for the Stage* (1992); William Ingram, *The Business of Playing: The Beginnings of the Adult Professional Theater in Elizabethan London* (1992); and Andrew Gurr, *The Shakespearean Stage, 1576–1642*, 3rd ed. (1992) and *Playgoing in Shakespeare's London*, 2nd ed. (1996).

The Globe Theatre

Studies of the Globe include C. Walter Hodges, *The Globe Restored* (1953, reissued 1989); John Orrell, *The Quest for Shakespeare's Globe* (1983) and *The Human Stage: English Theatre Design, 1567–1640* (1988). Herbert Berry, *Shakespeare's Playhouses* (1987), examines the major documents relating to the Globe. Franklin J. Hildy, ed.,

New Issues in the Reconstruction of Shakespeare's Theater (1990), a collection of essays, examines specific questions about the early buildings. The best studies of how the plays were staged at the Globe are Bernard Beckerman, *Shakespeare at the Globe, 1599–1609* (1962); Peter Thomson, *Shakespeare's Theatre* (1983); and Alan C. Dessen, *Recovering Shakespeare's Theatrical Vocabulary* (1995). Two books about the new Globe are Andrew Gurr and John Orrell, *Rebuilding Shakespeare's Globe* (1989); and J. R. Mulryne and Margaret Shewring, eds., *Shakespeare's Globe Rebuilt* (1997).

Censorship and Governmental Regulation

Janet Clare, *Art Made Tongue-Tied by Authority: Elizabethan and Jacobean Dramatic Censorship*, 2nd ed. (1999); and Richard Dutton, *Mastering the Revels: The Regulation and Censorship of English Renaissance Drama* (1991).

Critical Studies

These categories are often overlapping. Many studies could also be listed in other categories.

HISTORY OF SHAKESPEARE CRITICISM

John Dryden, *Of Dramatick Poesie* (1668); Samuel Taylor Coleridge, *Coleridge on Shakespeare*, ed. by R. A. Foakes (1971); Samuel Johnson, *Johnson on Shakespeare*, ed. by Arthur Sherbo (1968); J. Frank Kermode, *Four Centuries of Shakespearian Criticism* (1965); and Brian Vickers, *Appropriating Shakespeare: Contemporary Critical Quarrels* (1993).

CRITICISM OF SHAKESPEAREAN CHARACTERS

Maurice Morgann, *An Essay on the Dramatic Character of Sir John Falstaff* (1777); and Edward Dowden, *Shakspere: A Critical Study of His Mind and Art* (1875).

HISTORICAL CRITICISM

Alfred Harbage, *Shakespeare and the Rival Traditions* (1952, reissued 1970); Henry Ansgar Kelly, *Divine Providence in the England of Shakespeare's Histories* (1970); Bernard Spivack, *Shakespeare and the Allegory of Evil* (1958); Elmer Edgard Stoll, *Art and Artifice in Shakespeare* (1933); and J. A. K. Thomson, *Shakespeare and the Classics* (1952, reissued 1978).

NEW CRITICISM

Robert B. Heilman, *This Great Stage: Image and Structure in King Lear* (1948, reissued 1976); G. Wilson Knight, *The Wheel of Fire: Interpretations of Shakespearian Tragedy*, 4th rev. and enlarged ed. (1949, reissued 2001), *The Imperial Theme: Further Interpretations of Shakespeare's Tragedies, Including the Roman Plays*, 3rd ed. (1951, reprinted with minor corrections 1989), and *The Shakespearian Tempest, with a Chart of Shakespeare's Dramatic Universe*, 3rd ed. (1953, reissued 1971); L. C. Knights, *Some Shakespearean Themes* (1959); F. R. Leavis, *The Common Pursuit* (1952, reissued 1984); and Derek Traversi, *An Approach to Shakespeare*, 3rd ed., rev. and expanded, 2 vols. (1968–1969).

SHAKESPEARE'S LANGUAGE AND IMAGERY

Miriam Joseph, *Shakespeare's Use of the Arts of Language* (1947, reissued 1966); M. M. Mahood, *Shakespeare's Wordplay* (1957); and Caroline Spurgeon, *Shakespeare's Imagery and What It Tells Us* (1935).

PSYCHOLOGICAL, ARCHETYPAL, AND MYTHOLOGICAL CRITICISM

Janet Adelman, *The Common Liar: An Essay on Antony and Cleopatra* (1973); C. L. Barber, *Shakespeare's Festive Comedy* (1959, reissued 1990); Northrop Frye, *A Natural Perspective: The Development of Shakespearean Comedy and Romance* (1965, reissued 1991), *The Myth of Deliverance: Reflections on Shakespeare's Problem Comedies* (1983, reissued 1993), and *Fools of Time: Studies in Shakespearean Tragedy* (1967, reissued 1991); Norman Holland, *Psychoanalysis and Shakespeare* (1966); and Ernest Jones, *Hamlet and Oedipus* (1949, reissued 1976).

NEW HISTORICISM, CULTURAL MATERIALISM, MARXIST CRITICISM, AND POLITICAL THEATER

Jonathan Dollimore, *Radical Tragedy: Religion, Ideology, and Power in the Drama of Shakespeare and His Contemporaries*, 2nd ed. (1989); Terence Eagleton, *Shakespeare and Society* (1967) and *William Shakespeare* (1986); Stephen Greenblatt, *Renaissance Self-Fashioning* (1980) and *Hamlet in Purgatory* (2001); Jean E. Howard, *The Stage and Social Struggle in Early Modern England* (1994); Jan Kott, *Shakespeare, Our Contemporary*, 2nd ed. (1967, reprinted 1988; originally published in Polish, 1961); Leah Marcus, *Puzzling Shakespeare: Local Reading and Its Discontents* (1988); Steven Mullaney, *The Place of the Stage: License, Play, and Power in Renaissance England* (1988); Stephen

Orgel, *The Illusion of Power: Political Theater in the English Renaissance* (1975, reissued 1991); Annabel Patterson, *Shakespeare and the Popular Voice* (1989); Alan Sinfield, *Faultlines: Cultural Materialism and the Politics of Dissident Reading* (1992); and Robert Weimann, *Shakespeare and the Popular Tradition in the Theater* (1978, reissued 1987; originally published in German, 1967).

FEMINIST CRITICISM AND GENDER STUDIES

Juliet Dusinberre, *Shakespeare and the Nature of Women*, 2nd ed. (1996); Peter Erickson, *Patriarchal Structures in Shakespeare's Drama* (1985); Kim F. Hall, *Things of Darkness: Economies of Race and Gender in Early Modern England* (1995); Lisa Jardine, *Still Harping on Daughters: Women and Drama in the Age of Shakespeare* (1983); Coppelia Kahn, *Man's Estate: Masculine Identity in Shakespeare* (1981); Ania Loomba, *Gender, Race, Renaissance Drama* (1989); Carol Thomas Neely, *Broken Nuptials in Shakespeare's Plays* (1985); Karen Newman, *Fashioning Femininity and English Renaissance Drama* (1991); Marianne Novy, *Love's Argument: Gender Relations in Shakespeare* (1984); Gail Kern Paster, *The Body Embarrassed: Drama and the Disciplines of Shame in Early Modern England* (1993); Carol Rutter et al., *Clamorous Voices: Shakespeare's Women Today*, ed. by Faith Evans (1988); Bruce R. Smith, *Homosexual Desire in Shakespeare's England* (1991); and Valerie Traub, *Desire and Anxiety: Circulations of Sexuality in Shakespearean Drama* (1992).

POSTSTRUCTURALISM AND DECONSTRUCTION

Linda Charnes, *Notorious Identity: Materializing the Subjective Shakespeare* (1993); Joel Fineman, *Shakespeare's Perjured Eye: The Invention of Poetic Subjectivity in the Sonnets* (1986); and Patricia Parker, *Shakespeare from the Margins: Language, Culture, Context* (1996);

BROAD-SPECTRUM CRITICISM: LANGUAGE, THEMES, THOUGHT

Stanley Cavell, *Disowning Knowledge in Six Plays of Shakespeare* (1987); Rosalie L. Colie, *Shakespeare's Living Art* (1974); Philip Edwards, *Shakespeare and the Confines of Art* (1968, reprinted 1981); Lars Engle, *Shakespearean Pragmatism: Market of His Time* (1993); T. McAlindon, *Shakespeare and Decorum* (1973); A. P. Rossiter, *Angel with Horns* (1961); Wilbur Sanders, *The Dramatist and the Received Idea: Studies in the Plays of Marlowe and Shakespeare* (1968); Robert N. Watson, *Shakespeare and the Hazards of Ambition* (1984); and W. Gordon Zeeveld, *The Temper of Shakespeare's Thought* (1974).

SHAKESPEAREAN COMEDY

Robert G. Hunter, *Shakespeare and the Comedy of Forgiveness* (1965); Arthur Kirsch, *Shakespeare and the Experience of Love* (1981); Alexander Leggatt, *Shakespeare's Comedy of Love* (1974, reprinted 1990); W. Thomas MacCary, *Friends and Lovers: The Phenomenology of Desire in Shakespearean Comedy* (1985); and Leo Salingar, *Shakespeare and the Traditions of Comedy* (1974).

SHAKESPEAREAN TRAGEDY

Janet Adelman, *Suffocating Mothers: Fantasies of Maternal Origin in Shakespeare's Plays* (1992); Philippa Berry, *Shakespeare's Feminine Endings: Disfiguring Death in the Tragedies* (1999); A. C. Bradley, *Shakespearean Tragedy,* 3rd ed. (1992); Arthur Kirsch, *The Passions of Shakespeare's Tragic Heroes* (1990); and Maynard Mack, *King Lear in Our Time* (1965), and *Everybody's Shakespeare: Reflections Chiefly on the Tragedies* (1993).

SHAKESPEAREAN HISTORY

David Scott Kastan, *Shakespeare and the Shapes of Time* (1982).

DRAMATURGY AND SHAKESPEARE IN THE THEATER

Anne Righter, *Shakespeare and the Idea of the Play* (1962); and Meredith Skura, *Shakespeare the Actor and the Purposes of Playing* (1993).

Credits